Ray Berwick's Complete

TRAINING YOUR CAT

By Ray Berwick and Karen Thure

ABOUT THE AUTHORS

RAY BERWICK'S animal-training résumé is unmatched in Hollywood. For years the official animal trainer at MCA Universal studios, he has more than 50 movie credits — including "The Birds," by Alfred Hitchcock, "Birdman of Alcatraz," "Jonathan Livingston Seagull," and "Eye of the Cat."

On television, he's known for training the cockatoo on "Baretta," the dog Boomer, canine star of "Here's Boomer," and Bandit, the dog in "Little House on the Prairie."

He has trained many animals for commercials, including soaring hawks for Kodak and curious cats for Friskies. In 1984, he received a Cleo Award for a Friskies commercial costarring a cat and an all-bird marching band.

In addition to movie and TV work, Ray is executive producer of the bird and animal shows at San Diego Wild Animal Park and Lion Country Safari. He has been featured in numerous articles and has made frequent appearances on national talk shows as a personable spokesman for humane animal training.

KAREN THURE, a long-time cat lover and owner, has been a writer and editor for many years. She was on the editorial staff of *Playboy* magazine and McGraw-Hill magazines before becoming an editor for 13 years for the University of Arizona Press. As a freelance writer in recent years, Karen has written for many magazines, including *Smithsonian, Arizona Highways* and *The American West.* Karen and photographer Gill Kenny recently co-authored a beautiful travel book, *Arizona!,* published by Oxford University Press. She is currently a senior editor of technical publications for Bell Technical Operations, Systems & Software Engineering Department.

Publisher: Rick Bailey
Executive Editor: Randy Summerlin
Editors: Judith Wesley Allen, Judith Schuler
Art Director: Don Burton
Managing Editor: Cindy Coatsworth
Book Assembly: Kathleen Koopman
Typography: Michelle Carter
Director of Manufacturing: Anthony B. Narducci
Photography: Robert Pearcy, T. Thure
Illustrations: Arlene Dubanevich
Technical Consultant: Juliet Rathbone, D.V.M.

Published by HPBooks
A division of HPBooks, Inc.
P.O. Box 5367
Tucson, AZ 85703
(602) 888-2150
ISBN: 0-89586-423-1
Library of Congress Catalog
Card Number: 85-81841
©1986 HPBooks, Inc.
Printed in U.S.A.
2nd Printing

Note: We use the masculine pronoun "he" when referring to a cat. This is for convenience and clarity and does not reflect a preference for either sex.

Notice: The information in this book is true and complete to the best of our knowledge. All recommendations are made without guarantees on the part of the authors or HPBooks. The authors and publisher disclaim all liability in connection with the use of this information.

CONTENTS

Chapter 1: Berwick on Cats 5

TRAINING BASICS

Chapter 2: Preparing to Train 38

BEHAVIOR TRAINING

Chapter 3: Changing Your Cat's Behavior 64

TOILET TRAINING

Chapter 4: Toilet-Training Preparation 94

Chapter 5: Step-by-Step Toilet Training 122

Chapter 6: Solving Toilet-Training Problems 150

TRICK TRAINING

Chapter 7: Beginning Tricks 168

Chapter 8: Advanced Tricks 184

BERWICK'S ANIMALS WITH HOLLYWOOD FRIENDS .. 212

INDEX 221

Ray Berwick with a favorite, Jiggs.

Berwick on Cats

Making the decision to own a cat shouldn't be taken lightly. Not many people realize what it means to own or be owned by a cat.

It's true you must take on certain responsibilities in exchange for the love and companionship that come with owning any pet. But what you give in money and time is nothing compared to what you get in return. Did you know some people spend more time with their household pet than with any person in their family? They know the right kind of pet can soothe the hurts and disappointments of life and make life more full and meaningful.

Probably the most adaptable of all pets is a cat. If you live in an apartment or condominium, a cat is easier to keep than a dog. This is also true if everyone in your house is away during the day at work or school. A cat doesn't mind being left on his own — he can entertain himself.

A cat is housebroken more easily than any other pet. He can even be trained to use the bathroom toilet in much the same way you do. You'll learn more about this in Chapters 4, 5 and 6.

A cat can be your ears. If you are hard of hearing, you can train your cat to let you know when the doorbell or telephone rings. And if you choose, you can train your cat to put on a delightful show as he performs a collection of unusual tricks. You will learn all about the trick-learning ability of cats when you read of their antics in the *Hollywood Cat Tales* scattered throughout this book.

But most important is what a cat can give you in love, companionship, fun and entertainment.

A cat can be a playmate.
Courtesy of Pets Are Wonderful Council.

OLD PREJUDICES

Even if you are feeling down, you can't help but smile when you watch your cat do something as characteristic as exploring the mysteries of an empty grocery bag. I write this sheepishly because during the earlier part of my life, I really didn't understand—or even like—cats. As a child, one of the first things I remember hearing about these animals was that they sometimes smothered babies by draping themselves over their faces.

"Keep those darned cats out of the house and away from me!" my grandpa used to snap. My father, my uncles and all the other men I came in contact with as I was growing up felt the same way.

As a boy, I had a vague notion that cats were fascinating and mysterious. I knew they had been held sacred in some ancient societies. But I remained influenced by the male adults in my family. I took it for granted that cats were pretty useless critters, endowed with all sorts of undesirable qualities.

In retrospect, I think this negative, erroneous attitude is the reason for the long history of cat abuse in Europe and in

America. Cats have been burned as witches, drowned with criminals and shot in archery tournaments. It's a major tribute to cats that they've survived at all.

Stroking my 27-year-old cat Hot Rod as he languishes in his easy chair on the front porch, I feel a strong pang of guilt because I fell into disliking his species without question. Even though I had always loved animals and spent most of my life with pets in the house, it never occurred to me to include cats in my affections.

A Movie Opens My Eyes—I didn't begin to seriously question my dislike of cats until I became a professional motion-picture animal trainer. A number of years ago, Universal Pictures asked me to train a group of cats for an eerie thriller, "Eye of the Cat." My work on this picture quickly taught me that either cats had undergone a radical change since I was a boy, or I had been a real dummy.

I embarked on the project with considerable trepidation. I had trained and worked with many types of animals—dogs, birds, primates, rodents, even wild animals—but never with cats! The film was unusual. Many cats had to work together—acting and attacking humans. The concept didn't sound difficult, because I had just completed Alfred Hitchcock's epic, "The Birds," using thousands of birds flying free and playing villainous roles.

My main doubt was about the cats themselves. Could these notoriously independent animals be trained to do anything at all? And more doubtful, could they be taught to work together?

In no time I had my answer, and it came from Hot Rod. He was as remarkable then as he is today—a seemingly ageless orange ball of energy.

Cat antics make you smile.

He had been a gift from friends who were moving east. I had been reluctant to accept him because he was 10 years old—quite a ripe old age for a cat to start in show business. But my friends had raised him from a kitten, and they were convinced that Hot Rod had the drive to become a star.

To my surprise, they were right. Hot Rod proved to be 6 pounds of super-charged energy—and he was willing to try anything. He was good-natured, but not shy. He never allowed himself to be pushed around. Among the cats I had to work with on this movie, I felt Hot Rod showed the most promise.

How Do You Train a Cat?—As I had done in the past with birds, lions, badgers, wolverines and a whole parade of other critters, I began to work out a training strategy. I sat back and watched my cats interact with each other. Trainers call this "reading your subject."

It wasn't long before three things became obvious. First, cats react strongly to certain sounds—that is, sounds they wish to hear. They are able to tune out sounds they aren't concerned about. Second, cats discipline each other with a hiss and a push or paw-slap in the face. Third, cats react involuntarily to very quick, unexpected movements.

Starting with this knowledge, I built a waist-high small table 2 feet square. Experience had already shown this to be a great back-saver when working with a small animal. It also served another important function. An animal on a table is much less intimidated than one on the floor, where he must gaze up at a human monster several times his own size.

Lesson from Hot Rod—I started with Hot Rod. He and I took our positions, with him on the table and me in front of it. As I knew would happen, after about 3 seconds, he started to jump down. I put my hand directly in front of his face and hissed like an old tomcat. He looked up at me in amazement as if to say, "What is that? Where did you learn cat talk?"

Hot Rod looked confused and tried again to leave the scene, but I raised my hand and hissed again. This time he got the message—I was commanding him to stay put. I think I was more surprised than he by our sudden communication.

Within 5 minutes I could walk any place in the room and wait for Hot Rod to make a move. Without a hand gesture, with nothing more than a low hiss from me, he would go back to the center of the table. Soon he began to lower himself to his haunches and accept the behavior of lie-down-and-stay. My heart was pounding with excitement! I felt as if I were exploding an old myth. In just a few short minutes, Hot Rod and I had proved cats *can* be trained!

From this simple behavior, my trainers and I went on to teach Hot Rod to perform a complex series of tricks, including retrieving an object. Other cats, such as black-and-white Pinto and battered yellow Hopeless, soon joined Hot Rod as outstanding film actors. You'll hear all about these cats later. Together and alone they performed convincing dramatic close-ups and difficult, intricate, long shots. And they executed their scenes with all of the cooperation and aplomb of any of our movie-star dogs.

Instead of the training disaster I had secretly anticipated, our cats turned out to be a smashing on-screen success. While "Eye of the Cat" never enjoyed the box-office popularity of "The Birds," its feline stars were certainly not to blame.

During the months I spent working on this movie, I learned not only to train cats, but to love them as well. I decided that someday I would write a book to pass on everything I had discovered about these exceptional animals.

You and Your Cat—My years of working professionally with cats have taught me these little animals have fantastic potential for companionship and training. I believe this is particularly true of the modern indoor cat, who places greater emphasis on his relationships with humans.

Because a well-cared-for indoor cat spends almost no time or energy on survival, he begins to develop sophisticated

Berwick cues Hot Rod for his role in "Gremlins."

behaviors. This is good. But like a child, he is happier and more content if he learns something about obedience and responsibility. His "bonding" to you as his owner becomes stronger when he learns to communicate with you. Training is the key to communication. When your cat learns to perform obedience behaviors and to do tricks on cue, the two of you are communicating.

In short, training can be an exciting learning experience for you both. Because this is a relatively new field of animal training, you and your cat will be among its pioneers. Believe me, you'll never have a better opportunity to "meet with the mind" of one of nature's most appealing species of animals.

YOU CAN TRAIN YOUR CAT

With the exception of hard-to-train cats described on page 13, *any* cat can become a well-behaved household companion. He can learn to come when called, walk on a leash and perform at least a few simple tricks. In addition, he can learn to use the bathroom toilet. He'll become a closer and more affectionate pet in the process.

I can assure you this is true because of my experience with my co-author Karen Thure. Karen and her family have no more professional animal-training background than you do. But by using the methods we present in this book, they have been able to train their cat Ivanhoe to do all the things mentioned above and more.

Keep Ivanhoe's example in mind to build

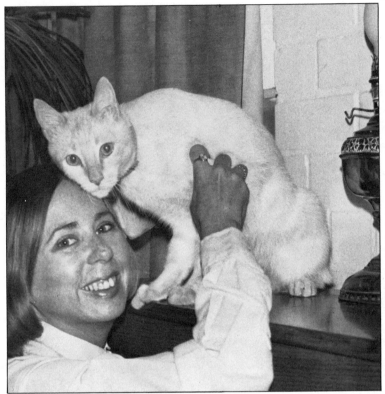

Karen Thure with trained cat
Ivanhoe.

your confidence as an animal trainer. You
·don't need the medical knowledge of a vet
or the lifetime experience of a circus professional. If you are patient and follow the
instructions in this book, you'll have success. So relax and enjoy the adventure of
making your cat a household star!

CHOOSING A CAT

You may already own a cat that you want
to train. If you don't, you should select one
that has strong training promise. The factors that influence how trainable a cat is
include age, neutering, breed, personality
and innate learning ability.

AGE AND SEX

If your cat is too young or too old, or of
either sex and unneutered, he will be difficult to train.

Kittens—Because of their appealing cute-
ness, kittens are often adopted before they
are 8 weeks old. This is a serious mistake
that may later interfere with the kitten's
training program.

A kitten adopted before the age of 8
weeks may not have had his basic instincts
reinforced by his mother's teaching. In
many ways, he may remain psychologically infantile. Excessive kneading
and drooling, sucking on blankets and
clothing, and refusing to use a litter box are
common infantile behaviors seen in kittens

Like a human baby, tiny 6-week-old kitten needs its mother. Kittens should not be adopted before 8 weeks of age.
Courtesy of Pets Are Wonderful Council

adopted before the age of 8 weeks.

Older Cats—You can adopt a cat at any age and find you have a delightful companion. But if you are planning on extensive training, you may not want to adopt a cat over 6 years old. On a human scale of aging, a cat between 1 and 6 years is between his teens and his 40s. His body is healthy and agile, and his mind is open and receptive to learning new behaviors. He is also usually willing to accept new toilet habits.

A 7- or 8-year-old cat is in his 50s and 60s in comparable human years. He has become more "set in his ways" and is generally reluctant to change. His training will probably go more slowly than a younger cat's.

After he has reached the age of 9 years, your cat has moved into the elderly years on a human scale of aging. His muscles begin to deteriorate, and his joints slowly grow stiff. He spends much of his time sleeping and is uninterested in learning new behaviors. Training an old cat is usually difficult, although there are exceptions. One of them is Hot Rod, who is 27 years old and still performing in movies.

Male or Female—Unless you plan to breed your cat, gender isn't an important factor when it comes to choosing a cat. Neutered male and female cats can be trained with equal ease. This applies to all types of training, including toilet training.

Unneutered male and female cats show definite gender-linked personality traits. Males are usually more aggressive. Females are often better hunters, and motherly and protective toward their kittens.

If your cat is neutered by the age of 6 months, gender-linked personality traits virtually disappear. Both males and females will have well-adjusted, human-oriented personalities. They are equally

Siamese are intelligent and easy to train.

anxious to learn new behaviors to please you. Neutering is discussed further in Chapter 2.

LEARNING ABILITY

Any well-adjusted, intelligent, domestic cat between the ages of 4 months and 6 years can be trained successfully. Siamese cats are the easiest domestic breeds to train, followed by Burmese and Himalayan.

Mixed-breed cats with Siamese, Burmese or Himalayan blood are often delightfully intelligent and eager to please. But so are many domestic shorthairs with no pedigreed ancestry. A combination of unplanned matings can produce a special kind of energy called *hybrid vigor*.

Highly independent breeds, such as the Abyssinian, and extremely relaxed breeds,

Cat's curiosity leads him to explore cranny.

such as the Persian, may take longer to train than other kinds of cats. However, both types are smart and friendly. They are capable of learning if you let them proceed at their own pace.

Cats with Physical Problems—Deaf cats are difficult to train because they can't hear important sound cues. Blue-eyed, white cats are often deaf. So are cats from highly inbred litters. A good test for deafness is described on page 16.

Cats who are sick cannot be effectively trained. Cat diseases range from serious nerve and organ disorders to simple parasitic infestations. Have a vet examine your cat to be sure he is healthy before you begin any training program.

Cats with Mental Problems—Some cats are mentally retarded or emotionally disturbed. These conditions are often the re-

sult of inbreeding to obtain attractive physical qualities.

No reputable breeder, animal shelter or pet store will sell a grown cat or kitten that has demonstrated he has mental problems. But take precautions and examine each prospective pet with a critical eye, as described in the following section.

If you accidentally acquire a retarded or disturbed cat as a stray or as a "gift" from a friend, you'll know it's a problem cat within a few days. Extreme listlessness, aggression or nervousness are not present in a mentally healthy cat. A cat who has serious mental problems *cannot* be successfully trained.

PERSONALITY FACTORS

Cat personalities vary as greatly as those of dogs—or even people. Choose a cat that suits your personal tastes for best training results.

Basic Characteristics—Some basic characteristics are common to all breeds of cats. Look for them in the animal you plan to adopt. If he doesn't exhibit common basic personality traits, he may be mentally retarded or emotionally disturbed.

The most recognized characteristic of cat personality is *curiosity*. Almost all cats explore open cupboards if given the chance. Your cat's instinctive curiosity makes him delightful to watch, but this trait can be dangerous. Cats have been locked in closets, shipped in boxes and shut in drawers as a result of curiosity.

Your cat's *independent attitude* is another basic personality trait. He may be deeply devoted to you, but he doesn't mind being left alone. His ability to amuse himself makes him a perfect pet for people who work.

Domestic cats are born with a *natural*

affection for human beings. Only cats raised in the wild fail to respond to a friendly human gesture.

Breed-Related Characteristics—Breed-related learning ability has been discussed, but don't choose a cat according to learning ability alone. To work well together as trainer and trainee, you and your cat must like each other. Ensure a good training relationship by choosing a breed with personality traits that conform to your preferences. Common personality traits of some of the most popular breeds are discussed below.

The Siamese is generally considered the most trainable of all breeds. These loyal, devoted animals may demand a lot of attention, often with a loud, persistent meow. Some Siamese "talk" a lot, which bothers some people. If you want a quiet, undemanding cat, *don't* choose a Siamese.

Because the Burmese is a close cousin of the Siamese, it has similar personality characteristics. Besides being smart, Burmese are usually playful, affectionate and gentle.

Long-haired breeds, such as the Persian, are often docile—so much so that some people call them lazy. They appear dignified and regal, but this impression may come more from elegant looks than any inbred personality trait.

The most unique trait of the Russian Blue is its loyalty. Self-reliance characterizes the Abyssinian. The Manx is brave and patient, and the Havana Brown is quiet and exceptionally clean.

The most common breed of cat—the domestic shorthair—is almost always a good bet for training and companionship. This cat is sensitive, intelligent, lively and alert—and often endowed with a sense of humor.

Activity Levels—Activity varies from cat to cat. Some animals are hyperactive to the point of being destructive if they must stay inside for long periods. Other cats curl up and sleep most of the day.

Neither of these extremes is ideal for a pet you want to train. For best training results, look for a cat that is alert but relaxed.

Shyness and Friendliness—An outgoing cat has no qualms about starting a friendly game with you at first meeting. A timid cat draws back, sometimes as far as possible.

Your first impulse may be to take the friendly one, and in many cases this is the best decision. It will probably be easy to train him to perform tricks in front of strangers. If you want to show him or teach him to perform on-camera, he may be unafraid of strange places and bright lights.

But an extremely outgoing cat may turn out to be a training problem. The bossy leader of a litter may become a bright, but independent, rebel who is difficult to teach. If you choose a less-aggressive litter mate, you'll have better training results.

Sometimes you fall in love with a very shy cat or kitten. Don't dismiss him as a possible choice because you think he'll be hard to train. The opposite may be true.

It's likely that once a shy cat or kitten gets to know you and your family, he'll be very loyal. He will be more loving and more devoted than most pets and less likely to stray and be picked up by strangers. He also may prove to be easy to train. His loyalty makes him extra-eager to please you by learning new behaviors.

There's no guarantee a shy cat will be loyal and eager to please, but it often turns out that way. If you don't care if your pet gives performances in front of an audience, a shy cat might be the perfect cat for you.

Lively domestic shorthair kittens have good training potential.

MAKING THE CHOICE

Don't let a breeder make the selection for you. Take time to make the right decision on your own.

Before you go out to select your cat or kitten, make some decisions about what kind of looks and personality you want in a cat. This keeps you from making impulsive decisions you may later regret.

You may have to neuter your cat for training, so don't let yourself be persuaded to buy a high-priced pedigreed animal with a championship physique. If the cat won't be bred, pedigree does not matter. Instead, choose a lower-priced cat with features that are less than show-perfect. Mixed-breed cats are also excellent choices for training.

Where to Go—Newspaper ads are a good source for kittens. Unpedigreed litters are often offered for free. Pedigreed kittens are priced competitively with those in pet shops.

Pet shops offer pedigreed and un-pedigreed kittens. Sometimes pedigreed litters are listed in a pet shop, and you must go to the breeder's house or kennel to pick out your pet.

The Humane Society and other local animal-protection groups usually have a wide selection of cats and kittens. The adoption fee they charge usually includes the cost of neutering your pet at a later date.

Wherever you make your selection, be sure the premises look and smell clean. If

Observing a litter at play helps you select the kitten most suitable for training.

they don't, leave and select your cat or kitten elsewhere.

Avoid buying a pet from a breeder who raises the animals in outdoor pens with little human contact. A cat from this environment may shy away from people and have trouble adjusting to life indoors.

Watch with a Critical Eye—If you choose a kitten from a litter, watch the litter at play for about half an hour. Watch for the looks and personality features you've decided on.

Beware of behavior that is inconsistent with the present time and place. Avoid a kitten that shows extreme aggressiveness or hyperactivity.

Inspect kittens closely for signs of good health. A healthy kitten has a glossy coat and clear eyes, and he is peppy and playful. A sickly kitten has a dull coat and may

have discharge from his eyes. He may be listless, smaller than his litter mates and refuse to join in litter play.

Test Him—After you select a cat or kitten, stroke him gently until he feels comfortable in your presence. When he's comfortable, give him the following simple tests.

Place him in a corner of the cage or pen. Make a friendly beckoning gesture with your hand and at the same time softly call "kitty, kitty." Most normal animals have the instinct to come to your call. If your prospective pet approaches you, you've learned three things—he is friendly, reasonably intelligent and probably not deaf.

Test further for deafness by clapping your hands at a distance of 3 feet *behind* the animal's head. He should react with surprise or fear. If he shows no reaction, test him with a loud finger snap, whistle or

Test cat's intelligence and alertness by playing with string.

shout. If he still doesn't react, he is probably partially or totally deaf.

A final test involves playing with the pet you have selected. Sway a handkerchief or piece of string above his face, and see if he tries to bat it with his paw. Jerk the handkerchief or string along the floor, and see if he tries to attack it. Give him a crumpled piece of paper or cellophane, and watch him play with it on his own.

If the pet you have chosen shows an active interest in these play activities, you can take him home with the knowledge he is normal and intelligent. If he doesn't show any interest, it may be a sign he's sick or mentally retarded. Make another selection.

JERRY'S WORLD

Cats must see the world quite differently than we do. It's hard to imagine the way they think, but once in awhile you find a special friend whose mind seems to reach out to you. I have such a friend in my little cat Jerry. I didn't find her — she found me. That was my lucky day. I'll let her tell her own story:

The first thing I remember about that day is being carried by a woman into a big room filled with kitties of all sizes.

"You pitiful stray kitty," she said, "you sure don't have much of a future. How am I ever going to find you a home? You're a female, and you're skinny. No telling what kind of cats your mama and papa were."

It didn't sound like I was in for much fun. Then I heard a loud knock on the door. The lady opened it, and a man came in. As he walked through the door with a lively step, I got a little tingly feeling. This was my kind of person. I started toward him, but he stepped right over me. He and the lady went to the back of the room where a few huge kitties were in cages.

"This is the cat — the best in our animal adoption agency," the lady said. "He is so sweet. He's full of kisses. Watch this." She stuck her hand out and the big gray started licking it.

The man took the cat from his cage and put him on the floor. The cat slinked away. The man didn't seem too happy about that.

"Don't worry — he just has to get to know you," the lady said. She handed the man the cat, and they walked to a desk and sat down.

I felt like it was time to make myself known. After all, I liked this man. Just three skips and a hop, and I was on his shoulder. He twisted his head and smiled at me. It was a good feeling, but the lady put me back on the floor.

"I'm sorry," she said, as I jumped back on the man's shoulder.

"That's okay. I like his spunk," the man said.

"She's a girl," the lady informed him.

"Then I like her spunk. How much will you take for her?"

"Oh, I'll just give her to you. I picked her up in a parking lot this afternoon to keep her from getting run over. Who knows how long she's been a stray?"

The man smiled. He put the big cat in a metal box, and the three of us left with me riding on his shoulder.

The man took us to a big colorful place with hundreds of people milling around. I didn't know it then, but it was the tour area of Universal Studios. We made our way through the crowd to an area that was full of kitties, dogs, birds and chimpanzees. I soon found out that these animals were trained for motion pictures and live shows. The man put me in a cage and called to another man.

"Hey, Steve, take a look at this brat. I might be wrong, but I think she's really something."

A young man with a little moustache came over and took me out of the cage. I jumped up on his shoulder, and he grinned from ear to ear.

"I think you're right, Ray," he said. I guess I have a way with people.

We walked out onto some kind of stage. The man put me on a table and started showing me things. I tried to do everything he wanted. I couldn't understand it all, but I tried. He seemed pleased. It was the beginning of my training.

The next chapter of my life — training — was a whirlwind of fun. I loved what I was doing so much that I couldn't wait for each training session. Ray and Steve began to call me "Jerry" instead of "kitty."

To make a long story short, in a little while I was working in front of an audience as Jerry, the only cat in the world who could do a backward somersault.

Steve would tell the audience that he was going to show them the world's greatest rat trap. On that cue, I would come rushing out and jump onto the high end of a teeter-totter. Spring! My jump would send a large toy rat on the other end of the teeter-totter flying into the air. I would leap up and catch the rat in my paws, doing a backward somersault in the process. Then I'd put the rat in my mouth, scamper up a ladder to a little house labeled "Rat Bank," and drop the rat into a slot in the top. My act brought the house down!

You can see me doing my famous backward somersault on page 202 of this book. That day I did it just for Ray and the photographer, but I really prefer a big audience and lots of applause!

Ray Berwick

INTRODUCE YOUR CAT TO YOUR HOME

First impressions are important to your cat. If you quietly introduce him to your home and allow him to explore, he will soon feel confident and happy. If, on the other hand, you expose him to loud noises or rowdy play, he will feel frightened and insecure. Make sure that your cat has the advantage of a quiet introduction to your home.

You can further increase your new cat's feeling of security by purchasing the food and equipment that are exactly right for him. Find out what to purchase by questioning his breeder or your vet.

FOOD

Before you take your cat home, ask about his feeding schedule and the types of food he is accustomed to eating. During his first week in your home, feed him on his familiar schedule. If you decide to change your cat's original diet, do so gradually. Sudden changes in diet almost always cause diarrhea.

Your vet is an important source of advice regarding your cat's diet. Veterinary help is especially important if you have a cat who is over 6 years old. Cats in this age bracket can become dehydrated quite easily. Your vet may advise against dry food and prescribe a vitamin supplement.

Choosing the right foods is an important part of your role as a responsible cat owner. You can buy commercial food or make your own cat food from recipes in a cat-care book. Grocery stores carry a wide variety of canned, dried and semimoist foods. Most cat owners buy food from grocery stores because of convenience.

When trying to decide among the many brands of commercial foods, keep in mind that most national brands are made from formulas based on the results of extensive taste and nutrition tests in large research kennels. Unknown brands or generic products may not be backed up by such testing. If you choose a generic or unknown brand of cat food, check the list of ingredients on the label for wholesomeness and balance.

A well-balanced cat food includes various sources of protein, carbohydrates, minerals and vitamins. Meat or fish protein, cereal or refined food starch, copper oxide, and vitamins A, D and E are examples of important ingredients to look for on a cat-food label. A nutritious food should contain at least 15% protein.

If you decide to make your own cat food, don't be misled by fads, such as a vegetarian cat diet.

Whatever you choose, confine offerings to two or three kinds of food. Otherwise your cat may become a finicky eater. Occasionally you can add *small amounts* of table scraps and other supplements for variety. If you choose to do this, mix these additions with a serving of cat food. Otherwise, your cat may come to prefer the supplements and table food to cat food. Supplements that promote bowel regularity become especially important during toilet training.

EQUIPMENT

Some items, such as food dishes or a litter box, are essential to owning a cat. Other items, such as blankets, a scratching post, and grooming tools, make cat care easier and increase your cat's enjoyment of his surroundings.

Litter and Litter Box—These are two of the most important items you can have for

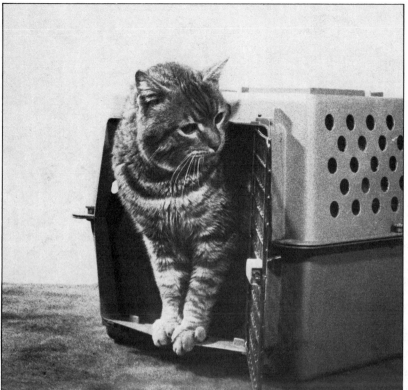

Portable kennel is essential for care and training.

your cat. If you don't plan to toilet train your cat, you may want to buy a covered litter box to reduce smell and mess. If you plan on toilet training, buy the training toilet described on page 101.

Find out what kind of litter your cat is accustomed to using. Use this type during his first week in your home. After this, you can begin to gradually introduce another type of litter.

Kennel and Miscellaneous Items—A portable kennel is necessary for traveling and for trick training. Pet stores sell many types of portable kennels. The plastic, airline-approved kind is perfect for traveling. Choose one that has room enough for a fair-sized litter box. A water dish is usually attached to the door.

Other cat-care items include a bed box with soft blankets, a scratching post, food and water dishes, and a brush and comb. A collar, name tag, harness, leash and tether are also important.

Get a comprehensive cat-care book, such as *How to Choose & Care for Your Cat,* published by HPBooks. Read it from cover to cover before you get your new cat. Consult it when you have problems regarding his care.

Toys—A variety of toys help make your cat happy in your home. When you play with him and his toys, you help establish the bond of friendship that is essential for training success. Grocery-store pet departments and pet shops carry many cat toys, with and without catnip. *Don't use*

Follow cat as he explores home.

catnip toys during your cat's first month with you. Catnip has a mind-altering effect that is undesirable while you become acquainted.

Homemade cat toys often turn out to be your cat's favorites. Make them from common household objects, such as spools, small bells, string and yarn. Crumpled cellophane makes a perfect cat toy. The rustling noises it makes resemble the sounds made by small prey.

BRINGING HIM HOME

Bringing a new pet into your home is one of life's most delightful experiences. To establish immediately the one-to-one relationship that you'll need in training, introduce yourself to your new pet on a one-to-one basis. Ask other family members or roommates to leave the two of you alone together during your cat's first hour in your home. Later they can share the pleasures of stroking and playing with him.

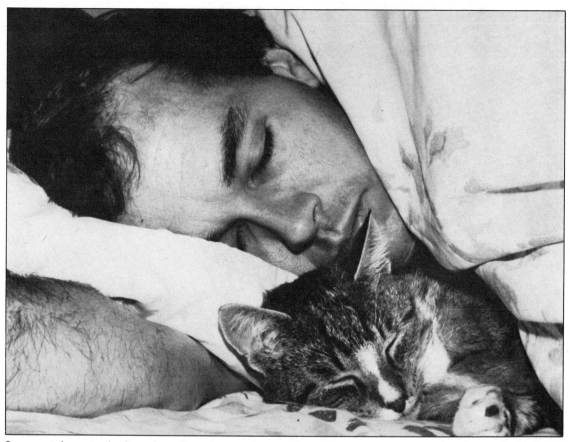

Some cats have cat beds—others share their owner's.
Courtesy of Pets Are Wonderful Council

The First Hours—After you enter your home, set your new cat's kennel down in the room that contains his litter box or other toilet facility. If you plan on toilet training him, the toilet facility will be the training toilet in the bathroom.

Before you let your cat out of his kennel, put other pets outdoors or in another room. Be sure children understand the new pet must not be exposed to roughness or loud noises.

Your first urge may be to hold the cat or kitten, but it's best to allow him his freedom until he has investigated his new environment. Let him jump out of his kennel on his own. Watch him as he begins to explore.

Before your cat leaves the room containing his toilet facility, gently place him on the litter. If he's been away from a litter box for a long time, he may use it immediately. If he doesn't, follow the instructions on page 116.

Berwick on Cats **23**

Wait until pets are friends before you leave them alone.

After you've introduced your new pet to the litter box, carry him into the room where you will feed him. Let him watch while you prepare his food and water. This lets him know you are replacing his former owner or mother as a source of nourishment.

Don't be disturbed if your cat refuses to eat or drink. Moving is an ordeal, and it may be several days before he regains his normal appetite.

Follow your cat when he leaves his food to explore other rooms in your home. If he performs an undesirable behavior, gently interfere and redirect his attention. *Don't administer discipline during his first day!*

His first impression must be one of comfort, care and kindness.

After your cat has explored your home alone for at least half an hour, take him in your lap and stroke him. If he closes his eyes, carry him to his sleeping place and stroke him for a brief period. Then leave him alone, and allow him to nap.

Hours that Follow—Stroke your cat frequently during his waking hours. A strong sense of mutual trust comes from frequent handling and contact. Even if your cat seems skittish and afraid, he will become friendly and even affectionate after a day or two of gentle stroking.

Allow other members of your household

to introduce themselves to your cat one at a time. They can watch him as he explores or take him into their laps for stroking. If they want to play with him, warn them not to be loud or rough.

Allow your cat to nap when he wishes. Put him in his sleeping place if you don't want him to get into the habit of lying on the furniture. If you are going to allow your cat to sleep on your bed, take him with you when you go to sleep.

Weeks that Follow—Gradually introduce your new pet to pets you already own. When you leave home, confine the pets in separate rooms. When you return, put each pet in the room the other one was in before. This helps them become familiar with the other's scent.

If the animals show hostility toward each other, you may want to use one of the introduction methods described on page 154. Don't leave them alone together until they have become good friends.

Don't allow your new cat outdoors for at least 1 month, unless he is with you on his leash. Otherwise, he may become disoriented and lost.

Take your cat to the vet for a checkup and shots *as soon as possible*. The importance of a checkup can't be overemphasized. Many diseases can snuff out a cat's life in a matter of days. Nearly all these diseases can be avoided by making certain shots are current.

Establish regular household routines to help your cat feel cared for and content. Groom him at a regular time each day. If you plan to toilet train, begin to feed him for regularity as discussed on page 96. Give him affection and stroking regularly. If your cat feels happy and secure in his routine, training will be relaxed, enjoyable and rewarding.

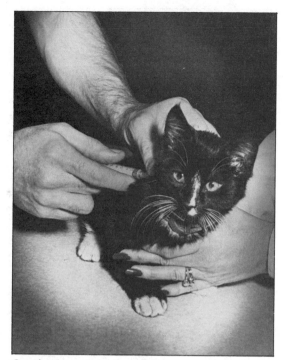

Get shots as soon as possible.

GETTING TO KNOW YOUR CAT'S BODY

A knowledge of how a cat's body works makes you an understanding trainer. Your cat's body is a streamlined, living machine. **Inside**—In many ways, your cat's body resembles your own. His skeleton includes many of the same bones, such as a skull, backbone and ribs. Bones are shaped and arranged to allow him extraordinary flexibility. Any dancer would love to have a cat's agility.

Your cat has many internal organs you have, including a windpipe, lungs, heart, veins and arteries. Everything is smaller and adapted to the needs of a cat.

Backward somersault shows off cat's agility.

Your cat's digestive system includes the same organs as yours. Food passes from his throat to his esophagus, into the stomach and intestines. His liver and kidneys help cleanse his body of wastes.

Your cat's body has a bladder and rectum. When he needs to eliminate wastes, he feels the same pressures you do. This is important to remember if you plan to toilet train him.

Outside—The outside of your cat's body is covered by skin and hair. His skin is similar to your skin. It has oil glands, hair follicles, blood vessels and nerves. The pads of his paws have sweat glands to help him keep cool in hot weather.

Despite these similarities, your cat's skin differs from yours in several ways. It has pigment cells around the oil glands. These cells lend color to the hairs that grow out of the skin. The skin is almost entirely covered by a thick coat of hair to protect him and keep him warm.

Your cat's hair grows out of thousands of follicles in his skin. Follicles are equipped with small erector muscles that make your cat's hair stand on end when he is angry or afraid.

Many cats appear to show great pride in their coats. They spend hours grooming. After a long grooming session, they may strut about as if they were showing off.

SENSES

Three of your cat's senses are so much more acute than yours that they deserve to be called "super senses." These are the senses of *hearing, smell* and *balance.*

Hearing—Nature has given your cat phenomenal hearing capabilities. His ears pick up a wide range of noises you can't hear or imagine. His world is filled with tiny crackles, rustles and squeaks that come from animals, plants and insects. He moves his flexible outer ears to direct the sounds that interest him into his sensitive inner ears.

One unusual aspect of hearing may be totally unique to cats. They can actually shut off sounds that are uninteresting to them. They can do this and remain amazingly alert to sounds they want to hear. For example, your cat may decide not to hear the din of conversation at a lawn party, but he will tune in loud and clear to a bird chirp from a tree above the guests.

Smell—Like his sense of hearing, your cat's sense of smell has a far greater range than yours. His world is filled with aromas

Cats have an amazing sense of balance.

of the earth, animals and food that your nose cannot detect. He sends messages to other cats by "marking" things with his urine and scent glands. In addition to his nose, he has a special smelling organ in his mouth to pick up message-bearing odors from other cats.

Balance—The feline sense of balance is legendary. Many people believe cats can instinctively right themselves so they land on all fours, whether they fall from a height of a few feet or several stories.

The sure-footedness your cat shows in high places comes from his confidence in the balancing mechanism of his inner ear. But despite this confidence, he still can slip and fall.

Other Senses—In a way, your cat's vision is a super sense. He can see at levels of light that would be darkness to you. However, he probably does not see things with sharp clarity and color. It's impossible to picture exactly the world his eyes see, but even in daylight it's probably fuzzy and undetailed compared to your own. Colors are probably muddy and dull.

Your cat has taste buds that may convey most of the same taste sensations you experience. His teeth are designed for ripping, not chewing. Because he doesn't chew his food, he doesn't keep it in his mouth as long as you do. Despite this fact, he may have strong personal likes and dislikes about tastes.

Your cat's sense of touch is as sensitive as your own, if not more so. Besides the nerve endings in his skin, he has long, touch-sensitive whiskers at the sides of his mouth. He uses his whiskers like an insect uses its feelers—to explore the world. Whiskers also protect his eyes. Touch your cat's whiskers, and his eyelids often close.

Extrasensory Perception—Because cats sometimes get nervous before natural disasters such as tornadoes and earthquakes, some researchers believe cats have means of perception we don't know about. They believe cats can detect changes in the electric and magnetic qualities of the air.

There are occasional reports of "incredible journeys," in which cats have found their owners by tracking them over hundreds of miles. These reports have given rise to the idea that cats may have a sense of direction similar to a homing pigeon's.

Cats have been associated with magic since they became domesticated. In some cultures, they have been linked to good magic. In other cultures, they have been related to evil. In either case, various superstitions may have arisen out of cats' sensory perceptions that we don't understand.

GETTING TO KNOW YOUR CAT'S MIND

Popular cartoons about cats are fun, but they don't really depict the way your cat's mind works. A cat doesn't think and feel in the same ways you do. He thinks and feels in ways unique to a cat. Your cat's brain is 30 times smaller than yours.

Brain Structure—In terms of complexity, your cat's brain falls halfway between a rat's and an orangutan's. Like all mamma-

Cat's brain development is between rat's and orangutan's.

lian brains, it is similar in structure to a human brain.

The lower part of your cat's brain controls muscle coordination. This part is proportionately larger than the lower part of your brain.

The upper part of your cat's brain controls different functions, such as memory and learning. This part is proportionately smaller than the upper part of your brain.

Specific centers of your cat's brain control senses. Some of these, such as the center for smell, are proportionately larger than those in a human brain.

Other centers of the brain control feelings, such as fear, pain and pleasure. These centers are proportionately about the same size in your brain and your cat's.

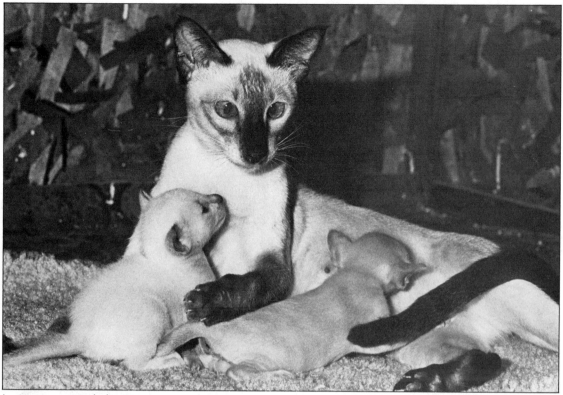
Instinctive nursing behavior.

You each have a lower brain that is the center of the autonomic nervous system. This system controls muscle coordination and basic body functions, such as circulation and digestion. It does its job quietly and efficiently, without conscious knowledge on the part of the main brain. Remember this if you plan to toilet train your cat—he has no more conscious control over digestion than you do.

Instincts—It's hard for us as human beings to understand what strong instincts are like. The few we have are mixed with emotion and intellect, and we barely recognize them as instincts.

The way a newborn human or animal nurses is a good example of *instinctive behavior*. Babies don't have to be taught to eat to survive. The automatic flight-or-fight response to danger is another instinct. All animals and human beings are born with a strong urge toward self-preservation.

A wide variety of stimuli trigger automatic behaviors in your cat. The sight, smell and sound of a mouse make him automatically crouch and stalk. The sight and smell of a bowel movement make him scratch in the dirt to bury it.

Some instinctive behaviors are not triggered by outside stimuli. Your cat performs them because he has a strong inner urge to do so. Such behaviors include grooming, marking with urine or scent glands, and sexual and maternal activities.

Some cats learn on their own to switch on lights.

This cat has figured out how doorknob works.

Reason and Memory—Most cat owners can tell stories about their pets that prove cats have some degree of reason and memory. On their own, cats sometimes learn to open doors, flick on lights and ring doorbells.

Such self-taught behaviors demonstrate your cat has some understanding of cause and effect. He has enough memory to learn from experience and to retain behaviors he has learned.

But your cat doesn't have the brain power to perform complex reasoning tasks. He can't solve problems that require more than one or two simple decisions.

Abstract Thought—Anyone who has seen a kitten at play knows he has something akin to imagination. He jumps at nonexistent houseflies and pounces on make-believe mice. In his mind, he must picture these as phantom prey.

Because he doesn't have a verbal language, much of your cat's thoughts must be in some type of pictures. When he's hungry, he might envision food. When he expects you home from work, he might envision you. However, researchers have no clear idea of how this process works in his brain.

Your cat has a strong sense of time when

it comes to daily routine. If you get up at 7 a.m. each morning, he may soon become a living alarm clock. If you return home at 6 p.m. each evening, he'll be waiting for you in the window.

Your cat probably doesn't understand the future in any abstract way. Except for his grasp of daily routine, he lives in the present moment.

Your cat almost certainly does not understand good and bad in the way you do. His actions are governed by his instincts and by what gives him pleasure or discomfort. It's important to remember this point when you begin training.

EMOTIONS AND ATTITUDES

Some animal behaviorists are reluctant to state that cats have feelings akin to those of people. They say that cats are animals, so their feelings must be unique. This may be so, but any cat owner knows that cat feelings often appear humanlike—especially feelings of affection.

Emotions—Your cat can't show emotions through facial expressions like yours. His lips are not equipped with muscles that allow him to smile or frown. A layer of reflective cells enhances his night vision, but it often makes his eyes appear blank and expressionless.

Because of this lack of facial expression, some people believe cats don't have feelings. Anyone who has owned a cat knows this isn't true.

By his actions, your cat shows he feels affection, pleasure, fear, anger and aversion. Many of these feelings seem linked to instinctive likes and dislikes. Other feelings may be unique to the personality of your cat.

Moods—Your cat may seem to respond to the weather in the same ways you do. Hot,

Like every species, cat sees the world in unique ways.

humid days make him lazy. Clear, crisp days make him frisky and anxious to go outdoors.

Some cat owners believe their pets become agitated on nights of the full moon. No one knows why this occurs—or even if it really does—but some researchers think it might be due to the moon's magnetic pull. The fluids in your cat's body and brain may be affected by magnetism.

Some cats become hyperactive for a brief period every day. They run around wildly and meow restlessly. This behavior may be inherited from wild ancestors who used to waken from long naps to begin hunting.

Because you feed him, your cat may see you as a mother figure.

If your cat becomes hyperactive in the evening, take him for a walk on his leash. If his agitated mood continues, consult your vet. Unusual behavior may be a sign of illness.

Dreams—Sleep studies show cats experience the kind of deep sleep that produces dreams in humans. During this type of sleep, his whiskers, ears or legs may move as if he were chasing phantom prey.

Experiments cannot prove your cat is actually dreaming the same way you do.

There is no way to know if he has dreams that contain fantasies and emotions. He certainly seems to enjoy his sleep—he spends well over half his lifetime in the sleeping state.

How He Sees You—Your cat recognizes you by your walk, voice, personal aroma and face. In a room full of people, he can pick you out.

He is probably aware you are another species of animal. It's almost certain he doesn't think of you as another cat.

Unlike a dog, your cat doesn't see you as his boss. Instead, he treats you as a kitten treats his mother. He shows affection by allowing you to stroke him and by rubbing his head against your body. He may purr and knead your lap when you stroke him, just as a nursing kitten purrs and kneads his mother.

Most researchers believe your cat sees you as a mother figure. He has a need for your affection and may grow unhappy or ill if he is deprived of it. He has a deeper friendship with you than he can ever have with another cat.

CAT TALK

As mentioned earlier, sounds are very important to your cat. He singles out for special attention sounds that are important to him. The sounds he makes also have special meaning. If you listen to them carefully, you can learn to interpret what they mean.

Meow—Your cat is equipped with vocal cords that allow him to make his characteristic "meow." He can vary the sound of his meow, just as you can vary the sound of a hum.

As you become acquainted with your cat, you will learn the meaning of various meow sounds. He may give a little chirping meow when he greets you, a loud demanding meow when he wants food and a long, complaining meow when he's frightened or in pain.

Your cat usually uses his meow to communicate with human beings. He makes other sounds when communicating with other cats. Some researchers think he can make ultrasonic noises you aren't capable of hearing.

Hissing and Howling—Your cat's solitary nature makes him instinctively hostile to strange animals. When he sees another cat, he probably hisses to express his hostility. If the confrontation ends in a fight, he may growl, spit and scream. He may make ultrasonic noises you can't hear.

The most elaborate vocalizations come from unneutered cats just before mating or on the night of a full moon. The long, drawn-out howls have been the subject of thousands of cartoons. Most cats stop howling after they are neutered, but some continue this behavior—especially when the moon is full. Siamese cats are most inclined toward occasional howling.

Purring—Purring is a sound all cat owners love. Your cat began purring when he was a nursing kitten. As an adult, he purrs to express contentment and friendship.

The source of your cat's purr has always been a mystery. The latest theory is that the sound results from the vibration of a major blood vessel in his chest. When the vibration rises into his windpipe and throat, it produces a purr.

Body Language—The position of your cat's ears, tail and coat tell you a lot about what he thinks and feels. When he's comfortable and content, his ears are erect, his tail is vertical, his back is relaxed and his coat lies flat. When he becomes angry or afraid, his ears lie back, his tail becomes stiffly erect, his back arches and his coat stands on end.

Between these two extremes, your cat has many forms of body language. His waving tail expresses annoyance. A butt with his head is a call for attention or a gesture of affection. The gentle touch of a paw on your cheek expresses friendship.

Be aware of your cat's body language when training him. It helps you understand his changing moods and makes training fun for you both.

CASTE OF CATS

Cats are essentially loners who tolerate each other *only* after they've worked out a strict social order. This fact was dramatically demonstrated when I decided to add a contingent of more than 100 cats to my stable of animal actors.

The group was a mixed crew I had assembled from all parts of Los Angeles. They varied from streetwise strays from the pound to pampered pets given to me by friends. You can imagine what happened when I put all these guys together in one large pen. Wow! The fur flew!

As hissing turned to snarling and claws began to pop out, I realized that something had to be done fast. Wearing heavy gloves, I divided the angry cats into groups and put them in smaller cages, where I kept them until a certain level of tolerance prevailed.

The first thing I noticed was what appeared to be a concerted hunger strike. Most of the cats seemed to gather themselves up into hunched-up balls of fur and turn off the world.

Because they refused to eat, I started weighing them carefully on an accurate scale. It was strange — their weights were staying almost the same, despite their self-imposed starvation. They were simply drawing into themselves and shutting down, waiting for less traumatic times. They were also working out a very subtle form of "scratching order."

After a few days, signs of this order began to emerge. Dominant members of the group began asserting themselves, and a full set of rules became established for each individual.

As I watched my cats create this complex society, I became fascinated with the minds of these beautiful, intelligent animals. As time went on, I started to establish friendships with several members of the group.

I soon realized that cats are wonderfully sensitive. They have a depth of feeling and capacity for love and loyalty like other animals I've known.

They aren't all good, or even nice, but most are. And then there are some very special ones, like the few irreplaceable best friends you find in your lifetime.

Ray Berwick

TRAINING
BASICS

Chapter 2: Preparing to Train

I'm ready but are you?

Training is based on three important pet needs—hunger, affection and the desire to avoid bad feelings. These same principles apply to household, trick and toilet training.

The rewards in this system of training—food treats, praise and stroking—meet your cat's hunger needs and supply affection. Your cat strives to earn his rewards in order to earn things that make him feel good.

Discipline, on the other hand, creates bad feelings, which your cat seeks to avoid. He performs desired behaviors in order to avoid discipline.

Pushing your cat into training before he is ready can create a serious problem. If he is forced to try to learn a behavior at a time when he is not capable of learning it, he may not be able to acquire that behavior later when the time is right. His bad memories of the first experience make him resist your second attempt at training. For this reason, make sure your cat is ready for each new step that you introduce.

AGE AND SEX

If your cat is too young or too old, training will be difficult. Young kittens want to play and sleep most of the time. Most old cats just want to sleep.

Male and female cats learn with equal ability, but neutered cats learn far faster than unneutered ones.

Age of Kittens—As discussed earlier, kittens younger than 8 weeks should not be adopted. If your kitten is at least 8 weeks old, you can begin his household training as soon as you take him home.

Wait until he is at least 4 months old before you begin his toilet or trick training, however. By that time, your cat has well-developed motor skills. He is large enough to jump on the toilet seat and balance without falling. He is mentally alert and can perform tricks with precision.

Age of Grown Cats—The relationship between age and training was discussed in Chapter 1. New behaviors are usually learned fastest by cats between 1 and 6 years. Older cats may learn more slowly.

Cats who are older than 9 years may be difficult to train. They don't have the agility and eagerness to learn that a younger animal has.

SEX FACTORS

Male and female cats can be trained with equal ease for household behaviors, tricks and toilet usage. Even though their urinary organs are different, both sexes can eliminate their wastes in the bathroom toilet.

Have Him Neutered—If you are going to successfully train your cat, you probably should have him neutered—especially if you are going to toilet train him. An unneutered cat sprays his strong-smelling urine on a vertical target 1 or 2 feet above the floor. The rank, unpleasant odor of cat spray will permeate your bathroom if you share it with an unneutered male or female cat.

Spraying mainly occurs in unneutered males, but some unneutered females and neutered cats of either sex may indulge in spraying activity. If your cat has been neutered at the age of 6 months or younger, he is less likely to spray than a cat who is neutered later in life.

A spraying male cat backs up to a target and raises his tail. His tail trembles as he releases the spray of urine on the target. A female cat sprays in a crouch, with her forelegs down and her hindlegs elevated.

Unneutered cats are also restless and difficult to teach. Males especially are more interested in mating and fighting than in learning new behaviors from you.

Take your cat to the vet for neutering, or call your local animal-control center to ask about county-supported neutering clinics. Some animal-protection groups offer neutering services at substantial discounts. The female neutering operation usually costs about twice as much as the operation for the male.

If your cat is a female, have her neutered between 5 and 6 months of age. If she is older than this when you adopt her, have her neutered as soon as possible.

Neutering requires a surgical incision in her abdomen. Allow the stitches from her operation to heal before you go on to a new step of training. After stitches are removed, your cat's operation won't affect her training progress.

If your cat is male, have him neutered between 6 and 8 months of age. If he is older than this when you adopt him, have him neutered as soon as possible. The neutering operation for males is less complicated than the one for females and requires no abdominal incision or stitches.

Proceed with a male cat's training soon after surgery. His operation won't affect his training progress.

YOUR CAT'S HEALTH

Your cat learns best when he is mentally and physically healthy. It's important to make sure he feels good before you begin his training.

Two of the most common cat health problems are parasites and skin diseases. Because some of these are contagious to people or cause excessive shedding, they are described in this book. Contagious diseases are very important to avoid if you plan on sharing your toilet with your cat.

Diseases that are not contagious to human beings, such as distemper and feline leukemia, are described in detail in any good book on cat care. Acquaint yourself with the symptoms of these serious diseases so you can recognize them if your cat become sick and needs to see the vet.

PARASITES

Your cat must be free of parasites—especially if you choose to toilet train him. Take him to the vet for a parasite check before you begin his training. Parasites cause discomfort that distracts him and seriously impairs his learning ability.

Worms—Cats can be hosts to several types of worms, and some can infect human beings. To determine if your cat is affected, take a fresh sample of one of your cat's bowel movements to your vet. Ask to have it analyzed for worms. If tests show there are worms in the sample, your vet will prescribe medicine to kill them.

Don't try to treat your cat for worms with a commercial worm-killer from a pet shop. Let your vet prescribe the medicine that's most effective against the worms that infest your cat.

If you toilet train your cat, have his bowel movement examined for worms ev-

ery 6 months. This precaution ensures the safety of you and your family.

Toxoplasmosis—This rare, one-celled parasite reproduces in your cat's intestines. At one stage in its life cycle, it can pass out of his body with his bowel movements.

The toxoplasmosis parasite can harm an unborn human baby. For this reason, a pregnant woman should *never* handle dirty cat litter. She should wait until after her baby is born before she begins to toilet train her cat.

Fleas—These tiny, wingless, hopping insects are most common during summer. Your cat picks them up from dogs, wild birds or rodents. Look for them on his head, neck and tail. One type of flea sticks tightly to the skin of the inner ear.

Treat your cat for fleas as soon as you discover them on his coat. Use a flea powder formulated for cats. Place your cat on a newspaper, and apply the flea powder as directed on the package. Don't get powder in his eyes or nose. When finished, burn the newspaper.

If your cat immediately begins to lick the flea powder off his coat, wrap him in a towel and hold him gently for 15 minutes. After the powder has done its work, let him go free.

Sprinkle a small amount of flea powder on your cat's sleeping place. This will kill any flea eggs that may have dropped off his coat. If you let flea eggs hatch, the fleas will invade your entire home. You or a professional exterminator will have to fumigate the rooms with insecticide.

In addition to invading your home, fleas can give your cat tapeworms. Some types carry tiny tapeworm eggs that your cat may swallow after he licks them off his coat.

As soon as you find your cat has fleas,

take one of his bowel movements to your vet for a worm check. Take your cat along so the vet can fit him with a flea-and-tick collar that's safer and more effective than the kind sold in pet stores and supermarkets.

Ticks—Ticks are small, blood-sucking insects with round bodies and large jaws. They are usually brown. In the Rocky Mountain states, one type of tick can give human beings Rocky Mountain spotted fever.

A feeding tick burrows its head and jaws into your cat's body. As it sucks blood, its body swells to several times its normal size.

Don't pull a feeding tick off your cat with your fingers. You may accidentally leave the insect's head inside your cat's body. To remove a tick, dip a cotton swab in rubbing alcohol, and press it against the tick's body. The fumes from the alcohol will drug the insect, causing it to relax its gripping jaws. Use tweezers to gently pull the entire tick from under your cat's skin. Immediately crush it, and flush it down the toilet.

Don't try to remove a large infestation of ticks from your cat. Take him to your vet for treatment, then have him fitted with a flea-and-tick collar.

Lice—If your cat has a dull coat and scratches a lot, he may have lice. Flea powder can usually destroy them. If it doesn't work for your cat, take him to the vet.

Ear Mites—These tiny parasites can cause your cat a great deal of discomfort. He scratches his ears and shakes his head in an effort to get rid of the irritation they cause. Your vet will prescribe medicated ear drops for you to put into your cat's ears each day. Treatment may last for several weeks.

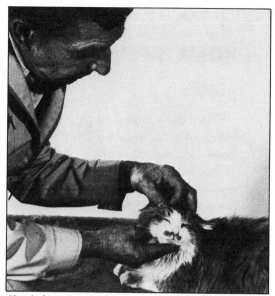

Check for ear mites if cat shakes head or scratches ears often.

SKIN DISEASES

Most cat skin diseases are not contagious to people. Ringworm and scabies are exceptions.

Ringworm—This fungus-caused disease can be hard to diagnose because sometimes infected cats show no lesions. Lesions are scabby, circular, raised patches without hair. Ask your vet to check your cat for ringworm and other fungus infections. Most fungus infections can be cured rapidly with medicine.

Mange—This disease is caused by a tiny mite that burrows under your cat's skin. One type, called *scabies,* can be spread to people.

Hair falls out around the area invaded by the mites. The bald skin patch becomes dry, red and encrusted. Your cat may scratch it frequently.

Take your cat to the vet if you suspect he has mange. All forms of the disease respond to medicine.

Preparing to Train **41**

HOME SWEET HOMES

Illness can cause strange, uncharacteristic behavior in a cat. I learned this from a sweet loyal cat named Winn Strathern, whom I initially mistook as a "love-'em-and-leave-'em" heartbreaker.

The first time I saw Winn, he was lying on the front steps of a house at the end of my block. The name of the street was Strathern. The cross junction was Winnetka, the abbreviation of which became his name.

He was very unusual-looking. He had orange splotches starting at his ears and cropping out at regular intervals down the center of his face. He also sported Fu-Manchu-moustache marks of the same color that started under his nose and ran out of sight on either side of his chin.

Because of my animal-training business, I had an eye for cats, and I was impressed. Winn's bearing and fascinating markings made him stand out. He also projected a certain sense of character that's hard to define — an intangible air of kindness and integrity.

From Winn's size, I was sure he was a male. Most big cats like him spend their time out tomcatting — not sitting docilely on the steps of the same front porch. I assumed his front-porch position meant he was very loyal to his family. I was full of admiration for him.

I was surprised when, on my way to work on a Friday morning, I spotted Winn sitting on the front steps of a house four doors down from the previous one. As I drove by, a man came out the door. Winn greeted him affectionately, brushing back and forth against his leg.

I was puzzled by Winn's strange switch. Every morning he was in position at his new house. His loyalty seemed so strong — he never appeared to move more than a few feet from the front door.

A few days later the mystery deepened. I awoke to see Winn settled on the steps of the house across the street from me, wearing his characteristic contented expression. Dumbfounded by this latest switch, I began to feel disenchanted with the cat. Instead of the faithful animal I had envisioned, he was the most fickle beast I had ever seen!

But a surprising event soon showed me my judgment was too hasty. One morning I was leaving for an early call at the studio. As I walked out to my car, a blur of color in the middle of the street caught my eye. I watched it as it streaked across the road and began to race in circles near the curb.

I stepped closer and saw Winn in a frenzy of incoherent movement. I recognized his plight. He was having what I had learned as a child to call a "running fit."

The cat flew past me, leaped the curb and collapsed on my front lawn. As I kneeled over him and rubbed his head, his muscles gradually started to relax. He lay still for a few seconds, then opened his eyes and looked up at me with a sort of worshipful expression. Struggling to his feet, Winn gazed around my yard as if he needed orientation. Then he walked slowly and a little unsteadily up to my front door, where he settled down exactly as I had seen him at his previous temporary homes. I offered to let him in the house, but he refused. So I left him at the door and went to work.

On the way to the studio, I pondered Winn's problem. Perhaps he had epilepsy. The rest seemed fairly obvious. He evidently had some sort of memory loss after his seizures and felt wherever he recovered was his home.

He was faithfully awaiting me when I got home from work, so I took him to the vet for an examination. Winn's problem turned out to be a small, treatable brain tumor. It was safely removed. When I brought him home 2 weeks later, he was a new cat. Most importantly, he now had a home that could be permanent.

Winn decided to accept my invitation to live in the house. Once he got used to the idea of indoor life, his affection grew by leaps and bounds. He made me feel like some sort of superbeing by his constant show of gratitude.

I soon gave Winn a part on "The Rockford Files" and used him on two other series in quick succession. He was a big hit each time, and by now was one of my most reliable animal partners. He went on to appear in many other productions, including "Little House on the Prairie" and a feature film called "Beast Master."

Winn is with me still. He has repaid me many times with affection and gratitude for the small effort of taking him to the doctor.

Remember Winn. If your cat ever begins to exhibit strange behavior, don't hesitate to take him to the vet — your action may save his life.

Ray Berwick

Daily grooming prevents a variety of problems.

Other Skin Diseases—Eczema, dry skin and baldness are other skin diseases that may affect your cat. They are usually caused by a hot, dry environment, poor diet, allergies, aging or hormonal disturbances.

All these conditions involve the flaking of dry particles of skin. Your cat scratches the dry areas, and scratching causes inflammation and infection.

Your vet can advise you about changes in diet and environment to help cure your cat's skin condition. He or she will show you how to brush your cat's coat to stimulate oil glands. In some cases, medication may be necessary.

DAILY GROOMING

Grooming is essential to your cat's good health. Daily grooming keeps your cat's coat smooth and shiny. It keeps cat hairs from collecting on clothes and furniture.

When grooming your cat, check him for health problems. Inspect the areas around his eyes and ears for parasites. Separate his coat with a fine-tooth comb to look for skin diseases. Check the area around his rectum for tapeworm segments. If you detect problems early, you can keep them from becoming serious.

Daily grooming prevents your cat from getting hairballs of swallowed hair. Hairballs can cause constipation.

Where and When—Groom your cat while he's relaxing on a bed or sofa, or put him on a table or dresser and brush him standing up.

Grooming your cat in your lap while you are watching television can be pleasant for you and your cat. Put a towel on your legs to catch loose hairs.

If you groom your cat at a specific time of day, he'll look forward to his daily grooming sessions. He may meow for you to get the brush and comb if you are late.

If your cat resists grooming at first, groom him in several short sessions instead of a long one. Stop grooming if he begins to claw, bite or complain. If you are patient and persistent, he'll soon enjoy his grooming sessions.

Groom kittens for at least 2 minutes each day. Grooming sessions for grown cats should last at least 5 minutes. If your cat has long hair, you'll have to spend 10 to 15 minutes on his grooming each day.

Grooming Tools—Your most important grooming tool is a good brush. A man's natural-bristle hairbrush is excellent for a short-haired cat's coat. So is a natural-bristle cat brush. These are available in your pet store.

Long-haired cats require brushes with long, firm bristles. Rubber or plastic bristle brushes may be better for long-haired cats than natural-bristle ones.

Some cat brushes come with soft bristles on one side and stiff bristles on the other. Use the soft side for grooming tender areas, such as the stomach, and use the stiff side for grooming your cat's back and flanks.

Metal cat combs are available in pet stores. Buy one with medium-fine teeth for removing loose hairs. Buy another with very fine teeth for inspecting your cat's skin and removing fleas. Long-haired cats need several sizes of combs.

Other cat-grooming aids include a chamois, special claw clippers, cotton swabs, cotton balls, baby oil, petroleum jelly and scissors. Some cats don't mind if you use a vacuum cleaner to remove loose hair from their coats between grooming sessions.

Brushing and Combing—Brush your cat's coat in the direction the hair grows. For most of his body, this is downward, but you can use an upward motion on his chest and chin.

Gently brush your cat's head and stomach. Brush more vigorously on his back, flanks and tail. Work on a small area of your cat's body at a time. Clean accumulated hair from the brush before you proceed to each new area.

Combing follows brushing. Use the comb in a slanted position, and clean it frequently. Don't try to comb through mats and snarls. Stop and untangle them with your fingers.

After you brush and comb your cat, you may want to rub his coat with a chamois to bring out the shine. If you don't have a chamois, stroke your cat gently with the palms of your hands. If you wish, lubricate your palms with a drop of baby oil.

Eyes, Ears and Rectum—Some cats have a watery discharge from their eyes. This may be caused by infection or it may be normal tearing. Take your cat to the vet if his eye discharge is dark or puslike.

Remove normal eye discharge with a cotton swab dipped in warm water. You may have to have someone hold your cat's head to prevent him from resisting treatment.

Gently clean dirt and wax from your cat's ears with a swab dipped in baby oil or petroleum jelly. *Don't put the swab into your cat's delicate inner ear.*

To trim claws, unsheath them by pressing pads.

Your cat may sometimes have bowel-movement residue around his rectum after he eliminates. Clean this with a cotton ball dipped in warm water. If his rectum is red, apply a small amount of petroleum jelly. If the condition persists, report it to your vet.

Claws—Every 3 or 4 weeks, you may have to trim your cat's claws. It's best to have a helper. He or she can hold your cat's hind legs while you trim his front claws, then hold his front legs while you trim his back ones.

Unsheath the claws on your cat's paw by gently pressing the pads with your fingers. Look for the vein that extends halfway up each claw. The vein ends in a pink line that is the quick of the claw. If you cut the quick, it will bleed.

Use small cat-claw clippers to trim each claw slightly in front of the quick. Don't forget the high claw on the side of each front foot.

If you feel uncomfortable about trimming your cat's claws, take him to a professional cat groomer or a vet. Your cat may sense your uneasiness and become frightened and nervous. He may jerk his paw and scratch you or cause you to accidentally cut the quick.

TRAINING DECISIONS

Before you begin to train your cat, you should outline a training plan. You should set training goals and decide exactly how you want to achieve them. The section that follows gives you a range of possible training goals and provides guidelines on how to make training decisions.

WHO SHOULD TRAIN?

The people around you should help, not hinder, your cat's program. Before you start any type of training, be sure the people who are close to you understand what you are doing. Let them know you are serious.

Explain to friends and family that during the next few weeks or months your cat's training may take a lot of your time. Assure them you aren't deliberately neglecting them—you are temporarily preoccupied.

Some members of your household may want to help with training. Encourage them to become involved if they are mature and like cats.

How Many Trainers?—Cat training is most effective when only one or two trainers are involved. Trainers become familiar with a cat's personal ways of communicat-

Training is usually best on a one-to-one basis.

ing and anticipate his positive and negative reactions. They learn the methods that work best with a particular animal.

With the exception of some basic behaviors and tricks that require two trainers working together, conduct most of your cat's training on a one-to-one basis. Conduct sessions in a place where you or another trainer can be alone with the cat.

As owner, you are the most effective trainer. Your cat strives to perform well because he loves you. A family member or roommate can help in training if he or she is loved and trusted by your cat. Plan together before scheduling daily training sessions so your cat doesn't become overworked by two trainers.

Unqualified Trainers—Don't let young children help with training. They may tease the cat or cause him to become over-

Start leash training when your cat has been in your home 1 week.

excited. They don't have the maturity to consistently follow the instructions for teaching each step.

Don't let people who dislike or fear cats help with training. Your cat can sense their negative feelings. He won't learn unless he feels surrounded by affection.

Remember Your Vet—Don't overlook your veterinarian as a valuable source of information and advice about cat training. Your vet is well-informed. He or she will probably be encouraging and helpful about training.

Some veterinarians have made pet psychology their specialty and have taken courses in animal behavior. You may want to select one of these specialists as a vet for your cat.

Negative Attitudes—You'll encounter people who insist you are wasting your time training a cat. They are strong believers in the old-fashioned idea that a cat is too wild and independent to learn new behaviors from people.

While general training and trick training are not as difficult as toilet training, all require determination and patience to produce successful results. Don't let the negative attitudes of misinformed people discourage your cat-training program.

WHAT TO TEACH

Before you decide what to teach, you must evaluate your available time and level of patience. Your training program can be as simple as teaching your cat not to eat house plants, or as elaborate as teaching your cat to do tricks like a circus star. It all depends on what you want.

Household Training—This type of training begins the day your cat enters your home. First, you establish desired behaviors, such as using a scratching post. At the same time, you stop unwanted behaviors, such as clawing furniture.

It's a good idea to complete your cat's household training *before* you begin trick or toilet training. You avoid confusing him with rewards and corrective discipline for too many different behaviors at the same time.

Leash Training—Begin to teach this important behavior after your cat has spent 1 week in your home. By this time, he has adjusted to his new environment and is ready to cope with the strangeness of the leash.

By learning to obediently follow you, your cat builds a foundation for future training. He begins to understand the principle of performing on command.

When your cat has learned to lead on a leash, he can enjoy the outdoors, safe from traffic and predators. You will develop your friendship as you take long walks together.

Other Basic Behaviors—Other desirable behaviors consist of coming when called and entering a portable kennel on command. You can begin to teach these immediately after you adopt your cat.

The habit of obediently responding to a call helps make your cat an enjoyable companion. You won't have to hunt for him all over the house—he'll come running when you want him. If you let him go outside, you can call him, even from a distance of several blocks.

Trick Training—If your main goal is to teach your cat to perform a collection of entertaining tricks, proceed to trick training as soon as you have taught him his basic behaviors and established desirable household routines. Be sure to read *all* of Chapters 7 and 8 before you begin.

Your cat may have limited learning ability. If this is the case, he may not be able to acquire many new trick behaviors. For this reason, it's important to read through the entire discussion of tricks, and make notes regarding what tricks you want your cat to learn. Teach these tricks first so your cat will acquire them before he reaches his learning limits.

Toilet Training—Chapters 4, 5 and 6 of this book are devoted to toilet training. Some people don't want to share their toilets with their cats. If you feel this way, don't read this section.

Many people are anxious to toilet train their cats because it saves money and reduces smell and mess. If you decide to toilet train, make sure your cat first acquires the three basic behaviors—coming when called, kennel training and leading on a leash. Also be sure that desirable household routines are well-established.

Decide whether you want to teach your cat to perform tricks before or after you toilet train him. *Don't try to teach tricks and toilet training at the same time!* Toilet training is difficult to accomplish if you are teaching other new behaviors. If you attempt this, you will confuse your cat.

You must also make a decision regarding the type of toilet training you want to undertake. It will probably be easy to train

Speak softly and approvingly to your cat to reward him with affection.

your cat to urinate in the toilet. Most cats are quite comfortable urinating perched on the toilet seat. To make toilet training brief and simple, you may decide to set your training goal for urination only.

Most cats initially resist having bowel movements in the toilet. They feel uncomfortable having bowel movements, which require a rear thrusting motion, while perched on the toilet seat. Most cats get over this discomfort, however. Once they establish this behavior, the convenience makes your training efforts seem worthwhile. If your cat easily learns to urinate in the toilet, consider continuing his training until he accepts the toilet for bowel movements.

TRAINING BASICS

To get your cat to do the things you want him to do, you reward him with stroking and special food treats. To stop him from doing things that are forbidden, you use negative cues that make him feel bad.

If you encounter training problems that are not specifically covered in this book, remember these training basics. These principles, along with your own common sense, will help you solve your unique cat-training problems.

REWARD OF STROKING

Your cat is independent and practical by nature. He sees no point in performing an action on cue unless he knows he will receive a reward. Because stroking is one of the rewards he loves best, you incorporate it into your training program.

What Happens—Your cat's body is built to allow him to enjoy being stroked. Every hair in his coat is surrounded by tiny nerve endings. When these nerve endings are stimulated by stroking, they convey a sensation of pleasure to his brain.

When you stroke your cat, his entire body relaxes. He purrs in contentment and may begin to drool. His digestive system is often stimulated by stroking.

Techniques—You and your cat will devise your own favorite ways of stroking. To increase your cat's enjoyment, stroke his coat smoothly downward in the direction his fur grows. Don't ruffle his fur. Scratch your cat on his ears. Gently stroke his nose in an upward direction with your index finger.

Speak softly to your cat as you hold him in your lap to scratch and stroke him. Call him by name. Let him know that you love him.

Scent Marking—You may have noticed

that your cat sometimes rubs his cheeks, forehead and tail against your body. He often purrs as he does this. Sometimes he rubs against door frames and furniture.

Your cat's rubbing is a type of scent marking. Tiny glands in the skin of his cheeks, forehead and tail convey his personal aroma to you and the objects he rubs against. You can't smell the aroma, but he can. It probably helps him feel comfortable with the people and objects he marks.

When stroking your cat, scratch him on his cheeks and forehead. Gently stroke his tail in the direction the hair grows. Allow his scent glands to transfer his personal aroma to you.

Wrestling Response—Your cat may roll over on his back while you stroke him. Unlike a dog, he probably isn't asking you to scratch his stomach—more likely he is inviting you to play with him. The play he has in mind is a form of wrestling—he indulged in this kind of wrestling with his litter mates.

Don't stroke or scratch your cat's stomach if you see it triggers the wrestling response. Encouraging unruly behavior detracts from your effectiveness as a trainer.

REWARD OF FOOD

Strictly scheduled feedings are significant in all types of training. To teach your cat new behaviors, you must be able to control his level of hunger.

Control Feedings—Unlike dogs, cats don't have an inherited desire to serve their owners. They usually show no interest in performing any unnecessary behavior unless they're hungry enough to want to earn a food reward.

Never set out a large serving of food for your cat to eat any time he wishes. This can result in several serious training problems.

Cats who try to get into food cupboard may need larger meals.

Cats who have access to a bottomless bowl of food often become lazy and listless. They have nothing to anticipate in their day and show little interest in learning new behaviors. They also frequently become overweight, a condition that can threaten their health.

Kittens need multiple feedings to nourish their rapid growth. Contrary to the advice of many cat-care books and vets, a healthy 1-year-old cat (or older), can get by well on *one good feeding a day.*

A cat who eats one meal a day is usually easy to train because he's anxious to earn food rewards. He stays vigorous and lean and will probably live much longer than a cat who eats three meals a day. His training rewards satisfy his natural nibbling instinct.

You don't want to starve your cat, so use good judgment about feedings. If he meows at his eating place or tries to get into the food cupboard, he may be trying to tell you he needs a supplemental feeding. If your cat demands a second feeding, offer it on a regular basis. Portion sizes and feeding times are discussed in detail on pages 97 and 98.

Types of Food Rewards—An effective food reward has three qualities. First, it is soft and easy to eat, so your cat won't be distracted from what you are trying to teach him. Second, it is not part of your cat's regular mealtime diet, so he understands it's a special treat for training. Third, your cat must enjoy its taste so he'll be anxious to earn it.

Pet stores carry a wide variety of soft treats made to appeal to the taste of cats. They range from milk-flavored drops to moist liver nuggets.

Commercially prepared cat treats are appealing to your cat and convenient for you. But they can be harmful if offered in excessive amounts. If you want to use commercial treats, cut them into small tidbits.

Professional trainers often cook tiny balls of hamburger or ground horsemeat. They bake them in big batches and freeze them. If your cat doesn't appear to like these meatballs, flavor them with garlic or onion powder.

Small pieces of fresh shrimp, fish, cheese or meat also make good training treats. Chicken, turkey, beef and liver are meats that cats like best. Some cats enjoy tiny morsels of hot dogs, which are convenient and easy to prepare.

Don't use canned tuna, salmon or mackerel to reward your cat. No matter how careful you are, these products flake into tiny, unmanageable pieces. The aroma gets on your hands, so your cat can't tell the fish from your finger. Many cat bites result from the mistake of using canned fish products as training rewards.

Be Consistent—When you find the treat your cat likes best, offer him *that treat only* during training. Don't substitute leftovers of a different variety.

You may make an exception to this rule if your cat begins to show a lack of interest in his food rewards. He may get bored with the same type of treat. Experiment with different treats until you find one he likes, then offer that treat only for the rest of training.

Your cat performs a requested action to earn a specific type of treat. Frequent substitutions can confuse and disappoint him.

Prepare Treats in Advance—For convenience, cook enough food rewards to last your cat at least 1 week. The size of a week's supply of treats will vary according to the step of training your cat has reached at the time.

Cut perishable cooked treats into small pieces. Treats used for household training and toilet training should be no larger than a quarter of a mouthful. For most cats, this is about 1/4 inch square. Treats used for trick training should be smaller—only about 1/8 inch square.

Store cooked, precut treats in plastic sandwich bags in your freezer. Put a bag in the lower part of the refrigerator each evening so it can defrost overnight. By morning, treats will be fresh and ready to offer as rewards.

How to Offer Food Rewards—Many people think they can offer their cat food rewards from their outstretched fingers. *This is a dangerous practice that can result in unintentional cat bites!*

No matter how sweet-tempered your cat

Avoid cat bites by offering rewards from top of inverted can.

can be, he may become overanxious to get his treat and bite your finger by mistake. When you try to pull it from his mouth, he will probably clamp down harder because he thinks you are trying to take away his reward. You may need the help of a second person to pry his clamped jaws from your finger.

Cat bites can penetrate to the bone. They often result in deep puncture wounds that get infected. An experience with a serious cat bite is described on page 60.

Avoid bad experiences by offering your cat his rewards on top of an inverted empty tin can. Flat cat-food cans are good for this purpose.

Put the can under your cat's nose, and let him eat his reward. He can easily see it on the shiny tin surface, no matter how small the treat may be. During trick training, your cat will be working on the training table. In this case, you can set the can beside your cat on the table, and allow him to help himself to his reward.

Catnip—Our system of training does *not* include using catnip as a regular reward. Catnip contains a chemical that makes some cats feel relaxed and happy. They roll

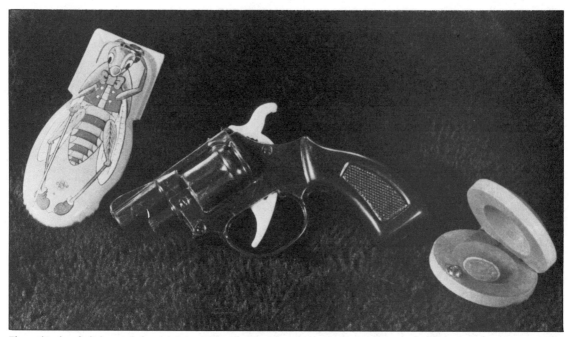

Three kinds of clickers: *(left to right)* cricket, clicking toy gun and castanet.

their bodies and purr in delight. Some full-grown cats play like kittens under the influence of catnip and may appear intoxicated.

The mood-altering properties of catnip interfere with training. You want your cat to learn new behaviors in a normal frame of mind. Save catnip treats for after his training sessions.

TRAINING CUES

Cats are very sensitive to sound. They react to sound cues more readily than to visual cues. To speed up training, you need a good noise-making training aid to use with other visual or verbal cues.

Clicker—The most important cue in cat training is a little noisemaker or *clicker.* Often called a *cricket,* it makes a sharp double-clicking sound that immediately catches your cat's attention.

Your cat soon learns to associate the sound of the clicker with the new behavior you teach him. He also learns the sharp double click is often followed by a food reward.

You can buy toy clickers at most party-supply stores. If you can't find one, look in the phone directory of a nearby city. Most stores take mail orders if you send the proper postage.

You may have to buy a dozen to get one clicker. They are inexpensive — a dozen usually costs less than $5.

CLICK, CLICK—THE SOUND OF SUCCESS

When I first decided to train cats for the movies, I got lots of discouragement from people who assured me that cats could not be trained. Luckily, I refused to believe that tired old bias. Even more luckily, I discovered the value of a simple little training tool that would help me shatter the old myth about cat training.

The tool was a small metal toy called a *clicker,* or cricket. I had long used this little noisemaker in training birds and other highly sound-sensitive animals. It seemed logical that it would work for training super-hearing cats.

The cat I chose to train was a 10-year-old orange male named Hot Rod. He was aggressive, energetic and super intelligent.

We began without the clicker. I stood in front of Hot Rod as he sat on the training table. With nothing more than a raised hand and a low hiss, I was able to cue him into place. Within 5 minutes, I could make him sit and stay by giving him these cues from any place in the room.

Now was the time to experiment with the clicker. I stood in front of Hot Rod as he sat on the table. I cut off small bites of a hot dog, clicked the clicker and offered him a tidbit. It took only three bites before he understood the clicker meant goodies.

Now came the big test. With Hot Rod still on the training table, I walked to the far side of the room. As he prepared to jump down, I hissed—and he froze. After 30 seconds, I clicked the clicker, and he catapulted toward me! What a simple way to teach a cat to come!

I was thrilled by Hot Rod's performance—and all my cats learned to respond to it almost as fast as he did. Before long that sharp little clicking sound would bring them running from all directions—whether they were hungry or not.

The clicker's effectiveness was especially dramatic in a movie with an outdoor cat mob scene. More than 100 cats were to chase an actor toward the camera. Standing behind the camera, I simply clicked the clicker—and the actor had all he could do to stay ahead of the cats!

Ray Berwick

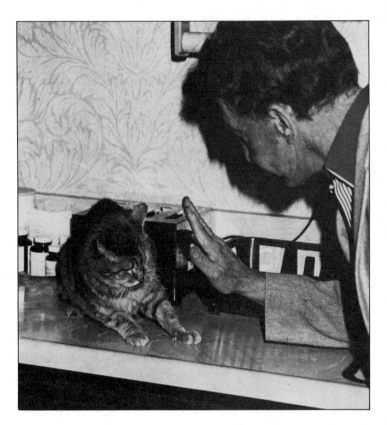

Negative cues include hiss and face-push.

If you can't find any place to buy a clicker, you can imitate the noisemaker's sharp double-click with a castanet from a store that sells musical instruments. You may have to buy a pair to get one castanet. They cost more than toy clickers.

If you can't find a castanet, browse through a toy department. Purchase any inexpensive metal or plastic toy that makes a sharp double-clicking sound.

Visual and Verbal Cues—During trick training, you use both visual and verbal cues. These are "show-off" cues that you use to demonstrate to an audience that you and your cat have a special form of communication.

In addition to the clicker, you use a different verbal and visual cue to demand each new behavior from your cat. For example, when you cue him to wave bye-bye, you say "bye-bye" and wave your hand. Gradually you phase out the sound of the clicker and use only verbal and visual cues to demand trick behaviors from your cat.

Negative Cues—Negative cues are used during training for the sit-and-stay behavior and for corrective discipline. They include a hiss, a push in the face, a flip on the nose and a firm *"No!"* Negative cues are discussed in detail in the section that follows.

BASIC CORRECTIVE TECHNIQUES

You can let your cat know that he is doing something you don't like by using negative cues. Because these cues make your cat feel bad, he stops performing the undesired behavior in order to avoid bad feelings.

The bad feelings that come from negative cues are not so strong that your cat resents them, however. Stronger measures that produce resentment can interfere with training.

No Pain or Humiliation—Severe physical punishment for cats is impractical and unnecessary. This basic principle cannot be overemphasized.

Your cat is a dignified animal who resents physical punishment. At first he may express his resentment by eliminating his wastes in inappropriate places. If you continue to punish him physically, he may run from you. In either case, your bond of friendship is broken, and training becomes almost impossible.

Imitate Mother Cat—When your cat does something you don't want him to do, immediately discipline him the same way his mother did when he was little. First hiss at him loudly. Hissing is a sound he instinctively understands. He does it himself when he's angry or threatening another animal.

If you can reach your cat before he runs away, imitate his mother in another way. Without stopping your angry hissing, place the flat of your palm in his face and give him a firm, but gentle, push. If days go by and your cat continues to perform the unwanted behavior, make the pushes a little stronger. *Always stop before the pressure of your hand becomes rough or painful!*

After a few seconds of pushing your hand in his face, flip your index finger on his nose. This isn't harsh or painful—it's a light little rebuke that imitates the way a mother cat disciplines a kitten with her paw.

Stop hissing immediately after the nose-flip. Firmly say *"No!"* This lets him know how unhappy you are with what he has done.

Discipline with Sharp Sounds—Sharp sounds are handy when you can't reach your cat to give him an immediate face-push and nose-flip. While your cat is on the run, hiss and say *"No!"* He soon learns the meaning of the word and stops what he's doing when he hears it.

A stronger disciplinary noise is the smack of a rolled-up section of newspaper against your palm. Reinforce the sound of the slap with your usual loud hiss.

Get as close to your cat as possible to make the slap with the paper, but don't use it for anything but sound effect. *Even when you are angry, physical punishment is not an effective way to train a cat.*

A variety of startling sounds can be used to train your cat to stay away from a specific place or piece of furniture. They are discussed in detail in Chapter 3.

Allow Him to Run—If disciplinary measures send your cat running from the scene, don't try to restrain him. His urge to run is part of his natural desire to avoid discomfort. It shows you he understands he has done something that results in bad feelings.

Stroke and Make Up—Your cat may want to be alone for a while after you discipline him. He may groom himself in what may be an effort to distract attention from his recent embarrassment.

When your cat finishes his isolation or grooming, stroke him gently and call him by name. This should occur within 10 minutes after you have administered the discipline. It's important to let your cat know you are unhappy with his actions, not his personality.

TIMING FACTORS

Discipline works best when administered immediately after your cat performs an unwanted behavior. If you delay even a moment, he may not understand what he has done to cause the discipline.

In the case of an unwanted household habit, such as scratching furniture or jumping on counters, you may have to hide and wait for your cat to perform the behavior. This may be time-consuming, but it's worth it. Your cat may never learn to break a bad habit if he isn't caught in the act and immediately disciplined.

Delayed Discipline—Sometimes you discover the result of an unwanted behavior after your cat has performed it. You see a misplaced bowel movement, for example, or a badly scratched armchair.

Delayed discipline is not as effective as immediate discipline. In fact, most animal-behavior specialists believe it has no effect at all.

Because you won't be using harsh techniques, you can administer delayed discipline if you want. Carry your cat to the place where he has performed the unwanted behavior. Discipline him as if he had just performed the act. However, remember that delayed discipline is unlikely to have much effect on your cat's future behavior.

SPECIAL TRAINING SITUATIONS

Some situations require special attention. At first they may pose a difficult challenge, but the challenge often can be turned into an advantage. Double-cat training is a good example. Although it can be difficult to train two cats together, one

Two cats can learn by watching each other.

cat may learn by watching another.

More than One Cat—You may want to acquire two kittens so the animals can play together, or you may already have several grown cats living in your home.

It is possible to train two or more cats at the same time. Conduct training sessions that include the introduction of a new behavior with each cat on a one-to-one basis. After the new behavior has been learned, do most behavior-review sessions one-to-one. But occasionally it's fun and helpful to review cats together.

During toilet training, keep all the cats you are training on the same feeding schedule. This will give them similar

Training techniques for dogs and cats are different.

elimination patterns.

It often helps to have a training partner when training two or more cats. This type of training is difficult, and a helper is often the key to success.

Training Dogs—Some people think they can use our methods to train a dog. While the methods may produce some success, they won't be as effective as techniques developed specifically for dog training.

Cats and dogs possess different sets of inherited personality traits. These differences call for different training methods. Don't try to use the training tech-

---

HOLLYWOOD CAT TALES

LIGHTS, CAMERA, OUCH!

Cats have been domesticated much less time than dogs. As long as they are not declawed, they are perfectly capable of surviving on their own in the wild. Their instincts to be possessive of their food are strong—a fact that I learned from a beautiful gray cat named Silver.

Long-haired and elegant, Silver was the picture of languid grace. He seemed every inch an aristocrat, incapable of wild behavior.

I learned quite the contrary one afternoon on a film shoot that required Silver to race along a sidewalk and duck into a store entrance.

Working even a single animal in a movie nearly always requires two people—one to handle the animal at the release point and another to call or cue him. An assistant trainer and Silver were at the corner of the block—the release point—and I was situated for cueing in a dark entryway down the street.

The director shouted "Action!" and I began clicking the clicker to cue Silver. As expected, he came bounding along the sidewalk toward the sound. He scooted to a stop. His ears told him the sound was coming from the dark area inside the entrance.

One leap and Silver was in front of me, nipping to get at the luscious hot dog I held as a reward. But instead of the hot dog, the cat clamped down on the third finger of my right hand.

When I started to yank it away, his sharp teeth immediately pierced all the way to the bone. I tried to pry his jaws apart, but it was no use. Silver was single-minded. In his view he had his food reward—my finger—and no one was going to separate him from it. My assistant trainer finally arrived. Between the two of us, we managed to pull his teeth from my finger.

I had been chewed on by dogs, raccoons, lions and bears, but never had I

---

niques in this book on your dog.

People often ask if they can train their dogs to use the toilet. The answer is "No!" Dogs don't have the agility to balance comfortably on the toilet seat. They don't have the strong natural instinct to scratch in the dirt to bury their wastes.

Some dogs occasionally scratch a small amount of dirt when they eliminate. This may be an effort to mark their territory. You can modify this scratching behavior to train a small dog to use an indoor litter box. Use the reward techniques outlined in a good dog-training manual.

experienced anything quite as painful as this cat bite. Surprisingly, there was little bleeding, even though I had felt Silver's fangs grind against bone. The punctures closed almost immediately. Eventually an infection developed in my arm.

Thanks to antibiotics, I recovered from Silver's bite, and I continued to work with him until the end of the shoot. After all—the bite had not been the cat's fault—he was only following his instinct to protect his food.

If anyone was at fault in the incident, it was I. I should have known better than to feed a cat from my hand in a dark entryway—especially since the food was a finger-shaped hot dog.

From then on, I always rewarded my cats from the top of an empty cat-food can. And I substituted cooked liver or horsemeat for hot dogs—a move that I'm sure has saved me from many a cat bite since.

Ray Berwick

BEHAVIOR TRAINING

Chapter 3:
Changing Your
Cat's Behavior

This chapter concentrates on ways you can make your cat a cooperative member of your household. The importance of such training cannot be overemphasized. A lack of it can undermine the quality of the friendship between you and your cat.

If you come home to find deep scratch marks on a favorite leather armchair, you feel very angry. But without behavior training, your cat doesn't know why you are angry with him. His confusion about your anger makes him draw away from you.

Use the tools and techniques described in this section to stop your cat from forming ingrained bad habits.

DEVICES TO CHANGE UNDESIRABLE BEHAVIORS

You have three options to use in trying to change or control your cat's undesirable behaviors: corrective discipline, which was discussed in Chapter 2; cat repellents; and protective measures.

Before you read this chapter, be sure to refresh your memory regarding basic corrective-discipline techniques. These are the hiss, face push and nose flip. Corrective discipline is an important way to change undesirable behavior. It lets your cat know he is doing something you don't want him to do.

Use the other two devices, cat repellents and protective measures, only when corrective discipline fails. If one week of regular discipline does not stop your cat from performing an undesirable behavior, it is time to try the techniques described below.

CAT REPELLENTS

Only four types of cat repellents are recommended—chemical preparations, bad-tasting substances, water from a squirt gun and noise-making devices.

Chemical Preparations—Pet shops sell chemical preparations that are specially formulated to repel cats. You can smell the unpleasant odor immediately upon application, but it soon becomes detectable only to your cat. Most chemical cat repellents come in aerosol cans and are fairly expensive.

Mothballs and vinegar are sometimes used as cat repellents, but we do not recommend them. Although they are less expensive than commercial preparations, they have unpleasant odors that linger for a long time. Further, if your cat eats moth-

balls or vinegar, it can make him sick. For these reasons, these substances are not good cat repellents.

Bad-Tasting Substances—Bitter or hot-tasting substances can be smeared on household items, such as electrical cords, to prevent chewing. The bad taste of the substance makes your cat want to leave it alone.

Some pet-supply stores sell a substance called *Bitter Apple®* that is used to keep pets from chewing dangerous things. Other bitter-tasting substances for people are sold across the counter in pharmacies for use in preventing nail-biting or thumb-sucking. Most cats seem to dislike bitter substances as much as people do.

If you are using the substance on a stainable surface, test the substance first to see if it stains. Smear a small amount on an unexposed place on the surface you want to protect. If the substance stains, choose another type of cat repellent.

Hot-pepper sauce is another bad-tasting substance that most cats dislike. Its use may seem cruel, because it can cause tongue-tingling and tears. However, one lick is usually enough for most cats, so the discomfort is brief.

Grocery stores sell several brands of Mexican-style and Louisiana-style hot sauce. Choose one that does not contain chopped onions and chilies. Some brands contain stabilizers that make them stickier, so they adhere well to surfaces. All brands of hot-pepper sauce stain, so don't use them on furniture, clothing or other stainable items.

Noise-Making Devices—You can use noisemakers to startle your cat so he runs away from a forbidden place. Noise-making devices can be as simple as strings of tin cans that clang or balloons that pop.

Behavior training makes your cat more lovable.
Courtesy of Pets Are Wonderful Council.

Hot sauce can deter your cat from chewing electrical cords.

Use your imagination to create other devices that make a loud noise when your cat sets them off. *Make sure they cannot injure him in any way!*

Water—This common cat repellent is often squirted from a toy water pistol. If your cat is a water-hater, a thin stream of squirted water may prove to be effective in keeping him away from a forbidden place. Only a few squirts may convince him that it's a spot he wants to avoid.

But some cats are water-lovers. These cats actually seem to enjoy getting wet. If your cat is one of these, a thin stream of water shot from a pistol may have little or no effect on his household behavior.

Find out your cat's attitude toward water by squirting him with a toy pistol whenever he is in a forbidden place. Continue to do this for at least 1 week. If he does not run from the squirtings or if he continues to frequent the forbidden place, choose another type of cat repellent.

Some people become determined to repel their cats with water. Instead of squirting a thin stream from a pistol, they douse large quantities of water on their pets from a garden hose or a pitcher. Sometimes they rig booby traps by precariously balancing water-filled tin cans in forbidden places. When their cats venture into those places, they upset the cans and douse themselves.

Such heavy dousings are frequently successful as cat repellents. But they can make a mess in your home and damage carpets and furniture. Dousings also can have bad psychological effects on your cat. They can make him feel nervous and insecure in your home. They can interfere with toilet training by giving him negative feelings about the water-filled bathroom toilet.

To prevent water damage to your home and to avoid bad psychological effects in your cat, don't use dousing as a cat repellent. Use water only if your cat hates it so much that he consistently avoids places where he's been squirted with a pistol.

Snapping Devices—Some people use mousetraps or other snapping devices to scare cats away from a specific area. Others shoot rubber bands or similar missiles when they catch their cats in the act of performing an unwanted behavior. Snapping devices can seriously injure a cat's tender nose or paws. Even rubber bands can inflict enough pain to make him feel insecure in your home. If you want to keep your cat's friendship, *never* use any type of snapping device in his training program!

Store breakables until cat stops climbing habits.

PROTECTIVE MEASURES

Use protective measures to stop problems before they arise. Protective measures include closed doors and covers or barriers to block your cat's access to things he can damage. These are excellent alternatives to corrective discipline when you cannot be present.

When you are present to administer discipline, eliminate the protective measures. Discipline your cat to teach him that his destructive acts are not acceptable in your household.

Closed Doors—One of the simplest protective measures is a closed door. If your cat is engaging in destructive activities in a certain room, close the room off to him during the night and when you are away.

When you are awake and at home, open the door. Watch your cat closely when he enters the room. As soon as you catch him in the act of performing his destructive behavior, immediately administer corrective discipline, as discussed on pages 56 to 58. In a short time, he will understand the behavior is forbidden, and you can stop closing the door.

Covers and Barriers—If you don't have a door that can be closed, use covers or barriers instead. Make them temporary and simple, so you can easily remove them. Do this when you can watch and catch your cat as he begins a destructive act. Administer corrective discipline immediately to let him know he's doing something you don't want him to do.

An inverted cardboard box can protect an area of floor. Inverted boxes also can cover breakable items on shelves, mantles and counters.

If your cat continues to damage breakables despite barriers, remove and store valuable items until you can train your cat to stay away from forbidden places. Kittens who jump on mantles and shelves often stop this habit on their own when they grow up.

The soil in potted plants can be protected with a window-screen shield cut to fit the pot and plant stem. Foliage can be covered with a loose sack of bird netting or nylon net from a fabric shop.

Drape a king-size sheet over any piece of furniture that has been the target of your cat's scratching. If he pulls it off, anchor the sheet with a Chinese jump rope. This long loop of elasticized cord can be bought in any toy department.

Use your imagination to employ other common household items to protect anything your cat may be damaging. Remove them when you are at home and awake. You want to catch your cat and administer corrective discipline when you see him performing a destructive act.

HOW TO ELIMINATE UNDESIRABLE BEHAVIORS

Because each cat is an individual, each develops his own set of behaviors—both desirable and undesirable. This section focuses on undesirable behaviors and offers suggestions to eliminate them.

The most common undesirable behaviors are: going into forbidden places, indulging in irritating personal habits, and showing aggression toward people and other animals. These are not all the undesirable behaviors a cat can exhibit, but the methods for changing them can be adapted for other undesirable behaviors.

If your cat has a behavior problem that is not discussed here, use what you have learned about basic techniques of animal training to eliminate the problem. Use corrective discipline and other strategies for changing undesirable behaviors. Reward desired behaviors with the clicker, a food treat and lots of love.

The following discussion of common behavior problems should give you good ideas about how to solve special problems that are unique to your cat.

FORBIDDEN PLACES

Use your imagination and common sense to combine cat repellents, protective devices and corrective discipline to keep your cat away from forbidden places.

Garbage Containers—The smells from a garbage container can be irresistible to a cat. Balloons are effective repellents to stop your cat from rooting through the garbage. Smear them with his favorite food so he is sure to pop them with his teeth or claws. When you are at home, reinforce the startling balloon pop with a hiss, a face-push, a nose-flip and a firm *"No!"*

Try smearing a bitter or hot-tasting substance on food in the garbage container. As soon as your cat takes a bite of it, he may decide that eating from the garbage is a very unpleasant experience.

Other Household Spots—Chemical cat repellents work well on drapes and furniture, but they are usually not suitable for closets or the kitchen. You don't want their temporarily unpleasant aroma on your clothes or kitchen counters. Strings of clanging cans or other noise-making devices are better for keeping your cat away from places in your closet or kitchen.

Noise-making devices are not good for keeping your cat off mantles and shelves. They may aggravate the problem. A startling noise may cause your cat to bolt and knock over breakable items. Chemical repellents combined with protective devices, such as inverted boxes, are best for keeping your cat off these places. It's a good idea to put away treasured breakable items until after your cat thoroughly learns the rules of your household.

These instructions are only examples of how you can combine techniques to keep your cat away from places you don't want him to go. Apply the same principles to devise solutions to problems that are unique to your household. Soon your cat will understand your rules and obey them without thinking.

PERSONAL HABITS

Cats, like people, often exhibit irritating personal habits. The most common include infantile behaviors, excessive meowing, messy eating, toilet problems and destructive scratching. This section is devoted to the first three. Problems with toilet habits are discussed in detail in Chapter 6, and destructive scratching habits are dealt with on pages 76 to 79.

Infantile Habits—Infantile behavior is most likely to occur with a cat adopted before the age of 8 weeks—but some cats who weren't adopted too early show these traits also. They include drooling, kneading, and sucking or chewing hair, wool or other soft materials in an imitation of nursing.

Some people encourage these habits because they consider them cute and kittenish. They are dismayed when they find the habits becoming destructive, especially if their cats extend their claws while kneading on blankets or clothing.

Unlike many unwanted behaviors, your cat probably indulges in his infantile habits only when he is purring in a location that's near your body. His view of you as a mother figure triggers his desire to nurse.

If your cat begins kneading, pick him up firmly and set him a foot away from you. Hiss and gently push his face. Don't flip his nose and say *"No!"* unless the hiss and face-push prove ineffective. Kneading, drooling and sucking are affectionate behaviors. You don't want to hurt your cat's feelings by rejecting him too strongly.

Excessive Meowing—Normally, your cat uses brief meows to communicate his moods or needs. Excessive meowing consists of a drawn-out howl or whine that a neutered cat makes for no apparent reason. Siamese cats are noted for this habit.

Stop excessive meowing from becoming a habit by refusing to reward whines or howls with food, stroking, a walk outdoors or other treat. If you think your cat is trying to communicate one of these needs to you, wait until he is quiet before you give in to him.

Don't teach a cat who indulges in excessive meowing the trick behavior of *speak,* described on page 185. He will assume meowing is a desirable behavior and whine and howl because he thinks he can earn rewards.

Messy Eating—Some cats persist in using their paws to remove food from their bowls so they can eat it from the floor. If your cat is one of these, you'll have to use your imagination to solve his particular problem.

Be sure your cat's bowl is stable and easy to eat from. If it slides or wobbles, he may be removing his food so he can eat in comfort.

If your cat persists in removing his food after you've provided him with a stable bowl, replace it with a bowl with high sides. That makes food removal more difficult. Heavy water crocks are perfect for this purpose. You can buy them in hardware stores, feed stores and pet shops.

Your cat may remove only one type of

food from his bowl. If this is so, offer another type of food to break his habit.

Whenever you see your cat removing food from his bowl, put his nose over the food so he can smell it, and administer corrective discipline. If you are consistent with this procedure, your cat should soon stop his messy eating habits.

Spraying and Urinating—When your cat sprays, a specially scented substance enters his urine. He sprays this urine onto household surfaces to send messages to other cats. Household spraying is described in detail on page 39.

Urination is the simple act of elimination. If it is done in an inappropriate place in your home, it can become an irritating personal habit. The floor of the bathtub or shower stall, the dirt in house plants, and the ashes of the fireplace are common places for problem urination. Ways to prevent this behavior are discussed on pages 152 and 153.

AGGRESSIVE BEHAVIORS

Your cat has a natural urge to assert himself. He may show aggression toward people, either playfully or intentionally, and begin to bite and scratch. He may dart outdoors to explore whenever the front door opens. Once outdoors, he may stalk prey or fight with other animals. Some of these behaviors are instinctive and normal—but you can teach your cat to hold them in check.

Darting Outdoors—After your cat has learned to walk on a leash, darting outdoors becomes an infrequent problem. Your cat understands he has the right to go outdoors—but only on his leash.

Before your cat learns to lead, darting can be a serious problem. This is particularly true if he lies in wait behind a locked

Infant security gate prevents darting outdoors.

door, listening for the sound of your key. The moment you open the door, your cat darts past you and runs outside.

Avoid this problem by entering your home through a room that can be closed off to your cat. If this is not practical, buy a 24-inch high, expandable, plastic-mesh infant security gate from a baby-accessory store. Choose one that can be pressure-mounted so you can fit it snugly into the outside frame of your front door. Your cat can jump the hurdle, but he will have to crouch to spring. This should give you a

THE GIANT

Because cats are much closer to their wild ancestors than dogs, training them can sometimes be a challenge. But it's even more of a challenge if the cat weighs 200 pounds and has teeth the size of jackknives!

Such was the case with Zamba, a lion who belonged to my friend Monte Cox. Monte had gotten Zamba as a playful, 20-pound kitten, and—through lots of patient training—made him into a well-behaved film actor. It was not so easy with his second lion, Feisty, who proved just how challenging big cat training can be.

It was hard for me to imagine Zamba as a kitten as I petted his mane one morning on an outdoor set for a commercial. Monte and I started walking, and Zamba followed along behind us like a faithful dog. All that was left of his kitten days was the affection that he showed when he rubbed against my leg.

Zamba's nickname was the Giant—his mane and withers were level with my chest. Glancing back at him, I smiled at the way he ambled along. I knew he was capable of unbelievable power and speed. On film he could look awesome.

"Before the camera crew gets here, how about giving me a hand with my new cat?" Monte asked. "I call him Feisty, but believe me, he's more than that. I don't trust him even a little. Just watch the Giant for me while I go get the devil."

So Monte drove off, leaving the Giant and me to roam around a wide clearing that was bordered by scrub brush. The lion sniffed around the bushes but made no effort to move far from me. My nerves tingled as I wondered if he might decide to become a kitten again and use me as a toy.

As the minutes passed, we began to feel comfortable together. The Giant allowed me to tag along, holding his tail as he prowled through the brush. It was getting to be great fun when he surprised me by suddenly spinning me around. Long before I heard a sound, he had heard Monte's panel truck coming down the hill toward us.

The Giant's eyes and ears were alert as the vehicle halted. Monte called him, and he loped across the clearing and obediently hopped through the back door.

The inside of the truck was sectioned off into two compartments. With the Giant safely locked away in one of them, Monte opened a side door and yanked a heavy chain. He stepped back to avoid the surly beast who leaped out at him.

Feisty lunged and took a swipe at Monte, who moved quickly to one side. Feisty was blocky and powerful, but not as tall as the Giant.

Using standard tactics for handling wild animals, Monte kept the upper hand by wrapping Feisty's chain around a nearby tree. With that leverage, he gradually curbed the lion in closer and secured the chain to a length of 20 feet. The lion's roar seemed to shake the ground.

"Pretty wild to start training, isn't he?" I asked.

"Now's as good a time as any," Monte said. He dropped a log between himself and Feisty, who looked like he was out for human flesh. The lion hunched and moved toward his trainer. As he reached the log, Monte shouted, "Whoa!"

Surprised, the lion stopped short. Monte walked to him instantly, patted him on the nose and told him he was a good boy. Stopping the lion at the log was the first step in teaching him to hit a mark. It was proper procedure. It was also proper procedure to show no fear, so Monte turned his back to walk away.

Immediately, Feisty crouched and sprung. His front paws hit Monte at shoulder level, knocking him to the ground. I shuddered as the lion tried to drive his huge fangs into the flat of Monte's back. It was only a question of seconds before the lion's mouth would move to Monte's side, where the lion could get a firm grip. As I grabbed a fallen tree limb and ran toward them, I heard Monte's desperate shout, "Let the Giant out!"

I couldn't believe my ears. "Two lions?" I yelled back. "Are you crazy!"

"Please Ray! Let the Giant out!" Monte choked out.

There was no time to reason it out. One trainer never questions another trainer about his own animals. I dropped the limb and raced back to pull open the back door of the truck. The Giant hit the ground with a roar. The two Goliaths crashed together in midair. Monte scuttled clear as the great feline bodies smacked together, the sound punctuated with heart-stopping grunts and snarls.

Monte appeared unscathed except for two rips in his leather jacket. Still panting, he backed away 10 feet and watched. The Giant upended the other lion and carved an 18-inch-gash in his flank, which began bleeding immediately. Feisty had had enough. He got back on his feet and retreated toward the tree, dragging his chain. The Giant stood his ground, his head lifted high in a grand victory pose.

"Zamba!" Monte called.

The Giant turned slowly and walked to Monte's side, ignoring the other lion as if he didn't exist.

"I just wish I'd thought of telling you about the Giant's ready rescue service a little earlier in the game," Monte said, trying to grin. I nodded numbly.

On that day I decided to confine my cat training to the domestic variety—they are challenging enough, thank you!

Ray Berwick

moment to step over the gate and close the door behind you.

If you are having a party, confine your cat in his kennel when guests arrive and leave. Don't risk the chance of his darting outside when the door opens and closes.

Catching Prey—Stalking and eating prey is a natural behavior for your cat. However, it can cause diarrhea and illness. If your cat goes outdoors only on his leash or tether, stalking prey can easily be prevented. Gently pull on the line to lead him away from his target before he begins to pounce.

If you allow your cat to roam freely, he may bring dead or injured prey into the house. If this occurs, don't allow him to eat it. As soon as he drops it from his mouth, pick it up and dispose of it outdoors. If you prefer, sweep it into a dustpan with a broom. In either case, put on leather gloves before you take the prey away from your cat. His anger at being deprived of his catch may cause him to bite and scratch.

If you are going to allow your cat to roam outdoors, you can avoid prey-capturing problems by attaching a small bell to his collar. Small bells are available in any pet store. A bell warns birds and other small animals that your cat is approaching. It allows them to escape and discourages your cat from hunting. If your cat is a house pet, this deprivation will be no great loss. He will be more dependent and friendly with you, which should make him more willing to accept behavior modification.

Fights with Other Animals—If your cat has a hostile encounter with another animal while he's on his leash or tether, pull him away as firmly as you can without dangerously straining his halter. Don't pick him up if he's hissing. He may express his anger and frustration by biting or

Discourage aggressive behavior.

scratching you.

If your cat has a hostile encounter when he's not on his leash, try separating the fighting animals with the soft end of a broom or mop. If you don't have one handy, try using a long stick.

Dousing with water—not recommended in other areas of cat training—may be the best way to break up an animal fight. Another trick involves covering one of the animals with an inverted crate.

Aggression Toward People—Stop aggressive behavior toward you or others *before* it starts by discouraging aggressive play. This includes the wrestling response and other forms of play in which your cat's claws are extended. When your cat extends his claws in play, firmly say *"No!"* Stop playing with him. Never encourage your cat to scratch or bite—even on a small toy.

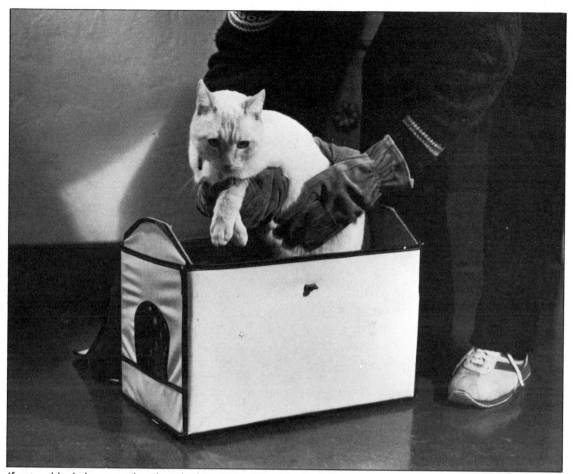

If cat suddenly becomes hostile, take him to vet. Wear leather gloves to pick him up.

Don't use your hands to play with your cat when he is on his back. This position is a natural aggressive or defensive position for him. It allows him to wrap all four feet around your hand. Even a friendly, gentle cat will sometimes revert to natural instinct in this position. He may severely bite or claw even his best friend.

If your cat shows aggressive behavior toward guests in your home, confine him in his kennel for half an hour or more. When you let him out, he may be ready to greet the strangers with a more friendly attitude.

Always introduce your cat to new members of your household in a quiet, gradual manner. This applies to new animals, adults and children—including a new baby.

If your cat suddenly begins to bite and scratch for no apparent reason, take him to the vet. Sick cats often allow pain and fear to develop into hostility. Use leather gloves to put your cat in his kennel. A cat in pain may unintentionally hurt the person he loves the most.

HOW TO PROMOTE DESIRABLE BEHAVIORS

You use negative techniques to stop your cat from indulging in undesirable behaviors, such as scratching, biting, excessive meowing and messy eating. Conversely, you use positive techniques to reinforce desirable habits.

Combine food rewards, stroking and cueing with a clicker to get your cat to do the things you want him to do. Throw in a little praise for extra success. These are the basics of behavior-modification training.

Good Habits—Your cat probably does a lot of things right, but more likely you notice things he does "wrong" (things that are annoying) first. The secret to successful training is to pay just as much attention—if not more—to reinforcing good habits as you pay to eliminating bad habits.

When your cat purrs without kneading, give him extra strokes and praise. When he gives a brief meow instead of a howl or whine, immediately give him whatever he is asking for. Stroke your cat and praise him when he eats neatly from his bowl.

The same principles can be applied to getting your cat to sleep and play in appropriate places. In addition to stroking and praising, click the clicker and offer him a food reward when he's in his bed or in a permissible play place.

Do this frequently at first, then phase out cues and rewards. Continue to stroke and praise your cat to let him know he's doing the things that fit in with the rules of your household.

Good Attitudes—Friendliness is the most-important attitude to encourage in your cat—especially if you want him to do tricks before an audience. Even naturally shy cats lose some of their reserve if they're introduced to strangers in a slow, quiet manner.

After friends have made his acquaintance, you can allow them to take your cat into their laps and stroke him. Tell them not to restrain him if he wants to jump down.

Make sure the people to whom you introduce your cat are glad to make his acquaintance. Don't force his company on people who fear or dislike cats.

When your cat discovers the people he meets are respectful, caring and playful, he'll begin to lose his fear and shyness. He will develop an open, friendly attitude based on confidence and trust.

GOOD SCRATCHING HABITS

For years it was thought that cats scratched objects merely to sharpen their claws. Animal-behavior specialists now believe cats also scratch to deliberately make a mark. Once a mark is made, they have a strong instinct to deepen it. This instinct is probably inherited from wild ancestors who scratch-marked trees to announce their presence to other cats.

Because of your cat's strong instinct to deepen a mark, it's important to redirect destructive scratching activity by training your cat to use a sturdy scratching post. Stop him from scratching furniture and other household items before he begins to mark them. Do this by setting up a sturdy scratching post *before* you bring your new pet home. Use the techniques in this section to let him know he has the right to indulge his natural scratching instincts—but only on his post.

Scratching Posts—Posts vary in size, shape and covering. Whatever you make or buy, it should be at least 1 foot taller than

Sturdy log makes good scratching place.

your cat when he is stretched full-length. The base should be broad and sturdy enough to allow him to lean his full weight against it without causing it to wobble. Many of the posts sold in pet shops do not meet these standards, so they are almost worthless for successful household training.

Carpeting is a common covering for scratching posts, but it doesn't allow your cat to make a mark. You may find a carpet-covered post only partially satisfies his scratching instincts. If he persists in scratching furniture or other things in preference to his post, use your imagination to make his post more suitable to his needs.

Many cats enjoy scratching on a rough surface such as *sisal*, a ropelike fiber grown in the tropics. Sisal-covered scratching posts are available in many pet stores.

If your cat is selectively scratch-marking household items made from a particular material, you may want to cover his scratching post with the same type of material. Frequent favorites are leather, velvet, wicker and bark.

If your cat enjoys scratching bark, use an oversized log that you can lean firmly in a corner. It should be at least 4 feet high and weigh at least 15 pounds. The bark should be soft and moist, so it does not crumble or splinter.

Changing Your Cat's Behavior **77**

If possible, get a freshly cut log so your cat is attracted to its fresh, natural smell. Many firewood suppliers can give you a large, fresh log custom-cut to your specifications. Another option is to get a permit from the National Forest Service, and cut a log with a chain saw in an approved wood-cutting area. After your cat has scratched most of the bark off his log, split it for firewood and replace it with a fresh one.

Instead of a log, you may want to give your cat a scratching tree that's secured to the floor and ceiling. It may have branches, platforms or hiding holes to make it fun and attractive. Cat magazines often publish articles with instructions for building a scratching tree. Magazines also advertise many items of "cat furniture" you can buy in pet stores or by mail. Before you invest in expensive, space-consuming items, try a simple scratching post. Your cat may be perfectly content.

Catnip—Putting catnip on a scratching post is one of the few times in training when this mind-altering herb may be helpful. Some cats show no reaction to catnip. Test your pet's reaction to catnip with a sample. If he seems to enjoy it, you may want to use it to make his scratching post more attractive to him.

Catnip comes in several forms. One of the nicest is the living herb, which you can buy in many nurseries. If you grow it as a house plant, you may have to keep it in a place that is inaccessible to your cat.

Crush the leaves of fresh catnip, and rub them on your cat's scratching post. The herbal oils will impart an attractive aroma that lasts several days.

Dried catnip varies greatly in freshness. If it's moist-looking and gray-green, it has been recently picked and is filled with herbal oils. If it's dry and dark or white, it has been on the shelf for a long time and may not be very effective.

If you decide to make a do-it-yourself, carpet-covered scratching post, put glue on the backing of the carpet and sprinkle dried catnip on it *before* you nail the carpet to the post. Once a week, rub the dried herb into the pile on the outer side of the carpet. Dried catnip also can be rubbed into the bark of a log scratching post.

Most pet shops sell essence of catnip in aerosol cans. If you choose this convenient form of catnip, spray it on your cat's scratching post at least once a week. Aerosol cans of catnip cost more than other forms of the herb.

Location—Put your cat's scratching post in a comfortable room that he often goes into on his own. Locate it in a place that's easily accessible—not in a corner blocked by furniture.

Make sure the post stands firmly against a wall, so it doesn't wobble or fall. If you are using a log, nestle it on a slight angle in a corner.

If you are trying to direct your cat's scratch-marking activity away from a particular household item, it may be helpful to locate his scratching post near that item. Immediately after you discipline him for destructive scratching, take him to his scratching post and encourage him to use it.

After your cat has learned to confine his scratching to his post, you may want to move his post to another location. See page 126 for techniques for moving your cat's litter box. The same methods can be used to move his scratching post.

Cues and Rewards—You can make your cat want to scratch his post by using clicker and reward techniques described in Chapter 2.

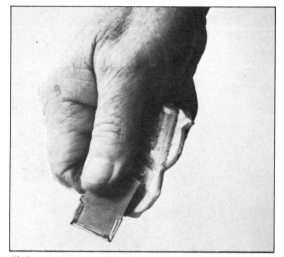
Clicker is important for correcting misplaced scratching.

With the clicker, the reward can and several food tidbits in hand, take your cat to his scratching post. Lift his front paws, and gently place them on the surface. If he doesn't begin scratching on his own, move his paws in a scratching motion. If he still doesn't begin to scratch, gently press his paws to extend his claws, and hook them into the rough surface of the post. At this point, click the clicker, and offer a food reward.

If your cat begins scratching on his own, click the clicker and offer another reward. If he doesn't begin to scratch, repeat the above exercise at least three times.

Repeat the scratching exercise at least five times a day for 1 week. In addition to rewarding your cat during training sessions, reward him when you see him scratching his post on his own. Stroke and praise him while he is scratching. Let him know you like what he's doing.

After a week has passed, begin to offer fewer rewards each day. Within a week's time you should be offering no rewards at all.

Resume offering regular food rewards at your cat's scratching post only if he begins to indulge in destructive scratching elsewhere. As soon as he redirects his scratching to his post, phase out rewards as instructed above. If you don't do this, your cat may become a compulsive scratcher, spending most of his waking hours at his post in an effort to earn rewards.

Claw-Clipping—Clipping your cat's claws is an important part of routine grooming, as discussed in Chapter 2. But claw clipping doesn't stop destructive scratching behavior. In fact, it may increase the behavior because your cat feels the need to sharpen the blunt ends of his newly clipped claws.

To prevent destructive scratching from beginning after you clip your cat's claws, reward your cat at his scratching post for a full day after clipping.

Declawing—This is one way to prevent destructive scratching, but it is a last resort. Use it *only* if your cat continues to scratch in forbidden places after you have used cat repellent and tried the reward techniques we have outlined for at least 1 month.

Declawing is an expensive operation. It costs more if you have all four paws declawed instead of just the front ones. Front-paw declawing is usually adequate to stop destructive scratching.

If you have your cat declawed, you must always remember he is a *handicapped animal*. He can't defend himself from enemies by fighting or climbing trees. He can't catch prey, which makes him completely incapable of surviving on his own outdoors. For these reasons, you must *never* allow a declawed cat outside unless he is with you on his leash or tether. He needs you to protect him from becoming lost or

Declawed cat can enjoy outdoors only on leash or tether. He needs protection from hostile animals.

attacked by hostile animals.

Such strong warnings about declawing may make the operation seem unfair or even cruel. Most vets disagree with this idea. Studies prove few cats show psychological reactions to declawing. Many of them continue to indulge in scratching behavior—almost unaware they no longer have claws.

When your declawed cat scratches most of your household items, he no longer can destroy them. Because his scratching doesn't make you angry, your friendship may grow stronger. When all other efforts fail to stop destructive scratching, declawing may be the right decision.

HOW TO TEACH THREE BASIC BEHAVIORS

You teach three basic behaviors—*come when called, kennel training* and *lead on leash*—differently from things you have just taught your cat. You are not modifying his natural animal needs. Instead you are introducing three new behaviors that are fundamental to future training. By teaching the basic behaviors, you begin an exciting new form of communication with your cat. You let him know what you want him to do, and he understands and obeys. You no longer live in two different worlds—animal and human. Your worlds are connected by the understanding you establish through the training experience.

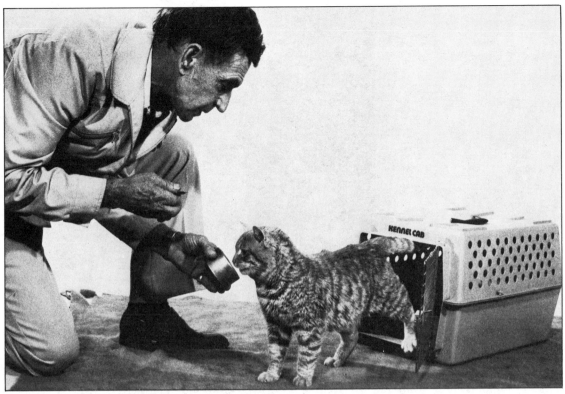

To teach come-when-called behavior, start cat from kennel.

COME WHEN CALLED

Most cats come when they are called at mealtime, but you want yours to come whenever you need him. Whether you want him to go for a walk on his leash or to come for a grooming session, the two of you are communicating when he responds obediently to your call.

His Name—Give your cat a simple name that's two syllables long. If you want to give him a longer name, make sure it can be shortened to a simple, two-syllable nickname. If you want to give him a shorter name, turn it into two syllables by adding the affectionate ending "-y."

Don't use the traditional "kitty, kitty, kitty" if you want your cat to come to the sound of his name. Call him by saying his two-syllable name or nickname in a repetitive chant similar to the traditional kitty call.

Say your cat's name frequently when you groom and stroke him. He will learn those two special syllables are somehow connected to him.

Start from Kennel—Before you begin training, assemble the tools you need—your cat's kennel, the reward can and 10 food rewards. At first you may think it's unnecessary to start name-call training from the kennel, but soon you will realize why this is important.

If you don't start your cat from his kennel, he may become an untrainable pest as soon as he learns that the come-when-called behavior brings food rewards. The

Place reward on can to motivate cat to come when called.

moment you put a reward on the can, he begins whining and weaving around your feet, begging for his treat before he has earned it by coming to you from another location.

Place your cat in his kennel, and close the door. Put a reward on top of the can, and hold it close to the door so your cat can see and smell it.

If you have a top-closing kennel without screen doors or windows, place the reward on the can before you close the kennel top. Let your cat see and smell it, then lower the top of the kennel.

Click the clicker to get your cat's attention. When he begins to make restless movements inside his kennel, start to call him by name. Open his kennel door, back away 3 feet and let your cat come to his treat. After he has eaten it, stroke him and call him by name. Make him realize it's worthwhile to come when he hears his two-syllable name.

Repeat the above exercise at least 10 times each drill session. Schedule at least three sessions at intervals throughout the day. As soon as your cat begins to expect his reward, eliminate the clicker and call him only by his name.

When your cat consistently comes out of his kennel to get his reward at the sound of his name, begin to make him follow you before you give it to him. Continue to call his name as he follows you a greater distance each drilling session. By the end of a week, he should follow you across the room before he gets his treat.

Training Partner—Begin this exercise after 1 week of training your cat to come to the sound of his name. Place a reward on the can, and carry it with you into another room. When you begin to call your cat by name, have your training partner open the kennel.

If your cat comes to you, give him his reward and praise him. If he doesn't, have your partner carry him to you. Lower the reward can to floor level, and have your partner hold your cat close enough to see and smell the reward. When you are certain he is aware of the reward, allow him to be released from 1 foot away. Let him enjoy his reward, and stroke and praise him. Repeat this exercise, if necessary, until he is no longer confused. He will soon learn to come to your call, even when you are not in sight. He will run to you when he hears his name, no matter where you are.

Phase Out Rewards—When your cat is thoroughly trained to come to the sound of his name, begin gradually to give him random food rewards. After a month of randomly rewarding your cat, phase out food rewards completely. Continue to stroke him when he comes when called.

Come to Clicker—If you are going to allow your cat to roam outside without a leash, he should be trained to come to a clicker. The clicking sound is more distinct and demanding than the sound of your voice, and the sound carries farther.

Your cat learns to come to the sound of the clicker faster than he learns to come to the sound of his name. Use the same techniques as outlined above, but shorten drilling length and frequency. One training session a day for 1 week should be enough to train your cat to come to the sound of the clicker. In addition to using various rooms of your home, drill your cat outdoors.

When calling your cat from outside, always give your cat at least three rewards for coming to the sound of the clicker. Never use the random-reward system. Remember that your cat has many compelling distractions outside. If he is sufficiently clicker-trained, that sound should override almost any other interest. He deserves a substantial reward for giving up

his explorations to return to the call of the clicker.

KENNEL TRAINING

There are many good uses for a cat kennel. You can put your cat inside it whenever you have guests who fear cats, dislike them or are allergic to them. People who are allergic to cats especially appreciate this.

You can stop children from playing rowdy, noisy games with your cat by putting him in his kennel. You can also prevent fights with visiting animals this way.

You will use your cat's kennel to take him to the vet, to cat shows and for other excursions in your car. Don't put the kennel on the car seat. Instead set it firmly on the floor. This prevents it from falling off during sudden stops and injuring or frightening your cat.

If your cat's kennel is airline-approved, you can use it for air travel. If it isn't, you'll have to rent a cat kennel from the airline you are using. Most airlines sell kennels if you prefer buying to renting.

Your cat's kennel is important to training in several ways. As discussed, it is the starting position for the come-when-called behavior. In addition, you will learn later how to use the kennel for hearing-ear training and for teaching a wide variety of tricks.

If you confine your cat in his kennel for 5 minutes before you want him to perform a behavior, he'll be ready and eager to do it for you when you let him out.

Alternatively, if he is tired after a performance or nervous in strange surroundings, you can use your cat's kennel as a kind of bait. In such circumstances, his familiar kennel may look so inviting he'll perform a behavior in order to receive the reward of going into his snug little home.

Positive Reinforcement—To give your cat positive feelings about his kennel, make it a pleasant place where he receives rewards. Pad the floor with a small blanket or towel to make it comfortable. When you introduce your cat to his kennel, open the door and allow him to explore it on his own. If he goes inside, click the clicker and offer him a reward on the reward can. If he does not go inside, gently place him inside, click the clicker and reward him.

Take your cat out of his kennel. Hold the loaded reward can near the kennel door, and call him by name. When he comes to get his treat, place the reward can on the floor of the kennel. When he goes inside to eat it, click the clicker and stroke him. Do this 10 times each drill session.

Schedule at least three kennel-training sessions a day during your cat's first week at home. During his second week, cut them down to once a day. Discontinue drills when your cat is consistently going into his kennel when you call him.

After you have discontinued regular kennel drills, reinforce what your cat has learned by occasionally offering him a meal inside his kennel. When he seems ready to take a nap, put him inside his kennel to sleep.

Keep the kennel in a comfortable corner in a room your cat often goes into on his own. Always leave the kennel door open so he can go into it any time. He soon will become fond of his home and come running when you call him to it.

LEAD ON LEASH

Many people think cats are too independent to learn to lead on a leash. They are amazed when they see an elegant Siamese strolling through a park on a leash at his owner's heels.

Actually, most cats adapt rather easily to leash training. They may take longer to learn this behavior than dogs do, but once they have learned it, they become quite comfortable with it.

Count on at least 3 weeks of regular training sessions before your cat begins to feel comfortable on his leash. If you give him enough time, he will gradually understand the principle of restraint.

At first, your cat may balk or bolt on his leash because he doesn't understand that his movements are limited. *Don't give up your cat's leash training because he doesn't seem to be learning.* Take the time to allow him to learn this important behavior at his own pace.

Leash training is important for several reasons. Once your cat has learned to walk on his leash, he can enjoy the outdoors, safe from traffic and predators. You and your cat will establish a special kind of communication when you share long walks together.

Equipment—Buy a sturdy, lightweight cat leash of leather, nylon or plastic. It should not be longer than 5 feet. Longer leashes can get tangled when your cat explores the outdoors.

Buy a cat halter to go with the leash. One strap fastens snugly around your cat's neck. The other goes around his body, directly behind his forelegs. The halter's body strap has a metal ring on top for attaching the leash.

Some people try to leash-train a cat without a halter. They fasten the leash to the metal ring on the bottom of a cat collar. This practice can be painful and dangerous for your cat. When he pulls backward or forward on the leash, the collar can choke him.

Start leash training indoors.

If you plan to train your cat to enjoy the outdoors on a tether, you'll need some special equipment. One option is to buy a ready-made, tie-out chain or cable with snap bolts attached to both ends. Such products make perfect tethers, but they are fairly expensive.

To save money, you can make your own tether with cotton rope (from a horse-supply store), flat tubular nylon line (from a camping-supply store) or parachute cord (from an army-surplus store). Most of these stores sell snap-bolt fasteners to tie or sew on both ends of the tether. One fastener attaches to an anchoring picket and the other snaps onto the ring on your cat's halter.

Don't tether your cat outdoors unless you have a large fenced area, or you plan to stay close by to fend off any aggressor. An aggressor can appear suddenly, and your tethered cat is at a severe disadvantage. You may also find yourself a victim in an animal-to-animal confrontation.

Another safety consideration is the length and location of the tether. The tether should not be longer than 20 feet. Your cat should be tethered in a comfortable area where he can reach shade if he gets hot. The kennel or another ground-level structure that provides shade is ideal.

Never tether your cat where he might climb a tree and get hung up in the branches, or climb over a limb and strangle. The same is true of fences or other tall structures that he can jump. With one leap, he could easily become entangled and hang suspended.

Changing Your Cat's Behavior **85**

Start Indoors—In your home, your cat has few distractions while he learns the basic principle of cooperatively following you when he feels a slight tug on his leash. Choose a room that's comfortable and large enough for practice.

Assemble 15 food rewards, the reward can and the clicker. Then put your cat's halter on him, and attach the leash to the ring on top.

Put a tidbit on the reward can, and hold the can in one hand. In the other, hold the clicker and a loop of your cat's leash. Allow a good amount of slack to remain on the leash, and step 3 feet away from your cat. Click the clicker, and bring the reward can down to his eye level. When he comes to eat his treat, stroke and praise him. Do this 15 times each drill session; schedule at least three drill sessions a day.

Continue this level of drill for at least 3 days. Then allow your cat to wander a bit until you begin to give sharp tugs on the leash. Continue to do so until you get his attention, and then click him to you for a reward. It is a feline characteristic to resist a constant pull. Sharp tugs are more effective for training until your cat becomes accustomed to the steady tension of the leash.

Teach Tug-and-Follow—Now your cat is ready to learn to follow you when he feels a slight tug on the leash. With the reward can in your hand, step slightly ahead of your cat and tug the leash sharply. Release the tension after each tug. Click the clicker and give your cat his reward if he comes to you, even if it is only a matter of inches. Reinforce his behavior with a reward and abundant stroking and praise.

Don't be surprised if your cat suddenly begins to yank away wildly and flops on his side. He is in a temporary state of rebel-

lion. Quickly release the leash pressure and wait for him to adjust. After a time he will get back on his feet. As soon as he does, move the reward very close. Coax him to move slightly toward you to receive his reward.

After 3 days of this drill, or at a time when you think your cat's response is fairly reliable, you may stop using the clicker. Allow the tug on the leash to be his only cue.

When your cat has learned the principle of responding to the tug, begin teaching him to follow. Don't give him a treat instantly, but continue to space the rewards at longer intervals of tug-and-follow.

Don't be discouraged if you need to go back to the clicker. If such is the case, start with your cat a short distance behind you. Give a slight tug on the leash and click the clicker. He will soon learn that the clicker and reward follow shortly after the tug-and-follow cue. Gradually lengthen the distance until he follows you the entire length of the room.

Balking or Trying to Run—At first your cat may balk when he feels tension on the leash. He may arch his back and stiffen his legs. Stubborn cats may lie down and refuse to follow at all. Don't be impatient. Wait for him to stand up on his own. When he does, gently call him to you and beckon him with the cue to come.

Never forcibly drag or pull your cat when he's balking! His resentment will increase and he may learn to strongly dislike the leash.

Don't pick your cat up when he balks. He will think that all he has to do is balk or lie down and he will be picked up. In his mind it may become similar to the way a baby cries so his mother will pick him up. Be calm. You may step behind him and pass

When cat responds consistently to tug-and-follow cue, allow him to explore on leash.

by with his reward just as a reminder. Eventually he will learn he gains nothing by balking. He will learn it's more comfortable and fruitful to cooperate and follow on the leash.

Your cat may decide he's tired of his lesson and try to run away. When he comes to the end of his leash, he may strain and try to bolt. In this instance, if there is no threat of danger, stop him by holding back on the leash. The harness does not promote choking and will cause him no real pain.

If your cat bolts, lean over him and guide him back to your side with your hands. Then back 1 foot away and call him to you. It is important to try to get him to come to you, if only a tiny distance. If this proves impossible, end the lesson for the day by picking him up and carrying him into the house.

When He's Ready for Outdoors—Put your cat's halter and leash on him when he's rested and calm. He should have an edge to his appetite. If he's toilet trained, make sure he's recently eliminated his wastes in the toilet.

Make each outside training session at least 10 minutes long. Try to schedule two sessions a day, one in the morning and one in the afternoon or evening.

Teach leash training in a place with a minimum of traffic noise and where there are no other animals. If possible, find a place reasonably free of trees and shrubs. Foliage often has scent and scratch markings from other cats. During these first sessions, you need your cat's full attention.

We recommend you use rewards and the clicker in your first sessions.

Keep Him Beside or Near You—Your cat

Changing Your Cat's Behavior **87**

Leash-trained cat enjoys outdoors in safety.

is independent by nature. He is also curious about most sounds or smells he encounters. For these reasons, try to keep him in a clear area in the beginning. You want as much of his attention as you can get.

Try to keep ahead of him or keep him by your side. Offer him random rewards for good sequences of following behavior. Stop frequently to stroke and praise him.

Don't make the first session too long. Your cat's attention span probably is no longer than 15 minutes. Try to stop on a happy note. When you see that your cat is becoming restless and uncooperative, pick him up or have him follow you inside the house. At this time, offer him three or more rewards. Leash training has been hard for him, and he has earned his treats.

Outdoor Safety—Challenges from another animal, traffic hazards or electrical storms are examples of frightening or dangerous situations that you may encounter outdoors. If any of these occur, immediately pick up your cat and take him indoors. His well being is worth having to back up a bit in your leash-training schedule.

Be Gradual—During the first portion of outdoor leash training, try to maintain control as much as possible. Keep the sessions short and end them on a pleasant experience.

After 3 days your cat should understand the feeling of leash restraint and know what is expected of him. You may phase out the reward procedure if you feel he is ready. You may also lead him to an area that will interest him, such as a grove of trees or shrubs. Make every effort to lead him there yourself. However, once he is investigating something of interest, relax the leash and let him explore. At such times you may follow him from a short distance away. Freedom on the leash is fine, as long as your cat is regularly responding to short tugs by obediently following. *Don't allow him freedom on the leash until his response to the tug is firmly established.*

Heeling—This sophisticated behavior requires your cat to obediently follow at your heels—without the help of a leash! Because it is so difficult, don't try to teach this behavior until your cat has cooperatively followed you on his leash for *at least 1 year.* Use the same techniques you used for leash training to teach him to follow you without his leash.

It's wise to carry the clicker and several food rewards with you when you expect your cat to heel. If his natural curiosity sends him off on his own, you can quickly call him back with the clicker.

Tether Training—A tether-trained cat has learned to explore the outdoors on a 20-foot tether. The end of the tether is attached to a picket or a heavy piece of furniture. When the cat comes to the end of his tether, he does not tug or strain. Instead he goes off to explore in another direction. In this way, a tether-trained cat shows that he understands the principle of restraint.

Patience is the key to success. If you wait until your cat is *completely* comfortable with the sensation of being restrained on a line, tether training comes naturally.

Attach the tether snap bolt to the ring on your cat's halter, and observe him as he explores the outdoors. Because your cat is comfortable and confident on his tether, you may be tempted to leave him alone outdoors. *This is a very dangerous practice!* The tether can become tangled and choke your cat. He may encounter a strange animal and begin to strain at the end of the line. If he's attacked by a predator, he can't escape.

You can spend many pleasant hours reading or talking with friends as you watch your cat explore the outdoors on his tether. Relax and enjoy these interludes. Your watchful presence ensures your pet's safety.

THE PRO

Training in the kennel is one thing, but training on the set is another — it is filled with distractions, such as lights, cameras and busy people. Despite all these things, a well-trained cat will perform on cue with perfect timing.

One of my cats proved this on an outdoor set several years ago. He obediently performed a difficult long shot in the presence of the greatest possible cat distraction — a pack of curious dogs.

The location was a pleasant, grassy park. At least 50 dogs were running around without leashes. This surprised me, because the city had a strict leash law. But inside the park, the police seemed to ignore the ordinance.

The director was apprehensive about the dogs, but I was sure my cat was sophisticated enough to perform without even looking at the dogs.

For one particular long shot in the park, I had to be yards away from my cat so the camera could follow him all the way. If I got close to do my cueing, I risked walking into the picture.

All cat actors can work easily in closeups. Working close, a trainer can be very near an animal actor and use all sorts of cues and persuasions. During long shots, however, cueing difficulty increases in direct proportion to the trainer's distance from the subject.

The long shot started with the cat sitting in a tree, approximately 200 feet from the street. When it came time for the cat to jump down and perform, the director held his breath and watched the crowd of dogs nervously.

On cue, my cat jumped down and began to sprint through the park, stopping at a curb to wait for a passing car. He casually crossed the street, hopped on a stone figure beside the driveway to the huge old mansion and waited for a limousine to pass him.

There is no way for me to judge whether a lay person would consider this a difficult sequence of behaviors, but to a professional trainer it's mind-boggling. The animal must follow a very narrow path and hit certain marks throughout his trip to accommodate camera focus and other dramatic considerations. Then he must hit a final mark and stay put, which is perhaps the most difficult of all. My cat performed this entire sequence to the simple, long-distance cues of the clicker and the hiss — nothing more.

Sure enough, the canine spectators didn't cause any problems. All the dogs seemed to know each other and were well-behaved. They stood on the sidelines, behind the camera, and watched the scene like people did. They didn't bother my cat, and my cat paid little or no attention to them as he performed his phenomenal series of traveling behaviors.

The director, believe me, was duly impressed — and so was the audience of remarkably polite dogs.

Ray Berwick

TOILET TRAINING

Chapter 4: Toilet-Training Preparation

Agh! What will my friends say?

The very idea of toilet training a cat brings to mind humorous images. Picture your cat reading a magazine as he perches on the seat of your toilet. "He can't really read," you tell a friend. "He just likes to look at the pictures."

Imagine yourself with your cat on a camping trip in the woods. You can almost hear him thinking, "I can't believe they expect an aristocrat like me to go potty out here!"

But on the day you are loading several dollars worth of kitty litter into your grocery cart, the idea might not seem so funny. It also might lose some of its humor when you are hauling a smelly litter box out to the trash in the middle of a snowstorm.

If your cat lives to be 10 years old, you are likely to spend from $1,000 to $2,000 on litter. If you change the litter in his box once every 3 days, you will make 1,200 trips to the trash can. Think about it.

Many people fail at toilet training their cats because they don't take the program seriously. This attitude causes them to give up easily when they don't succeed in a short time. Cat toilet training can be difficult, but it is worthwhile if it reduces your expenses and makes your home free of litter mess.

This book presents a straightforward, serious approach to cat toilet training. The step-by-step-training program, which is explained in detail in Chapter 5, is based on proven techniques of animal-behavior modification—not on gimmicks.

Behavior modification gradually phases the cat into toilet training by using rewards to reinforce steps that take him from the familiar to the unfamiliar. The steps are:

1. Putting his litter box into the bathroom so he becomes accustomed to that room as the place for his wastes.
2. Placing a lidless toilet seat on top of his box to accustom him to eliminating in a confined space.
3. Substituting the training toilet for the litter box. A training toilet is a round container topped by a lidless toilet seat.
4. Removing the training toilet and placing a container of litter in the bathroom toilet.
5. Teaching your cat to balance in the perch-squat position on the toilet seat.
6. Gradually using less and less litter until you are using none at all.
7. Removing the litter container so your cat uses the bathroom toilet in the perch-squat position.

As mentioned earlier, you should begin your cat's toilet-training program after household behavior training, and before or after trick training. Don't try to teach your cat additional new behaviors while he is learning to modify his instinctive elimination habits.

Before you begin toilet training, your cat should be neutered, in good health, and at least 4 months old (but not older than 9 years).

PREPARE YOURSELF

The most important aspect of preparing for toilet training involves preparing yourself. Decide whether you will train your cat for toilet urination only or for urination *and* toilet bowel movements. Cats can usually be trained easily to urinate in the toilet, but they are more resistant to having bowel movements in the toilet. However, this level of training produces maximum convenience for you.

Once you decide how much training you want to undertake, prepare yourself for the fact that it may take weeks — or even months — to accomplish your goals.

Before you begin toilet training your cat, read carefully through this chapter and the next. This overview will give you a thorough understanding of the training program. Review the information often as training progresses.

Don't allow the jokes of friends to shake your serious attitude. Cat toilet training may seem funny at first, but the results can save you considerable time, mess and money. Once you succeed, the skepticism of others will change to admiration. Your friends may even want to know your secrets. So picture yourself pushing your grocery cart past those bags of litter. Good luck!

ENJOY TRAINING

Cat training is not always easy, but a healthy, realistic outlook helps make cat training fun.

Training your cat gives you a unique opportunity to communicate with your animal. You may discover new things about the ways your cat sees and thinks. He discovers new things about you. If training is done with patience and calmness, you de-

Serious attitude toward toilet training leads to success.

new conditions and expectations. Your affection helps him through difficult steps of training. He wants to learn new habits to please you.

Use Imagination—Every cat is an individual. Each one reacts to the steps of toilet training in his own unique way.

If your cat has a reaction not covered in this book, use your imagination to change the step of toilet training so it suits your cat. Devise your own solutions to unique problems. If one solution doesn't work, experiment with another. When you finish, you'll have a toilet-training system designed especially for your cat.

Don't Overwork—All types of training, especially toilet training, can require a lot of energy. Schedule each major step at a time when you aren't overworked in other areas of your life. Overwork can make you tired and discouraged. Your cat may sense your discouragement and refuse to cooperate. This setback may discourage you enough to abandon his training program.

Don't waste weeks of good progress by imposing unreasonable demands on yourself. Your cat learns new behaviors best in a calm, relaxed atmosphere.

velop a deep mutual understanding. Enjoy this special relationship.

As your cat progresses in his toilet training, enjoy each success. Congratulate yourself on your ability as a trainer. Take pleasure in the positive impression you are making on your friends. You've earned the right to be proud.

Offer Extra Love—Showing your cat that you love him is more important in toilet training than in other types of training. During the toilet-training weeks, provide your cat with extra affection. Stroke him frequently. Speak to him gently and affectionately. Call him by name.

Toilet training can be a mental strain for your cat. He needs to constantly adjust to

PREPARE YOUR CAT

By toilet training your cat, you are asking him to change instinctive behavior. That is a lot to ask of any animal, and you can take steps to make the process easier and less stressful for him. In addition to providing extra love during the training process, you can change feeding patterns and adapt your cat's household routines so as to give him the best chance for success. These steps are described in detail in the following sections.

SIMPLIFICATION

If you keep things simple, your cat won't get confused. Don't try to teach your cat other basic behaviors or tricks while toilet training. Your cat is learning to replace his natural instincts with a set of confusing new habits. He needs to put all his mental effort into making the adjustment.

Before you begin your cat's toilet training, teach him to lead on a leash, page 84, come when called, page 81, and go into his kennel, page 83. Be sure you have eliminated undesired household behaviors, as discussed on pages 69 to 75.

If you have trained your cat to perform a series of tricks, continue his review sessions, but don't introduce new tricks during toilet training. Save them for after your cat has been thoroughly toilet trained.

FEEDING FOR REGULARITY

Toilet training is easier if you feed your cat in ways that promote regular bowel movements. If his elimination follows a regular pattern, you can plan training sessions at times when you know he is likely to eliminate.

Ways to stimulate regularity include adhering to meal schedules, controlling food portions and providing bowel-stimulating foods.

Establish a strict feeding timetable. With the exception of food rewards, don't offer between-meal snacks.

Meal Schedules for Kittens—Begin feeding a kitten for regularity from the day he comes into your home. Give him at least five meals a day until he is 4 months old. At this time you can increase serving sizes and reduce the number of meals to four.

The reduction in meals coincides with the time your kitten can go on to Steps 2 and 3 (see pages 129 to 137) of toilet train-ing. Don't advance him to the new steps until he establishes a regular daily elimination pattern on a four-meal feeding schedule.

Ideally, you should feed your new kitten his five meals at regular times in the early morning, at midmorning, at noon, in late afternoon and in late evening. When he is 4 months old, drop the midmorning meal. When he reaches 6 months, drop the late-afternoon feeding. At 9 months, eliminate the noon meal, and at 1 year, discontinue the feeding in the evening.

If you must be away from home all day, feed your kitten a large breakfast. Leave a portion-controlled serving of dry or moist-packet food for him to eat during the day. Offer early-evening and late-evening meals.

Meal Schedules for Grown Cats—Begin feeding a grown cat for regularity at least 2 weeks before you begin toilet training. If you adopt a new grown cat, begin to feed him for regularity from the day he comes into your home. Don't advance to Step 3 of training until your cat has established regular elimination patterns.

A mature cat is easiest to train if he is restricted to one meal a day. Offer this in the morning, so he has plenty of nourishment for his daytime activities. Feed your cat at exactly the same time every morning. Don't make exceptions that aren't necessary.

If you find it inconvenient to feed your cat in the morning, establish a workable feeding time, and stick to it. Changing feeding times is bad for your cat physically and mentally.

If your cat is in a period of training in which he is receiving few food rewards, you may want to add a small supplemental second meal to your cat's feeding schedule.

Some cats need this second meal, even if they are receiving between-meal rewards. If you decide to offer your cat a second meal, wait at least 8 hours between feedings.

Always provide a bowl of fresh water at your cat's eating place.

Portion Control—Control serving portions so they are approximately the same size for each meal every day. Diet-scale accuracy is not necessary when you give meals to your cat. Simple measurements, such as half a can or half a bowl, are fine if you use the same size can and bowl each time.

Written records of serving portions can be helpful during the weeks you are establishing feeding patterns. Make sure notes include everything you feed your cat at his mealtime. If you offer regular food rewards, take these into account.

Your cat's age, size, sex, health and level of activity influence the amount of food he needs each day. Use your good judgment to give portions that are large enough to fill your cat but not so large as to stuff him.

Watch your cat at his mealtime. If he doesn't finish the portion of food you gave him, begin to give him less. If he demands more food by meowing, give him more. If your cat starts to lose weight, give him more food. If he continues to lose after you have increased his portions, take him to the vet.

Most adult cats do well on a total of 3 to 6 ounces of canned food a day. Portions of dry or semimoist food weigh less because they contain little or no water.

Portions for a kitten on a five-meal feeding schedule should weigh 1 ounce each. As you reduce his number of meals, increase the size of his portions. By the time he's a year old, settle on a standard portion size to feed him throughout his adulthood.

Provide Bowel-Stimulating Foods—In addition to commercially canned, dried and semimoist foods, your cat needs various laxative nutrients to keep his bowels regular. *Vegetables* and *whole grains* are the best sources for these nutrients.

Many people are surprised to learn that cats need and like non-starchy vegetables. The fiber in vegetables helps promote regular elimination, and their vitamins are important to good health.

Cats usually prefer vegetables cooked and finely chopped or mashed. Carrots, green beans, peas, cauliflower and broccoli are often favorites. Add small amounts of these vegetables to portions of your cat's canned food. He will soon develop a taste for them.

If your cat goes outside, he may eat grass. This is a healthy natural appetite you should encourage. Indoor cats often satisfy this appetite by eating house plants.

Discourage your cat from eating house plants by including plenty of vegetables in his diet. Another method is to grow grass in a plastic pot, and put it in his eating area to enjoy at will. Some pet shops sell "instant" grass that matures in a week.

Most canned and dry cat foods contain processed starches, but it is wise to supplement these foods with wholesome natural grains, such as wheat germ. Wheat germ promotes bowel regularity and provides protein and vitamins.

Sprinkle 1/4 teaspoon of wheat germ a day on the main serving of your cat's favorite canned food. After he develops a taste for it, sprinkle at least 1 teaspoon of wheat germ on all of his supplemental feedings.

Whole-wheat or bran cereals also make good dietary supplements. Crush them, then sprinkle them on your cat's canned food. You may try offering ready-to-eat cereal pieces. Your cat may enjoy playing with a tidbit of cereal before he eats it.

Check with your vet before giving milk to your cat. Some cat-care books state milk is a necessary part of a healthy cat's diet, but many vets disagree with this idea.

Milk gives many cats diarrhea. So do cheese and other dairy products. After a kitten is weaned from his mother, he may lose the ability to efficiently digest milk. A balanced diet of meat, grains and vegetables gives him the nutrients he needs without dairy products.

ELIMINATION PATTERNS

Regular feedings produce regular elimination patterns. This makes toilet training your cat easier. You can more readily predict when you should take your cat into the bathroom to attempt elimination.

Urination Patterns—Urination frequency and predictability vary with diet, season and age of the cat.

Because you must always give your cat free access to fresh water, his urination will fluctuate with his thirst. If you give him lots of dry food, he will drink large quantities of water to compensate for the lack of moisture in the food. Water consumption is likely to produce three to four urinations during the day.

If he has only occasional dry feedings, urination will occur two or three times a day. In either case, urinary frequency may increase in summer.

A kitten who drinks lots of milk may urinate as many as 10 times a day. Because his bladder is small, he can't store liquid wastes for long periods.

A neutered cat's urine is pale green or pale yellow. It is clear—not cloudy—and it does not have a strong, offensive aroma. Grown cats eliminate from 1/4 to 2 cups of urine at a time. Kittens eliminate much less urine more frequently.

Bowel-Movement Patterns—A grown cat who eats on a regular, portion-controlled meal schedule usually has one bowel movement a day. It may occur in the morning or in the evening. A few cats have one large bowel movement every 36 hours.

A kitten on five feedings has three or four bowel movements a day. One almost always occurs in the morning, and one happens at night. The other two often occur within 30 minutes of a daytime feeding. The number of bowel movements decreases when you decrease the number of meals the kitten eats.

A healthy cat produces well-formed, moist bowel movements that are small enough to eliminate comfortably. If your cat eats a lot of meat, his bowel movements will be dark brown. If his main diet is fish, they will be tan. The odor may be quite strong.

Keeping Records—You may find it helpful to keep a daily record of the times your cat has bowel movements. If you feed him on a regular schedule, your records should soon reveal a regular elimination pattern. This helps you predict when your cat is likely to eliminate.

If your records show bowel movements regularly occur at times when you can't be present to train your cat, adjust his feeding schedule. For example, if a late-evening feeding causes your cat to have a bowel movement in the middle of the night, feed him earlier. Record the new elimination time that results. Continue to keep a record of your cat's bowel movements until a regular, convenient pattern is established.

Written records reveal
elimination patterns.

HOUSEHOLD ROUTINES

During toilet training, you and your cat may have to make a few changes in your daily habits. None of these changes are difficult or irritating, and most of them are temporary.

Keep Him Inside—Limit your cat's access to the outdoors while you are toilet training him. If allowed outside, your cat has the opportunity to scratch and bury his wastes in the dirt. He becomes reacquainted with the instinctive habit you are trying to help him change.

When your cat is confined inside, he is forced to accept each new step of toilet training as you introduce it. He can't wait until he goes outside to eliminate his wastes.

Provide toys, such as spools, balls and string, to keep your cat occupied in the house when you are gone. During times when you are home, be sure to play with him often.

If you want to let your cat enjoy the outdoors during training, take him for a walk on his leash immediately after he has eliminated his wastes in the proper place in the bathroom. If you wish, put him on his tether, and let him play for a brief period under your watchful eye. If he begins to scratch in the dirt, take him inside and place him on his toilet facility.

Allow Free Access to Bathroom—Many unnecessary accidents happen when trainers inadvertently close the door when they use the bathroom. They do this out of habit, forgetting their cats must always have free access to their toilet facilities.

An exception to this rule may be made immediately after your cat has deposited his wastes in the proper place. You can be reasonably sure he won't need to use the bathroom again for awhile.

If you want privacy at a time when your cat has not recently eliminated his wastes, take him into the bathroom with you and close the door. The more time he spends in the bathroom, the easier toilet training will be.

Keep Lid Open and Seat Down—During later steps of training, your cat needs constant access to the unlidded bathroom toilet. Never lower the toilet-seat lid and leave it down—you can't blame your cat if he has an elimination accident in this situation. Your cat may accidentally knock the lid down on his own. If this begins to happen often, solve the problem as described on page 152.

Men often lift the seat to use the bathroom toilet, then neglect to return it to its lowered position. Because your cat needs the stability of the seat to comfortably eliminate his wastes, this habit can be frustrating to him. To ensure the seat is always returned to a down position, put a note on the wall near the toilet in your bathroom.

ASSEMBLE TRAINING TOOLS

Make sure you have all necessary items on hand before you begin to toilet train your cat. These include a *training toilet,* a *toilet insert,* a *clicker* and several other small items.

TRAINING TOILET

During the first stage of toilet training— when your cat still uses litter to eliminate his wastes—you use a training toilet.

The training toilet consists of a litter container with a toilet seat on top. Gradually, you phase out the litter, and your cat learns to eliminate his wastes in water instead.

Litter Container—A sturdy round dishpan or washtub is an ideal litter container. The diameter may be from 12 to 15 inches, depending on the size of your cat. It should be 5 to 6 inches deep, with a rim that is 1/4 to 1/2 inch wide.

The litter container may be strong vinyl plastic or hard rubber. The bottom should be flat, not round. Appropriate containers can be found in most variety stores.

Some young kittens are small enough to use the *toilet insert,* which is introduced later in training, as a litter container. The toilet insert is described on page 102.

Training-Toilet Seat—Toilet seats come in two sizes—standard and elongated. Buy a standard-size seat to use on your cat's training toilet.

Hard vinyl plastic toilet seats are available in variety, hardware and discount department stores. They are inexpensive and easy to clean. Choose one with a dull finish.

If possible, buy a toilet seat similar to the color of the seat on your bathroom toilet. If you can't find one, buy any shade you wish. Although your cat is not completely color blind, he does not see shades of color in the same way you do.

When you have bought a toilet seat, use a screwdriver to remove the lid, and discard it. You now have an oval to use as the training-toilet seat.

Making a Training Toilet—The training toilet is made by placing the standard toilet seat on top of the litter container. Rest the toilet seat firmly on the rim of the litter container so it does not easily slide or wobble off the rim.

If you want to fasten the seat securely to prevent your cat from knocking it off, use a drill, ice pick or awl to make holes in two opposite sides of the litter container. Position each hole at least 1 inch below the rim. Use string or thin wire to firmly tie the training toilet seat to the litter container.

TOILET INSERT

A toilet insert is a device that fits into your toilet. It is used in Steps 3 through 5 of toilet training. At first you fill the toilet insert with litter to help your cat make the transition to the bathroom toilet. Later you phase out the litter, then eliminate the device itself.

You have three options for a toilet insert—a rimmed mixing bowl, a hospital sitz bath or a patented device especially designed for training cats to use the bathroom toilet.

Rimmed Mixing Bowl—Before buying a rimmed mixing bowl, measure the side-to-side diameter of your bathroom toilet bowl at its widest point. Don't include the porcelain rim in your measurement. Most toilets measure from 10 to 11-1/2 inches from one side to the other.

Take a ruler or a tape measure with you when you shop for the rimmed mixing bowl. A quarter of an inch makes a big difference when you fit the bowl into your toilet.

The rimmed mixing bowl should be 1/2 inch wider than the side-to-side diameter of your toilet. When you measure the diameter of the mixing bowl, include the rim in your measurement. The bowl should be 5 to 6 inches deep. Four- or 5-quart mixing bowls are usually the right size. Stainless steel and sturdy plastic are the best materials for the mixing bowl.

The rim of the mixing bowl should fit firmly over the porcelain rim of your bathroom toilet bowl. It should be balanced and not wobbly. The toilet seat should go down neatly over the rim of the mixing bowl. It is all right if the bottom of the mixing bowl dips slightly into the toilet water.

Hospital Sitz Bath—Plastic sitz baths are available from hospital or sickroom supply stores. If your town does not have such a store, your local pharmacist can order a sitz bath for you.

Size is not a problem if you use a plastic sitz bath because its bowl is designed to fit snugly into your toilet bowl. You will, however, have to make some modifications to the rim of the sitz bath in order to lower your bathroom toilet seat over it.

You may discard the solution bag and plastic tubing that come with the sitz bath. To modify the sitz bath, use a jigsaw to cut off the raised plastic tubing guide at the front of the bath bowl. Cut off the raised back rest at the back of the bowl. Cut off the inverted rim that runs along the sides of the bowl.

You now have a toilet insert that fits snugly into your toilet bowl. Your bathroom toilet seat closes neatly over the insert.

Don't be concerned about the raised tubing guide at the bottom of the sitz bath.

Training toilet consists of litter container and toilet seat.

Rimmed mixing bowl makes stable toilet insert.

Hospital sitz bath before and after modification for toilet training.

This won't bother your cat during early steps of training. For Step 5 of training, you will remove it with a jigsaw when you phase out the toilet insert.

Commercial Toilet-Training Device— You can buy a patented device especially designed to train your cat to use the bathroom toilet. The device is made by Sun Hill Industries, Inc., and is available in some pet stores.

You can order the device through the mail from Walter Drake, Colorado Springs, Colorado 80940. Request a catalog for current item number and price.

The toilet-training device consists of a thin, clear-plastic form with a broad rim that fits over the porcelain rim of your bathroom toilet bowl. The center of the form is a depressed oval, about 1 inch deep.

Because it is made of thin plastic, the depressed oval buckles when your cat stands on it. This may make him so uncomfortable that he chooses to eliminate his wastes in the perch-squat position on the bathroom toilet seat. That is ideal. Your goal in toilet training is to train your cat to eliminate his wastes into the bathroom toilet from the perch-squat position.

The Sun Hill device comes with a teaching brochure and a small packet of herbs. Discard both these items if you want to follow the slow-but-sure system of training outlined in this book.

It does not matter which type of toilet insert you choose. All work equally well.

BATHROOM TOILET

For successful toilet training, your bathroom toilet must flush properly and be fitted with an appropriate toilet seat.

Flushing—You will be flushing your toilet frequently when you share it with your cat. If the mechanisms in the tank are in good repair, you won't waste water or risk overflow.

If your toilet tank "runs" with a constant flow of water after flushing, you probably need to replace the float ball. Buy one at any hardware store. Follow the installation instructions on the package.

Seat—Some toilet seats can cause problems for your cat. For example, a shiny plastic seat can be slippery, especially when wet. This type of seat is often thin and lightweight. Your cat can easily knock the lid down with his paws.

A soft, padded seat is heavier, but it can be damaged by your cat's claws. Unless you are planning to declaw your cat, this type of seat is not recommended for training.

Some elongated toilet seats have a space of several inches in the front part of the oval. This space makes it difficult for your cat to perch on the front part of the seat when he uses the toilet. You can train him to perch on the side instead, but it's better to have a toilet seat that is a continuous oval.

The hard vinyl toilet seat you buy to use as a training seat is perfect for replacing any of the above types of seats. Keep the screws in a safe place after you remove the lid, and use them to reattach the lid when your cat is finished with the training toilet. Install the seat on your bathroom toilet according to package instructions. The familiar seat may help your cat make the transition to the toilet more easily.

LITTER

You use litter during the first steps of training, then gradually phase it out. Once your cat is completely toilet trained, you may never buy litter again.

Commercial Litters—Many types of commercial litter are available in grocery or discount stores. Absorbent clay is the main ingredient in most. Some litters are made from deodorizing chlorophyll, and some contain scented ingredients that mask the odor of body wastes.

Masking body-waste odors is not advisable during toilet training. We recommend neutral-smelling clay litters over scented or chlorophyll brands. After your cat has used neutral-smelling litter once, the odor of his body wastes encourages him to use the litter again. This encouragement can be important when he is making a major change in his toilet facilities.

If you already use chlorophyll or scented litter, gradually substitute neutral-smelling clay litter. Do this *before* you begin your cat's toilet training.

When you choose a brand of neutral-smelling clay litter, don't change to another brand during toilet training. A change in the smell and texture of his litter can confuse your cat.

Litter Substitutes—Some people save money by using sand or sawdust instead of commercial litter. These materials have two major disadvantages. First, they are not very absorbent. Second, they cling to your cat's coat and paws, and he tracks them around your home. Because of the mess they cause, sand and sawdust litters are not recommended for toilet training.

Litter Deodorants—Several types of scented litter deodorants are on the market. They are not recommended for use during toilet training for the same reason that scented litter is not recommended. Change your cat's neutral-smelling litter frequently to achieve odor control.

ADDITIONAL TOOLS

Food rewards, a clicker and a slotted spoon are essential to your cat's successful toilet training. The rest of the items discussed in this section are optional.

Food Rewards—Preparing and giving food rewards is explained on pages 52 and 53. Food rewards provide positive reinforcement for the behaviors you want to teach your cat. He performs each desired behavior to earn his reward.

In addition to food rewards, you'll need a screw-top jar or plastic refrigerator container for storing the rewards. Keep the container on a shelf or in a cabinet near your bathroom toilet. If you don't have a shelf or cabinet, install one before you begin your cat's toilet training.

Clicker—You will use a toy clicker as a cue during toilet training, as you did in behavior training, to produce desired behaviors.

Cueing in toilet training differs from cueing in behavior training or trick training because your cat can't always produce the behavior you are cueing him to perform. He must wait until his digestive system is ready to eliminate.

The clicker is still an important training tool. As training progresses, the sound of it will often effectively stimulate your cat's digestion.

Slotted Spoon or Scoop—During early stages of toilet training, a spoon or scoop is used to scoop bowel movements from litter into the toilet bowl. Any slotted spoon is good for this purpose. A special litter scoop, equipped with a little rake, can be purchased at a pet store.

Your slotted spoon may also work for cleaning up bowel-movement accidents. If the bowel movement is not well-formed, however, you will need an unslotted spoon for this purpose. Mark its handle with nail polish, and keep it separate from other utensils.

Special Training Aids—You may need additional training aids. These include barriers for the area around the toilet, wood slats, string or tape, a cardboard collar for the toilet insert, a double-sided suction cup, a nightlight and a plastic toy cat. These are discussed in detail later in this chapter. You may have to devise additional training aids to solve problems unique to your cat.

Cleaning and Deodorizing Aids—A plastic drop cloth may be necessary to protect the floor from accidents or to avoid litter mess. Use an inverted box or bowl to protect specific spots from repeated accidents.

You will want to keep a whisk broom and dustpan in your bathroom for cleaning up litter during early stages of training. An aerosol bathroom cleaner and a rough-sided sponge are good for cleaning the training-toilet seat. You use them for cleaning the toilet insert during later stages of training.

If your cat has strong-smelling bowel movements, you may want to keep a scented or unscented deodorant spray in your bathroom. Don't use aerosol sprays in your cat's presence. The hissing sound they make may frighten him.

Incense can freshen the air in your bathroom without making a hissing sound. Close the bathroom door, and burn incense immediately after your cat has used the toilet.

Specialized cleaning and deodorizing

aids are discussed in detail on pages 155 and 156. You will need them only if your cat has frequent urine or bowel-movement accidents.

Cat Repellents—Commercial chemical cat repellents can help discourage your cat from having accidents in a specific spot. They are discussed in detail on page 65.

Never become so discouraged about repeated accidents that you decide to try to repel your cat with snapping devices, such as mousetraps. Instead of resorting to dangerous devices, follow the instructions for stopping problem accidents on pages 151 to 155.

PREPARE YOUR BATHROOM

Use only one bathroom in your home for toilet training your cat. Take the following precautions to "catproof" your bathroom, ensuring his safety and well-being.

HAZARDOUS SUBSTANCES

Many substances that are commonly kept in the bathroom can be harmful or fatal to your cat. Read the list of ingredients on the label of every cleaning agent or drain opener that you keep in the bathroom. Many contain chemicals, such as lye, ammonia or acid, that are poisonous to your cat. Other hazardous substances include spray disinfectants, bleach, toilet-bowl cleaners and plant sprays.

If a product is poisonous, remove it from the bathroom or keep it out of your cat's reach. Take the same steps that you would take to protect your child from poison.

Disinfectants and Bleach—Most spray disinfectants contain toxic chemicals called *creosols.* Never use these products

For cat's safety, put away disinfectants, cleansers and bleach.

when your cat is in the bathroom.

Chlorine bleach is another serious bathroom hazard. Some cats are attracted to it. If it spills, they sniff it or lap it up. Bleach can damage your cat's coat, eyes and nasal passages. If he drinks it, it can poison him.

If you keep bleach and other poisonous cleaning agents in the bathroom, store them in a *locked* cabinet. Don't assume an ordinary cabinet latch can adequately keep out your curious cat.

Toilet-Bowl Cleaners—Because your cat will be using your toilet often, chemicals in toilet-bowl water are of special concern. Some toilet-bowl cleaners are advertised as "automatic." They release a small amount of chemical cleaning agent each time you flush the toilet. They come in

Use water-soluble root fertilizers to protect cats who eat bathroom plants.

solid and liquid forms, and you install them in the flush tank or in the toilet bowl.

Some of these products are labeled as safe for children and pets. Others are labeled as eye irritants.

No matter what the label says, avoid using automatic toilet-bowl cleaners. If your cat puts his paws or tail in the toilet water, dyes in these products can discolor his coat. If he licks them off his coat or drinks from the toilet bowl, the cleaning and deodorizing chemicals get into his system. Regular ingestion of chemicals is not good for your pet.

Many types of toilet-bowl cleaners are not automatic. They are intended for use only on cleaning days, and they come in liquid and crystal forms.

Almost all of these toilet-bowl cleaners

are highly toxic and contain corrosives that can chemically burn your cat's coat and skin. If he sniffs toilet water that contains one of these products, it can seriously damage his nasal passages. If he drinks the water, he may die.

Never use a strong toilet-bowl cleaner when your cat is in the bathroom. If instructions on the label tell you to allow the product to work in the toilet bowl for a period of time, close the bathroom door during the time it is working. Your caution can save your cat's life.

Plant Sprays—Many people enjoy growing house plants in the bathroom. Plants become lush from the high humidity from baths and showers.

If you grow plants in your bathroom, don't use chemical sprays on the leaves.

Many cats eat house plants. If they eat leaves treated with chemical spray, they can become seriously ill. Leaf sprays include fertilizers, insecticides and shine-enhancers.

Use only root fertilizers to feed bathroom plants, and never use leaf-shine products on them. If you need to treat the leaves with an insecticide, choose a nontoxic organic product made from vegetable substances.

Cosmetics—Many cats are attracted to sweet-smelling perfumes, shampoos, lotions and powders.

Most cosmetics won't kill your cat, but they can make him sick if he inhales or eats them. If he plays with them, he may cause expensive and hard-to-clean spills on your bathroom floor.

Broken cosmetic bottles can cut your cat, and stains from lipstick, nail polish or other cosmetics are difficult to remove from his coat.

Return all cosmetics to a firmly latched cabinet immediately after use. Never leave shampoo and cream rinse on the corner of the bathtub.

Medicines—Some cats love sweet-flavored pills and medicines. They will eagerly lap up cough syrup, for example.

Protect your cat by placing all medicine in a firmly latched cabinet. Buy prescriptions in childproof containers. Drugs that are safe for humans can be dangerous for your cat.

HAZARDOUS OBJECTS

Chemicals are not the only dangers your cat may encounter in your bathroom. Many standard bathroom objects can cut, shock or otherwise injure your cat. Examine your bathroom for the following hazards.

Sharp Objects—Keep nail clippers, scissors and shavers in a well-latched cabinet. If your cat plays with these sharp implements, he can be seriously cut.

Dispose of razor blades through the slot in the back of your medicine chest. If your medicine chest doesn't have a slot, use a coffee can with a slot in the plastic lid.

Glass objects become sharp hazards if your cat accidentally breaks them. The potential danger of broken cosmetic bottles has been mentioned. Keep hand mirrors and powder jars in a latched cabinet with cosmetics. Don't display glass or china knickknacks in the bathroom you share with your cat.

Electrical Appliances—Never leave appliances, such as shavers, electric rollers or hair dryers, plugged into a socket in your bathroom. You may find it convenient to leave a small appliance plugged in, but this practice can injure your cat if he chews the cord. A serious electrical shock can burn him badly or cause heart damage and psychological trauma.

If you find your cat in the state of being shocked by a chewed-through electrical cord, don't touch him with your bare hands. Use a dry washcloth to grasp the wire, and pull it from his mouth. Take him to the vet as soon as possible.

Cats also can be burned by electrical appliances that aren't plugged in. If you leave a hot curling iron in the bathroom, your cat may touch the heating unit before it cools. The same thing can happen with sunlamps, clothing irons and electric heaters.

Never leave electric heaters or fans on when you aren't in the bathroom. This rule applies to in-the-wall and free-standing units. A heater or fan may be protected by a wire grid, but your cat's paws or tail may

Hot appliances in bathrooms burn cats.

story of a house or an apartment building, windows can be hazardous if not securely screened. If your cat accidentally knocks the screen out of an open window, he can fall from the ledge to the ground below.

Cats have survived falls of more than 20 stories, but their bones and internal organs are frequently injured from the impact of landing. It's a good idea to take your cat to the vet for a checkup if he falls from a height of one story or more.

DISTRACTIONS

Some bathroom objects, such as towels, wastebaskets or toilet-paper rolls, can't hurt your cat. However, they can distract him enough to interfere with his toilet training.

Towels—If you have a towel rack on the wall beside your toilet, don't use it while you are toilet training your cat. Some cats play with hanging towels. Later in training, hanging towels may be targets for misplaced scratching.

If your cat accidentally pulls down a towel, it may block his access to his toilet facility. In any case, it may frighten or confuse him. The convenience of hanging towels on the rack beside the toilet isn't worth the risk of giving your cat negative feelings about the bathroom.

Wastebasket—Many people keep a small wastebasket on the floor beside the bathroom toilet. This is convenient, but it can also distract or confuse your cat.

Some cats eliminate their wastes in the bathroom wastebasket. This happens most often when the cat is making the transition from the training toilet to the bathroom toilet.

Some cats overturn the bathroom wastebasket and play with or scatter its contents.

be small enough to fit between the wires.

Bathroom Door—Closing the door behind you when you enter the bathroom poses another hazard to your cat. This is especially true if you are toilet training a young kitten. You may accidentally close the door on him as he follows you in, breaking his bones or injuring his internal organs.

Avoid injuries by checking to make sure your cat is not following you before you enter the bathroom. Never slam the bathroom door—close it gently behind you.

Bathroom Windows—Make sure your bathroom windows fasten securely in the raised position. Cats have been injured by windows that suddenly fell on them.

If your bathroom is located on an upper

Discourage toilet-paper play or it may become a nuisance.

To prevent messes, remove trash containers from bathroom during toilet training.

Avoid wastebasket-related accidents and messes by moving the basket to the top of the toilet tank. If your cat continues to play with it, put it in a firmly latched cabinet. Return the wastebasket to its location beside the toilet when your cat has completed toilet training.

Toilet Paper—Some cats play with toilet paper. They may unwind the entire roll and scatter it throughout the bathroom.

This may seem cute the first time it happens. But if you must clean up strewn toilet paper often, your amusement will rapidly turn to irritation.

In later stages of toilet training, some cats pull sheets of toilet paper into the toilet water in an effort to cover their wastes. They may pull so much paper into the toilet you have to scoop it out before flushing. Wads of soggy toilet paper can clog your toilet line.

Some cats use the toilet-paper roll as a target for misplaced scratching. They can destroy entire rolls of toilet paper.

If your cat causes any of the above problems, immediately remove the toilet-paper roll from the roller on the wall. Don't allow toilet-paper play or scratching to become habitual. Keep the toilet paper on a shelf or cabinet near the toilet until your cat has completed toilet training.

If your cat cannot resist playing with toilet paper after toilet training, consider a toilet-paper dispenser. This is a special toilet-paper holder, similar to ones found in public restrooms, with a cover that descends over the roll of toilet paper. You may order the device through plumbing-supply stores. The device will permanently end your cat's toilet-paper play.

BASIC TECHNIQUES OF TOILET TRAINING

Before you begin the step-by-step process of toilet training described in Chapter 5, you should understand some general principles that apply to toilet training your cat. Fix the following techniques firmly in your mind. Review them frequently during the weeks or months you spend training your cat.

LIMIT NUMBER OF TRAINERS AND SESSIONS

As in behavior training, limit trainers during toilet training to yourself and one or two training partners. More trainers than this may confuse your cat. Trainers should conduct sessions separately, not together. Your cat learns best on a one-to-one basis.

Arrange training schedules with your partners in advance. You don't want your cat to become overworked by two or more enthusiastic trainers who don't know how many sessions have already been held in a day.

HUNGER AND THIRST

The basic needs of hunger and thirst play an important part in your cat's successful training. Meal schedules and types of food were discussed on pages 97 and 98. Apply these rules strictly when you are toilet training your cat.

By controlling your cat's feedings, you help him establish regular elimination patterns that will help in toilet training. You also regulate his level of hunger, so he will be eager to earn food rewards.

Give Him Fresh Water—Always have a large bowl of fresh water in your cat's eating place. This discourages him from drinking from the toilet. During Steps 3

Discuss training plans with training partner.

and 4 of training, your cat doesn't have access to toilet water. After he progresses to Step 5, toilet water will often be contaminated with bowel movements and urine.

Drinking contaminated water won't hurt your cat, but it shouldn't be encouraged. A bowl of fresh water at your cat's eating place makes it unnecessary for him to drink toilet water.

REWARDS AND DISCIPLINE

Use basic behavior-modification techniques—rewards and discipline—in the same way you used them for other types of cat training. Rewards include food and stroking.

Food Rewards for Desired Toilet Behaviors—Food rewards are important in toilet training. Your cat accepts toilet behaviors that are unnatural to him to earn the tasty tidbits you offer.

Toilet-training rewards should be a little larger than the tiny tidbits used in trick training. But never make them more than a quarter of a mouthful in size. Prepare and store a week's supply at a time.

During Step 1 of toilet training, count on offering from 4 to 10 rewards a day. During Step 2, you will offer at least 20. During later steps, you may offer from 4 to 10 rewards, depending on how often you catch your cat in the act of eliminating his wastes.

Defrost prepared sandwich bags of food treats overnight in the refrigerator. In the morning, empty the bag of food treats into a small screw-top jar or plastic container.

Keep treats in a cabinet or on a shelf near the toilet in your bathroom. Make sure the storage place is easy for you to reach but inaccessible to your cat.

When you leave home, put the jar of treats back in the refrigerator to retard the growth of harmful bacteria. When you return, replace the jar in the bathroom. Food treats must always be on hand to offer as immediate rewards. Instructions for safely offering rewards on a can appear on page 53.

Food Rewards for Previously Learned Behaviors—If you followed the instructions for behavior training in Chapter 3, you are already offering your cat food rewards. You may occasionally give him treats when he comes when called or uses his scratching post. If you have trained him to perform tricks, you are also giving him miniature rewards on a random basis during trick-review sessions.

Throughout the period of your cat's toilet training, continue to offer him food rewards he is accustomed to receiving. You don't want him to lose well-established behaviors because he feels they don't pay off. If your cat is in a frequently rewarded step of toilet training, make the treats you give him for other behaviors smaller than usual. If possible, offer the treats less often. Frequent food rewards for other behaviors should not reduce your cat's hunger to the point he doesn't feel the need to earn food rewards by acquiring new toilet habits. Eventually you will entirely phase out toilet-related food rewards.

Stroking Rewards—Stroking not only gives you and your cat pleasure, but it strengthens your special bond of friendship.

Stroke your cat and call him by name after you have given him a food reward for performing a desired toilet behavior. Stroke him frequently between training sessions in the bathroom. If you must discipline your cat for eliminating his wastes in an inappropriate place, stroke him within 10 minutes after you administer the discipline. This will assure him that although you are unhappy with his action, you still love him.

Discipline for Toilet Accidents—Discipline techniques for toilet training are basically the same as those described in Chapter 2. But in toilet training, it is important to catch your cat performing an undesired toilet behavior. Discipline must be fast to be effective.

If you see your cat eliminating his wastes in a place you don't want him to, hold him so he can't run away. Put his head directly over his wastes so he can smell the odor. *Don't rub your cat's nose in his wastes.* This offends his instinctive desire for cleanliness. Making your cat smell his wastes is as effective as nose-rubbing, and it allows you to keep his affection and respect.

At the same time your cat is smelling his wastes, make a brief hissing sound, and place your upraised hand in front of his face. Then lightly flip him on the nose and firmly say *"No!"* If the accident is a bowel movement, scoop it up with a spoon. With your cat in your arms, take the bowel movement to the training toilet or the bathroom toilet, and place it inside. Put your cat on the training seat or the toilet seat. Let him see where his bowel movement belongs.

If the accident is urine, soak a facial tissue in the moisture. With your cat in your arms, take the urine-scented tissue to the training toilet or the bathroom toilet, and place it inside. Put your cat on the training seat or the toilet seat. Make him smell the tissue so he realizes where his urine belongs.

Delayed Discipline—Sometimes you may discover an accident after it has happened. As discussed previously, delayed corrective discipline is not as effective as immediate discipline. In fact, most animal-behavior specialists believe it has no effect at all.

Because you aren't using harsh techniques, you can administer delayed discipline if you want to. Carry your cat to the spot where he had the accident, and show him his wastes. Discipline him as described above. Keep in mind that the delayed discipline is unlikely to have much effect on your cat's future behavior.

Have Sympathy—You may not feel sympathetic when you are angry and disappointed about a toilet-training accident. It becomes easier if you try to see things from your cat's point of view.

Your cat doesn't understand right and wrong as you know it. He understands what feels comfortable and what doesn't. When he resists a step in toilet training, he isn't deliberately doing wrong. He is shying away from something that doesn't feel comfortable to him.

Don't get angry at your cat for doing what comes naturally to him. You can't expect him to understand why you are frustrating his desire to follow his natural instincts.

Your cat goes through the steps of toilet training because he has an affection for you and because you offer rewards. But some steps are difficult for him. Have sympathy with your cat when he has an accident—he's doing the best he can.

TRANSITION TRAINING

Toilet training is more difficult when your cat advances from one step of training to another. During these times, you need special knowledge and techniques.

RULES OF TIMING

Deliberate slowness is a major factor in successful transition training. Some steps may take more than a month to complete, but the time you devote is worth it. What your cat learns, he learns for good.

Weekends are Important—Make major changes in your cat's toilet arrangements on a weekend or when you have a lot of free time. You need to be close to administer discipline and offer rewards.

Don't plan demanding outside activities on a weekend when you are making a major step in toilet training. Your cat needs your full energy and attention.

Time Establishes Habits—Give your cat an adequate amount of time to become comfortable with each new step of toilet training. Don't allow enthusiasm to tempt you to shorten the time periods we recommend.

To master some steps, your cat may need longer periods than recommended. If this occurs, give him extra weeks or months to become comfortable with the difficult step.

Never go on to a new step of training until your cat has mastered the previous step. Take each step slowly but surely—there is no rush. Rushing makes your cat feel frustrated and rebellious. He may express his frustration by depositing his wastes in inappropriate places. He may regress to an earlier step of training. You gain nothing by rushing your cat.

Step Backward, If Necessary—A particular step of toilet training may be unusually difficult for your cat. He may accept it for a while, then suddenly rebel by eliminating his wastes in inappropriate places. You patiently coax him back into accepting the new step, only to have him rebel once more.

If you encounter repeated rebellions, go back to the step of training immediately previous to the one your cat is rejecting. Wait until he is comfortable with it, then introduce the new step again.

If your cat continues to reject the new step, go back to Step 1 of training. Spend at least a week on each succeeding step until you reach the step your cat has been finding difficult. He is likely to accept it when you introduce it the third time around.

Never feel that taking a step backward is a sign of failure. It's a technique based on a sound principle of animal training. You take psychological pressure off your cat by

Give cat time to become comfortable with each new step.

moving him back to a step he has already mastered. He is relaxed and ready when you introduce the difficult step a second or third time.

CAT'S POINT OF VIEW

No matter what step of training you introduce, it is always easier to teach your cat to accept the new step for urination. This is because of the different ways in which he perceives his liquid and solid wastes.

Urine—Physically, it is easy for cats to urinate. Neither male nor female cats have to exert special muscles to force urine from their bladders. The urine flows out easily and naturally.

Socially, cats in the wild use highly scented urine to convey important messages. They use it to announce their presence to other cats and to convey arousing aromas to attract mates. Urination is a comfortable act often done on voluntary command. Because your cat is at ease about urine, it's usually simple to teach him to urinate on the toilet.

Bowel Movements—In your cat's mind, a bowel movement is distinctly different from urine. You can tell this because he almost never has a bowel movement at the same time he urinates.

Once toilet-trained, your cat will jump onto the toilet, urinate and jump down to the floor. A minute later, he may jump back onto the toilet to have his bowel movement.

Physically, bowel movements often demand a thrust of the rectal muscles. At first, it's awkward for your cat to thrust his muscles while he is perching on the toilet. He may prefer to have the support of at least one foot on a lower surface.

Socially, cats in the wild always bury their bowel movements. This may be to conceal their presence from prey. Because your cat is not physically or socially comfortable about his unburied bowel movements, it is more difficult to teach him to have them in the toilet.

TRANSITION TECHNIQUES

Use these methods to help your cat get over his natural resistance to a major transition or change in his toilet facility. The same methods apply whether you are introducing the litter box, the training toilet or the bathroom toilet. For this reason, this section uses the term *new toilet facility* to refer to all three of these possibilities.

Acquaint Him with New Facility—If you are dealing with a newly acquired cat or kitten, acquaint him with his new toilet facility immediately after he has explored your home on the first day.

If you are dealing with a cat who's been part of your household, acquaint him with his new toilet facility on the morning of a day you can be home at all times. Allow

Let him explore new toilet facility.

your cat to watch you make the change in his toilet facility. Put him on his new facility, and encourage him to explore it on his own. If he shows no interest, guide him gently with your hands until he has seen and smelled every aspect of the new facility.

Throughout the day, repeat the get-acquainted process. Don't disturb him if he's eating or sleeping. He'll probably dislike the disturbance and may transfer his negative feelings to the bathroom.

Be Watchful—Keep a close eye on your cat during the first few days after you introduce a new toilet facility. Continue your watchfulness until he has used the new facility at least six times on his own.

Follow your cat every time he goes into the bathroom. Place him on his new facility

Closed eyes, arched back and lifted tail signal elimination.

or cue him onto it with the clicker. Try to elicit elimination with the techniques described below. If he does not eliminate, don't forcibly restrain him. You want him to think of the bathroom as a pleasant place with no associations with anxiety.

Confine Yourself with Him—If your cat doesn't eliminate, stay in the bathroom with him. Watch him closely for the signals of elimination described below. The moment you see one, pick him up and put him on his new toilet facility. When he uses it, click the clicker and offer a food reward.

If your cat is strongly resisting his new toilet facility, you may have to spend hours in the bathroom with him. He is suppressing his wastes so he can deposit them in an inappropriate place when he's alone. Eventually he won't be able to suppress his wastes, and you can make him use his new toilet facility. Once you have made him use it several times, his resistance will weaken and disappear.

Make yourself and your cat comfortable in the bathroom if you think you are going to have a long wait. If you have a training partner, arrange to take shifts.

If your cat meows at the bathroom door, try to distract him with stroking or play. If he continues to complain about his confinement, let him out for a break. Keep your eye on him at all times to avoid accidents.

No Extremes—Don't carry your watchful sessions in the bathroom to ridiculous extremes. Don't spend the night on the floor, for example. Such extreme behavior can give your cat stress-induced constipation. It can lead you into a bitter battle of wits with your cat.

When you tire of waiting in the bathroom, leave your cat alone there with the door closed. Check on him frequently.

Your cat may have been suppressing his wastes because of a desire to be alone. If this is the case, he may eliminate them in the new facility immediately after he's left alone. If he does, click the clicker and reward him with a food treat and stroking. When the time comes for his next regular bowel movement, confine him in the bathroom alone.

If confusion causes your cat to suppress his wastes, he'll probably eliminate them in an inappropriate place as soon as he's alone. If he does, discipline him as directed on pages 113 and 114.

When the time comes for your cat's next regular bowel movement, confine yourself in the bathroom with him again. Try to get him to use his new toilet facility. Don't allow him to establish the habit of having accidents in the bathroom.

ELIMINATION SIGNALS

It is important to know the signals that indicate that your cat is about to eliminate. When you see one of them, you can put him on his new toilet facility.

Normal Signs—Your cat may signal a need to eliminate by scratching the floor, the toilet seat or the toilet water with his front paws. This signal is most often seen when he has recently graduated from a litter stage of training.

Loud meowing may indicate your cat is uncomfortable because he needs to eliminate. During times of transition, he may meow loudly to indicate confusion about his new toilet facility.

You can tell urination is about to begin when your cat squats and lifts his tail. He may slightly arch his back and lay back his ears.

The squat, lifted tail, arched back and laid-back ears are also signals of a bowel movement. Your cat's body may contract, and his flanks may tremble as he eliminates his solid wastes. His outer or inner eyelids may descend over his eyes.

False Tries—Outdoor cats often make several efforts to have a bowel movement before they successfully eliminate. They dig a number of holes in different places before they finally deposit and bury their wastes.

Remember this natural pattern during transition stages of toilet training. Your cat's confusion about his new facility is likely to cause him to make false tries. Never get angry if he fails to have a bowel movement on his first few efforts. If you wait patiently, he will probably successfully eliminate.

Signs of Suppression—Your cat may pass gas while he is suppressing a bowel movement. If you smell the odor, be alert to the fact that he probably won't be able to suppress his bowel movement much longer.

Your cat may make several false tries to have a movement, then begin licking his rectum. He is imitating the way his mother used to stimulate his bowels when he was a tiny kitten. If the licking successfully stimulates his digestive tract, he is likely to have a bowel movement soon.

If your cat continues to make false tries, he may have stress-induced constipation. This condition is not unusual during transition stages of training. Constipation is discussed in detail on page 160. Be sure to use the recommended remedies—serious constipation can be a threat to your cat's life.

HOW TO ELICIT ELIMINATION

The following techniques can cut down on your waiting time in the bathroom. Try them when you suspect your cat is suppressing his wastes.

Scratching Motion—Stimulate both urination and bowel movements by gently moving your cat's front paws in a rapid scratching motion. Do this while he's on his new toilet facility. Use the training seat or the toilet seat as a scratching surface. Make him scratch for about 10 seconds.

Perch-Squat—The perch-squat position is discussed in detail on pages 129 and 130. This is the position in which your cat will use the toilet when he has finished his training. Occasionally you can stimulate elimination by guiding your cat into the perch-squat position.

Stroking—Stroking also may cause your cat's digestive juices to flow. As he gradually becomes relaxed, his system begins the process of moving his bowels. Stroking can be a valuable aid in toilet training because it naturally stimulates elimination.

Try reserving a special type of stroking for times when your cat is urinating in his new toilet facility. Scratch him under the ears or gently stroke under his chin. Your

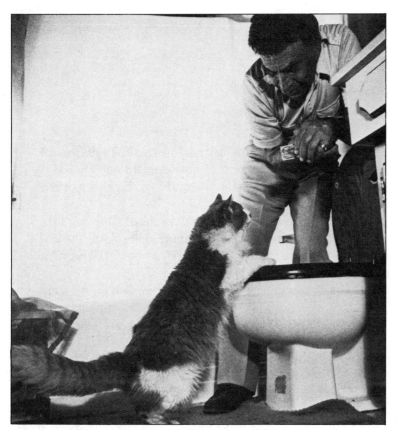

A clicker can help stimulate urination.

cat soon identifies this specific type of stroking with the act of urination. You may be able to elicit urination by stroking him in this special way.

Don't try to stroke your cat while he's having a bowel movement. He dislikes being disturbed at this time.

Food and Water—Drinking water stimulates your cat to urinate. Put a bowl of water on the bathroom floor if you think he's suppressing his urine. Encourage him to drink.

Eating stimulates your cat's bowels. If you think he's suppressing a bowel movement, bring a small bowl of food into the bathroom. Make sure it's not enough to disturb his regular feeding schedule. Encourage him to eat.

Sounds—The noise of running water sometimes encourages urination. Place a stopper in the washbowl drain, and turn on the tap. Let the water run at a trickle until the sink is partially full. Place your cat on his new toilet facility while the water is running.

The sound of the clicker is an excellent sound to stimulate your cat to have a bowel movement. If you regularly click it every time your cat eliminates his wastes in the proper place, he learns to associate the click with the act of elimination. He also associates it with the promise of a food reward. When he hears the click, he may eliminate to receive a reward.

NO SITTING PIGEONS

I wish I didn't have to say this, but it is true. Sometimes performing animals are not treated well in the movie industry. When I became a professional trainer, I made a vow that I'd never be a party to animal mistreatment—and I've stuck to it, even though it has sometimes cost me a job.

One job-threatening incident occurred on a feature-movie shoot. The shot that caused all the trouble involved a pigeon and a cat. According to the script, the cat was supposed to stalk across a long limb to the opposite side of a tree. From here he was to leap at the pigeon before the bird took flight.

Using the lure of a roast-beef treat, along with cues of the clicker and the hiss, my assistant trainer Karl got the cat to slink forward menacingly on the tree limb. He looked like a killer! I stood on the ground, cueing the trained pigeon, who performed with perfect timing.

The action was just what the script called for, and the shot was a "cut and print." Everybody seemed happy but the director. He merely grumbled and motioned for the camera to move on to the next shot on the opposite side of the tree.

Now the cat was to close in on the hapless pigeon. I was standing on a ladder, urging the cat toward the pigeon, when suddenly the director screamed, "Make him grab the pigeon!"

Without even thinking, I replied, "That's not the kind of work we do, sir."

"Don't give me any conversation," he shot back. "I'm the director. I want that cat to latch onto the pigeon."

"It doesn't say anything about that in the script," I said, trying to control my temper. As everyone in the movie business knows, the director is in charge. What he says goes, without question.

"Make him do it!" the director shouted.

Hoping to avert a confrontation, I suggested we cue the pigeon to fly and have the cat leap off camera right behind him. Without answering, the director turned and walked away. The director's first assistant and I looked at each other, wondering what to do.

"Go ahead and do it your way," the assistant said, glancing back at the departing director.

That kind of thing just isn't done on a set. All professionals know the rule that nobody does anything without the director's orders. The assistant and I knew both our fannies were on the line.

As we did the shot, the director and production manager huddled together in an ominous conference. The assistant was beckoned, then the cameraman. It became a full-scale war council.

Karl and I fidgeted nervously. Finally we were called over. "We're going to stop shooting for today," said the assistant. "The director says he won't work with you on this picture."

My mind churned when I heard those words. I knew this could be the end of my motion-picture animal-training career. A film production costs thousands of dollars every hour, whether it's shooting or not. This disagreement was costing the movie company a bundle—and Karl and I were likely to catch the blame.

Putting our cat in his kennel, we discussed the situation. The only thing that might turn things around was for us to crawl to the director and say we would do his shot. But we decided it wasn't worth it. If we agreed to put our bird in jeopardy, we would compromise everything we believed in. Dejected, we headed back to our hotel to wait for the ax to fall. Our mood was pretty grim as we packed our bags, sure we would be fired in the morning.

The next morning we sipped coffee and anxiously watched the coffee-shop entrance. Soon the production manager entered with another gentleman. The production manager was smiling. "Hey guys," he said, "this is your new director. You better get cracking. We've got a 9 a.m. call."

We inhaled the coffee and split.

The next weeks on that set were a pleasure. Even our cat sensed the change in atmosphere. While he had worked hard before, he now began to work with enthusiasm. Everyone's mood was upbeat and relieved—especially the pigeon's!

Ray Berwick

Chapter 5: Step-by-Step Toilet Training

OK. Let's hurry up and get this over with.

STEP 1. TRAINING TOILET

The training toilet is a round plastic container covered by a lidless toilet seat. It allows your cat to become accustomed to eliminating his wastes in a confined space. It also accustoms him to the presence of a toilet seat.

Locate the training toilet as close to the toilet as possible. If the training toilet fits into the space between the side of the bathroom toilet and the wall, place it there. This gives your cat some privacy and facilitates his transition to the bathroom toilet.

If the training toilet doesn't fit in the space between the side of the bathroom toilet and the wall, select a corner across from the bathroom toilet or a wall beside it.

Some people prefer to put the training toilet in the space under the sink. If you have a cabinet there, empty it and leave the doors open.

Shower Stall or Bathtub—Before you choose the shower stall or bathtub as a location, consider the following. These locations have two advantages. You can easily clean spilled litter from them, and you can draw the shower curtain to conceal the training toilet from guests.

A major disadvantage is that they may make your cat's toilet training difficult. Even after months of training, your cat may revert to eliminating his wastes in the shower stall or bathtub.

Don't take the chance of creating future problems. Locate the training toilet on the *floor,* close to the bathroom toilet.

NEW CAT OR KITTEN

From the beginning, your new pet should learn the bathroom is the place to eliminate his wastes. If your new cat is a stray, you have no way of knowing if he was trained to use a litter box. You do know he has been using the outdoors during the time he's been a stray.

Have your vet examine a stray cat for parasites and skin diseases. When you're sure he's healthy, introduce him to the training toilet in the manner described on page 116.

If your new cat is from an animal shelter, pet shop, breeder or friend, ask questions about his previous toilet training before you take him home. Has he been trained to use a litter box or the outdoors? If he's been trained to use a box, where was it located? What kind of litter was used?

If possible, take a look at the litter box before you take your new cat home. Un-

derstanding his familiar toilet arrangements can help you correct any problems that arise when you introduce him to the training toilet in your bathroom.

For example, if your new cat has been accustomed to using a litter box under a table, he may object to using the training toilet in the corner beside the bathroom toilet. Move the training toilet to a less-exposed location, such as the cabinet under the sink. Place it in the corner near the bathroom toilet after your cat has adjusted to your household. Instructions for gradually moving a litter box, pages 126 and 127, may be helpful when you decide to move the training toilet.

Litter—Buy litter that closely duplicates the type your cat has been accustomed to using. The familiar texture and smell will help him adjust to the strangeness of the training toilet.

If your cat's original litter was strongly scented, use that brand during his first week in your home. Each time you change the litter, mix the strongly scented brand with larger proportions of a neutral-smelling litter. Neutral-smelling litters are best for toilet training.

During your cat's first week in your home, fill the training toilet with at least 3 inches of litter. He may not use the training toilet if it doesn't contain enough litter to allow him to bury his bowel movements.

Your Cat's First Day—Quietly introduce your new cat or kitten to your home as described in Chapter 1. Show him his food and water. Take him into the bathroom to show him the training toilet.

If you're lucky, your cat will recognize the look and smell of his familiar litter in the training toilet. He will jump over the training toilet seat and eliminate his wastes.

Gently introduce new pet to training toilet.

If your cat does not jump into the training toilet on his own, pick him up and place him inside. Move his feet in a scratching motion. Stroke him and speak softly to him. If he doesn't eliminate his wastes, don't restrain him in the training toilet.

Wait for Him to Eat—Closely watch your cat during his first few hours in your home. When he finishes eating, take him to the training toilet in the bathroom. Confine yourself with him.

Use the transition techniques discussed in Chapter 4. Continue to use them until your cat has eliminated his urine or bowel movement in the training toilet. Click the clicker, and offer him a food reward before he leaves the training toilet.

Accidents—At first your cat might eliminate his wastes on the floor of a room that resembles the room that held his original litter box. He may object to the strangeness of the training toilet by eliminating his wastes on the floor beside it. He may find a hidden place to eliminate his wastes.

If accidents occur, don't move the training toilet out of the bathroom. From the first day in your home, your cat must learn the bathroom is the proper place to eliminate his wastes.

Discipline for accidents immediately with the techniques described earlier. Don't use physical punishment or scold your cat. He is not being bad—he's probably frightened and confused by his new surroundings.

FOLLOW-UP TECHNIQUES

After your cat has eliminated his wastes in the training toilet the first time, continue his toilet training by using the techniques described below.

Don't Change Litter—Wait until your cat has used the training toilet at least twice on his own before changing the litter.

Apply this rule until your cat has used the training toilet without accidents for at least 1 week. Every time you change the litter, wait until your cat has used it twice before you change it again. His body-waste odors attract him to the soiled litter.

Reduce Litter Level—When your cat is accustomed to using the training toilet in the bathroom, begin to use less litter. During training, you must overcome his instinct to bury his bowel movements. When the training toilet contains only a small amount of litter, his instinct is already partially frustrated.

One inch of litter is adequate after your cat has been using the training toilet without accidents for 1 week. Don't let him enjoy the sensation of scratching in deep litter.

Continue Rewards—When you see your cat eliminating his wastes in the training toilet, click the clicker and give him a food reward *before* he leaves the toilet. Stroke him, and speak softly to him after he eats the reward. Continue stroking after he has left the training toilet.

From the beginning of his training, your cat learns that eliminating his wastes in a toilet-seat-covered device produces rewarding results. He associates the sound of the clicker with two events—eliminating wastes and receiving a reward.

Sometimes your cat eliminates his wastes when you're asleep or away from home. You find them in the litter container hours after he has eliminated them.

Don't reward your cat for old wastes you find in the litter. He doesn't understand the meaning of long-delayed rewards, just as he doesn't understand the meaning of delayed discipline.

You may find your cat meows after he has urinated or had a bowel movement. He is calling you to come and offer him his reward. In this case, click the clicker and offer him a food treat. He has shown you he understands the reason he is receiving rewards.

Some cats wait until their owners are home before they eliminate their wastes. They know the act will produce a reward only if their owners are there to offer it.

Your cat's eager anticipation of his rewards is good. It will help him get through the steps of toilet training ahead.

LONG-TERM PET

Start your long-term pet's toilet training at a time when he's happy and healthy. Because toilet training can be a strain for him, he should start it in the best condition.

Advantages and Disadvantages—There are several advantages to toilet training a cat who has spent months or years in your home. The cat already knows you and loves you. You are well-acquainted with his habits and personality.

Begin to feed your cat to promote bowel-movement regularity at least 2 weeks before you begin toilet training. Keep records of the times when he has bowel movements in his litter box. Learn his regular elimination patterns.

There are two disadvantages to training a long-term pet. Unless his litter box is located beside the toilet in the bathroom, you will have to move it before you begin his toilet-training program. You will also eventually have to replace the litter box with the training toilet.

If you are training a new pet, on the other hand, you can start him out with a training toilet beside the bathroom toilet immediately after he arrives in your home.

Litter—If you have been using strongly scented litter, gradually change to neutral-smelling litter recommended for toilet training. Do this *before* you move your cat's litter box to the bathroom.

Each time you change the litter, mix more neutral-smelling litter with the strongly scented brand. Gradually reduce the amount of litter you put in the box until the level is reduced to 1 inch. When your cat regularly uses his box with 1 inch of neutral-smelling litter, you're ready to move his litter box to the bathroom.

Move Litter Box—Move your cat's litter box to a spot in the bathroom as close as possible to the place where you will eventually locate the training toilet.

Wait until the litter in your cat's box has been well-used before you move the box to the bathroom. Your cat's body-waste odors attract him to the box.

Move the box on the morning of a day when you can be home all day. Make the move immediately after your cat has eaten breakfast. Let your cat see you move the box.

Close the door to the room where the litter box was originally located. Keep the door shut for at least 2 weeks to prevent possible accidents. If the room has carpeting or a hardwood floor, use a plastic drop cloth to protect the area where the litter box used to be. Keep the drop cloth down for at least 1 month.

Encourage Elimination—When your cat has finished his breakfast, take him to his litter box in the bathroom. Place him in it. Move his feet in a scratching motion to encourage him to eliminate.

If you've been keeping records of your cat's regular elimination patterns, you can fairly accurately predict when he is likely to have a bowel movement. When the time comes, confine yourself in the bathroom with him.

Use the transition techniques discussed on pages 116 and 117. Continue to apply these techniques until your cat has eliminated his solid wastes in the litter box. Click the clicker, and give him a food reward before he leaves the litter box. Then apply the follow-up techniques on pages 124 and 125.

Accidents—Your cat may object to having his litter box moved. He may express his objection by eliminating his wastes at inappropriate places around your home. If you don't shut the door to the room where his litter box was originally located, he may eliminate his wastes on the floor

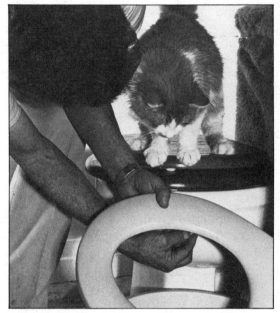

Toilet seat on litter box is transition step for long-term pet.

where the litter box used to be.

If accidents occur, don't move your cat's litter box back to its original location. As a first step in toilet training, your cat must learn the bathroom is the proper place to eliminate his wastes.

After accidents, discipline your cat immediately with the techniques described on pages 113 and 114. Don't use harsh physical punishment or loud scolding. Your cat is not being bad—he is simply confused. He cannot understand why you have suddenly moved his litter box.

Alternative Ways to Move Box—If your cat shows you by repeated accidents that he is confused by the move of his litter box, try one of these alternatives. After 1 week of frequent accidents, buy a new litter box. Put it where the original box was located. Keep the original box in the bathroom near the toilet.

Allow your cat to use both boxes as he

wishes. Click the clicker, and give him a food reward whenever he uses the box in the bathroom. Don't reward him when he uses the box in the old location.

When your cat is comfortably using both boxes, close the door to the room with the new box in it. Watch your cat closely. If he meows at the closed door to the room with the new box, put him in the litter box in the bathroom. Click the clicker and give him a reward when he eliminates his wastes there.

Remove the new litter box from the room where your cat originally eliminated his wastes. To prevent accidents, keep the door closed for at least 2 weeks as instructed above.

If the two-box method doesn't work with your cat, move his original litter box gradually. Place the box back in the room where it used to be. When your cat has used it consistently for 3 days, begin to move it along a wall in the direction of the bathroom. Move it a few feet each day.

Each time your cat eliminates his wastes in the box, click the clicker and give him a food reward. When the box is finally in the bathroom, wait at least 1 week before you introduce the training-toilet seat.

Add Training-Toilet Seat—Place the training-toilet seat on top of your cat's litter box in the bathroom. Align the front of the training seat with the front of the bathroom toilet seat. Show your cat his seat-covered litter box, and encourage him to explore it. Use transition techniques until he eliminates his wastes in it.

When the training-toilet seat is on the box, your cat has less room in which to eliminate his wastes. If you're lucky, this will cause him to perch on the training toilet seat and eliminate his wastes down into the litter. More likely, he will jump over the seat into the litter and eliminate his wastes on all fours there.

Do not be concerned about your cat's position in the litter box. You want him to feel comfortable about the presence of the training-toilet seat.

Replace Box with Training Toilet— Make this replacement after your cat has used his box with the training-toilet seat on it for at least 1 week. Because he has become accustomed to eliminating his wastes within the confines of the inner rim of the training seat, he should offer little objection to using the training toilet. It is merely a round litter container topped by a lidless toilet seat.

Put 3 inches of litter in the litter container, so he can thoroughly bury his bowel movements. Use soiled litter from the litter box, so the smell of his body wastes will attract him to the litter container.

Make the change to the litter container on the morning of a day on which you can be home all day. Do it immediately after your cat has eaten breakfast.

Let your cat watch you take his litter box out of the bathroom and put it in a closet or outdoors. Be sure he doesn't have access to the place where you put his box.

Encourage elimination by using standard methods. These include moving your cat's feet in a scratching motion, guiding him into the perch-squat position, and giving him food and water. You can also use sounds such as running water or the clicker. After your cat has used the training toilet, don't change his litter until he has used it again at least two times on his own.

If your cat resists the change in his toilet facility, use transition techniques until he feels comfortable about eliminating his wastes in the training toilet.

TRAINING-TOILET PROBLEMS

Because you are introducing an unfamiliar toilet facility, your cat may become temporarily confused. He may develop a variety of problem behaviors that you will have to take steps to eliminate. Don't become discouraged if your cat has problems. Most of them can be easily solved.

Soiling—Some cats stand on the training-toilet seat and urinate against the wall. If your cat does this, move the training toilet away from the wall so he doesn't have an inviting target. Then begin to teach him the perch-squat position as described on the opposite page.

When your cat has mastered the perch-squat, he will no longer urinate against the wall. His urine will be directed down into the litter.

Some cats repeatedly soil the training-toilet seat with their bowel movements. This problem can also be eliminated by teaching your cat the perch-squat position.

Litter Mess—Some cats scratch the litter vigorously, causing it to fly out of the training toilet. Put a plastic drop cloth or newspaper under the litter container to catch the mess. Reduce the amount of litter you use to minimize the problem.

If litter mess occurs because your cat knocks the training-toilet seat off the litter container as he enters or leaves it, fasten the seat to the litter container.

Kitten Problems—A small kitten may have trouble using the training toilet. A 5- or 6-inch-deep, tub-type litter container may be too high for him. He may have trouble climbing over the training-toilet seat. Kittens don't like to leap blindly over barriers.

Try substituting a mixing bowl or sitz bath toilet insert for the tub. Because the insert is smaller and shallower than the

Cats who eliminate on all-fours inside training toilet often soil seat.

tub, your kitten may prefer it.

If your kitten still has problems climbing over the training-toilet seat, put it away until later in training. Substitute a shallow dishpan or large cake pan without the training toilet seat. The pan must be round and no more than 12 or 13 inches in diameter. Your kitten needs to get used to eliminating in a confining round container.

Your kitten may stand too close to the edge of the low pan and urinate on the floor. Use newspaper or a plastic drop cloth to catch his accidents.

As soon as your kitten is big enough, replace the pan with the training toilet. Don't proceed to Step 2 of training until he is at least 4 months old.

Large-Cat Problems—Some large cats have trouble eliminating their wastes within the confines of the training toilet. They don't have enough space to scratch in the litter and bury their wastes.

Teach a large cat to perch-squat. After he has perched on the training seat and

Large round cake pan solves kitten problems.

eliminated, he can bury his wastes with his forepaws while his back legs rest on the training seat.

PREPARING FOR FUTURE STEPS

After your cat has learned to consistently use the training toilet in the bathroom, begin to do the following to prepare him for future training.

Scoop Solid Waste into Bathroom Toilet—After your cat has had a bowel movement, let him watch you scoop it into the toilet and flush it away. Do this only for bowel movements that are not heavily coated with clay litter. Large amounts of clay litter can clog your toilet line.

Keep the slotted spoon or scoop on top of the bathroom toilet. Encourage your cat in his natural curiosity about what you are doing with his solid waste.

It's not uncommon for a cat to come to expect this scooping service. He will have a bowel movement, then stand by the toilet and meow for you to come and scoop it into the toilet. Encourage him to do this. He is learning that toilet water is the proper place for his bowel movements.

Encourage Alternative Positions— When your cat becomes confident and comfortable about using the training toilet, he may stop climbing into the litter container to eliminate his wastes on all fours. Instead he may begin to assume one of several positions while eliminating. He may rest his two front paws on the training toilet seat. He may rest three paws on the seat, supporting himself with one hind leg in the litter container. He may put all four paws on the seat and eliminate his wastes in the perch-squat position.

Encourage your cat to adopt any of these alternative positions. The fewer paws he puts in the litter container now, the easier training will be later.

Introduce Perch-Squat on Training Seat—You may choose to introduce the perch-squat later in training. However, once your cat is regularly using the training toilet, you can acquaint him with the position at this early stage. Use your hands to guide your cat into the perch-squat on the training-toilet seat. Do this when he is not eliminating his wastes.

Always reward your cat with stroking when you drill him in the perch-squat. Do this for at least 3 days before you go on to Step 2 of training.

STEP 2.
PERCH-SQUAT ON BATHROOM TOILET

If you are training a grown cat, begin practicing Step 2 when your cat is regularly using the training toilet. If you are training a kitten, wait until he's at least 4 months

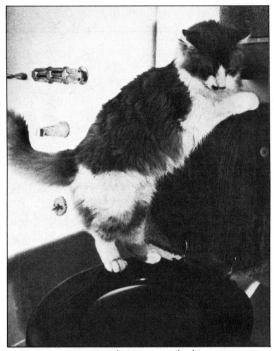
Your cat's curious explorations make him more comfortable with the bathroom toilet.

cat is becoming comfortable about using the training toilet, encourage his natural curiosity about the bathroom toilet. If he jumps up on the toilet seat on his own, click the clicker and offer him a food reward. Stroke your cat as he walks around on the seat.

Speak softly to your cat as he investigates the bathroom toilet. Let him dip a paw into the water. Let him put his two front paws on the sloping porcelain bowl and peer down into the bottom.

Your cat's curiosity about the bathroom toilet is good. He learns water is cold and wet. He becomes aware of the depth of the porcelain bowl. He learns to be sure-footed on the toilet seat.

Falling In—If your cat accidentally slips and falls in the toilet water, he won't drown. Unless he is an unusually small 4-month-old kitten, he is large and agile enough to immediately jump out and lick himself dry. The experience should not upset your cat so badly that he will not go near the toilet again.

Don't force your cat to let you dry him with a towel. Dry him if he seems to want you to, but give him the option of creeping off to care for himself in a secluded place. Cats are often uncomfortable after doing something clumsy. You don't want your cat to develop uncomfortable feelings about the bathroom toilet.

Drinking from Toilet—The importance of providing a bowl of fresh water at your cat's eating place has already been discussed. With plenty of fresh water available, your cat is less likely to drink from the toilet.

Drinking from the toilet may be part of your cat's early explorations. As his training progresses, he may continue to take an occasional lap of water from the toilet

old and large enough to jump onto the toilet.

Perch-squatting on the bathroom-toilet seat is more difficult than on the training-toilet seat. The bathroom-toilet seat is higher than the training-toilet seat. The toilet bowl is filled with water, not litter. These factors can make squatting on the bathroom-toilet frightening to your cat. For this reason, approach this step of training gently and gradually.

PREPARING FOR PERCH-SQUAT

Before you begin to teach your cat the perch-squat position on the bathroom-toilet seat, make him familiar with the bathroom toilet.

Encourage Him To Explore—While your

Getting wet is only a temporary setback.

bowl.

You can't effectively prevent your cat from drinking from the toilet without interfering with toilet training. If you discipline him for doing so, it may cause him to have negative reactions that will slow his progress in toilet training.

Drinking toilet water won't hurt your cat unless it contains toilet-bowl cleaner, as already discussed. Even if the water contains a bowel movement, the germs in it are so diluted that your cat swallows very few of them when he drinks. Many cats won't drink soiled toilet water. They wait for you to flush before they take a drink.

TEACHING PERCH-SQUAT

From this position, your cat will ul-timately eliminate his wastes on the bathroom toilet.

Use Your Hands—Place your cat on the toilet seat. Stand in front of the toilet, and manually guide him into the perch-squat position.

All four of his feet should rest on the toilet seat. His rump should hang out over the inner edge of the seat. His tail should be up and out of the water.

Remove your hands and allow your cat to balance in the perch-squat position on his own. If he does, immediately click the clicker and offer him a food reward.

Stroke and scratch your cat to keep him balancing in the perch-squat. When he becomes restless, allow him to jump down.

Use Front of Seat—Practice the perch-squat on the curved front section of the toilet seat. If your cat learns to use the front of the seat, he can use the sloping porcelain at the front of the toilet bowl for leg support during bowel movements. This support may be important to him when he comes to Step 5 of training.

Some cats find the elongated sides of the seat more secure for the perch-squat. If your cat does, let him have his way at first. You want him to feel comfortable in the perch-squat position.

Practice the perch-squat at least 10 times a day for about 1 week. Make your cat think of the toilet as a positive place where he receives rewards.

Possible Problems—Your cat may try to leap off the toilet seat immediately after he receives his reward. To continue his perch-squat training, restrain him with your hand on his shoulders and block his escape with your legs. Stroke him, and scratch him until he begins to feel content on the toilet seat.

Your cat may drop his tail into the toilet

water. Correct this problem by gently lifting it and placing it on the seat. Continue this until your cat gets the knack of holding his tail out of the water.

Your cat may lose his balance in the perch-squat position. His hind legs may accidentally slip into the water. Allow him to jump out of the toilet bowl and lick himself dry. Guide him back into the perch-squat position as soon as he is dry and comfortable.

CUEING WITH CLICKER

Until now, you have been clicking the clicker *after* your cat produces the behavior you desire. Now you reverse this procedure.

How It Works—In your cat's mind, the clicking sound has become the promise of a reward. He performs the actions he associates with the clicking sound because he expects to receive a food reward for doing so.

At this point in training, your cat has learned to associate the clicking sound with three activities: jumping onto the toilet, balancing in the perch-squat and eliminating his wastes in the training toilet. Now you can make him perform all three of these activities at the sound of the clicker.

Click the clicker, and wait until your cat performs any one of the desired actions. After he has performed it, you give him his reward.

Of course, your cat can't always urinate or have a bowel movement at the moment he hears the clicker. He must wait until his digestive system is ready to eliminate his wastes.

If your cat goes into the training toilet, watch for the signs of elimination described on pages 117 and 118. The moment you see one, click the clicker. The click should come *before, not after,* the act of elimination. This may initially confuse your cat, but eventually he will realize that the clicker is a *demand* for elimination, not just a part of the reward. After your cat has eliminated, give him a food reward.

If your cat does not eliminate, confine yourself in the bathroom with him. Use transition techniques until he shows signs of elimination. Click the clicker before he eliminates, and offer him a food reward after he does.

In Future—Throughout this step and all future steps of toilet training, click the clicker before your cat eliminates his wastes as often as you can. When you successfully do this, don't click it again before you offer him his food reward.

Sometimes your cat eliminates his wastes in the proper place at a time when you aren't in the bathroom. He may call you to come and give him his reward. When this occurs, don't click the clicker. He has shown you he understands there is a direct connection between eliminating his wastes and receiving a food reward.

Combine Jump and Perch-Squat—Stand beside the toilet, and click the clicker. Your cat will probably come running into the bathroom and jump onto the toilet. If he does so, give him a food reward. Use your hands to guide him into the perch-squat. Click the clicker once more and offer another reward.

If the sound of the clicker doesn't bring your cat running, try calling him into the bathroom. If this doesn't work, find him and carry him in.

Click the clicker. If your cat jumps onto the toilet, proceed as above. If he does not, lift him onto the toilet, click the clicker

After several days of training, cat perch-squats without assistance.

again and offer a food reward. Maneuver him into the perch-squat, click the clicker and offer another reward.

After a few days of practicing the perch-squat at least 10 times a day, your cat should eagerly jump up onto the toilet as soon as he hears the sound of the clicker. After he receives his first food reward, he should go into the perch-squat on his own because he knows this maneuver will earn him a second reward.

If he does not go into the perch-squat on his own, coax him into it. Offer him his first food reward for jumping onto the toilet. Then click the clicker to cue for the perch-squat. If your cat does not obediently go into this position, don't manually guide him into it.

Hold your cat's food reward in front of his nose. Make him think about what he has to do to get it. Wait at least 1 minute

before you manually guide him into the perch-squat, then reward him. Continue this drill until your cat obediently goes into the perch-squat at the sound of the clicker.

Combine Elimination with Perch-Squat—Practice this drill immediately after your cat has eliminated his wastes in the training toilet. Give him a food reward for elimination, then stand beside the toilet.

Click the clicker. When your cat jumps onto the toilet seat, give him a reward. When he moves into the perch-squat, offer him another.

When your cat proceeds to future steps of training, he will jump onto the toilet and go into the perch-squat position *before, not after,* he eliminates. This drill merely helps him associate the perch-squat position with the act of elimination.

When to Practice—The best time to drill

Three types of toilet inserts *(left to right):* rimmed mixing bowl; hospital sitz bath; patented toilet-training device for cats.

your cat on the perch-squat is just before a meal. He will be hungry and anxious to receive his food rewards. Make before-meal drills the longest and most-detailed drills of the day.

During periods of training when you are drilling frequently, you will have to space drills throughout the day. This keeps your cat from becoming bored. Choose times when he is awake, relaxed and happy. Never disturb your cat while he's sleeping or eating to practice the perch-squat. He will dislike the disturbance and transfer his negative feelings to the bathroom toilet.

Frequency—After your cat is comfortable in the perch-squat position, begin to drill him less often. After 1 week of drilling 10 times a day, reduce the number of drills to

seven. When your cat advances to Step 3 of training, reduce the drills to five. You briefly increase perch-squat drills to seven a day during the final step of training.

Continue offering food rewards for the perch-squat until your cat has mastered Step 4.

STEP 3. TOILET INSERT

Do not begin this step of training until *after* your cat has consistently used the training toilet in the bathroom for at least 2 weeks. He should also be familiar with the perch-squat position.

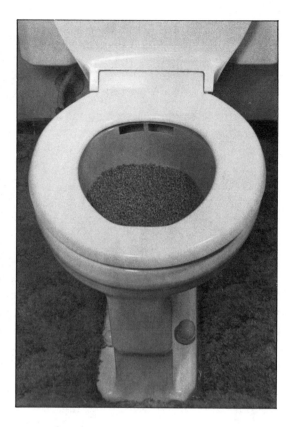

WHEN AND HOW

The three different types of toilet inserts are pictured above. The same training techniques apply to all three during this step of training.

Remove Training Toilet—Some young kittens can use the same receptacle as a litter container in Steps 1 and 2 and a toilet insert in Step 3. If yours is one of these, simply discard the training-toilet seat, and put the litter container into the bathroom toilet as a toilet insert.

Your kitten or grown cat may be too large to use the litter container as a toilet insert. If this is the case, discard the entire training toilet, and use the prepared toilet insert instead.

Make the change on the morning of a day when you can be home all day. Do it immediately after your cat has eaten breakfast. Let your cat watch you take the training toilet out of the bathroom and put it in a closet or outdoors. Be sure he doesn't have access to the place where you put it.

Add Toilet Insert—Fill the insert with 1 inch of litter (3/4 inch if you use the patented toilet-training device). Use soiled litter from the training toilet so the smell of his body wastes will attract your cat to the toilet insert.

Lift the seat on your toilet and lower the toilet insert into the toilet bowl. The rim of the toilet insert should fit firmly over the porcelain rim of the toilet bowl. Lower the toilet seat.

Let your cat watch you put the insert into

the toilet. When you have finished, stand beside the toilet, and click the clicker so your cat jumps onto the toilet seat. Give him a food reward. Click the clicker for the perch-squat. Reward your cat again.

Encourage Exploration—Let your cat move out of the perch-squat to explore the new situation on the toilet. His curiosity may prompt him to scratch his forepaws in the litter. He may go into the insert and scratch with his hind legs.

If your cat goes into the insert, click the clicker to elicit elimination. If he eliminates, give him a food reward. Continue to offer rewards for elimination throughout this step of training.

BODY POSITION

Ideally, your cat should perch-squat on the front of the toilet seat and drop his wastes into the toilet insert. It is unlikely this will be the case at first.

Four-Foot Position—Unless your cat mastered the perch-squat position while using the training toilet, he is accustomed to the security of having all four feet planted in the place where he is eliminating his wastes. He is unlikely to give up this security without additional training.

Young kittens are especially prone to eliminate their wastes with all four feet in the toilet insert. This is because they are small enough to fit comfortably within its confines.

Don't force your cat or kitten to eliminate his wastes in the perch-squat position at this early stage of training. You want him to think of the bathroom toilet as a comfortable place to eliminate.

Continue Perch-Squat Training—Drill your cat in the perch-squat at least five times a day. For the first three days, do your drills with the insert in the toilet. This helps familiarize your cat with his new toilet arrangement and encourages him to begin to eliminate his wastes in the perch-squat position.

Don't be concerned about encouraging elimination during perch-squat drills. Concentrate on making your cat familiar and comfortable with the body position. If he does happen to eliminate during a drill, however, be sure to take advantage of the opportunity to reinforce this behavior. Immediately click the clicker and offer a reward.

On the fourth day, do half the drills with the insert and half without it. This variety keeps your cat from becoming too attached to the security of the toilet insert.

Your cat may surprise you by showing you he suddenly feels insecure in the perch-squat position without the toilet insert. He may put his hind feet in the toilet water, expecting the support of the insert's bottom. He may let his tail get wet.

Don't be discouraged if your cat seems to have lost his ability to confidently maintain the perch-squat. Several days of drilling should get him over his confusion about the two situations he is experiencing on the toilet.

PRACTICAL CONSIDERATIONS

This stage of training requires some changes in your personal habits. When you need to use the bathroom toilet, remove the toilet insert. Put it on top of the toilet tank or in the sink. Never put it on the floor.

If you put the toilet insert on the floor, your cat may eliminate his wastes in it. This is a regression, and the experience may cause him to begin to have accidents on the floor.

Give your cat access to the bathroom when you use the toilet. Show him your wastes, and let him watch you flush them away.

Food Rewards—This step of training and the step that follows require giving frequent food rewards. You are rewarding your cat each time he eliminates his wastes in the toilet insert. You also reward him for jumping onto the toilet seat and going into the perch-squat position.

You may find it necessary to cut down the amount of food you give your cat at his regular feedings. Although rewards are small, they provide him with extra nourishment. You don't want to overfeed your cat.

Messing—This is the messiest step of toilet training. Even if your cat is quite neat, he will probably scratch a certain amount of litter onto the bathroom toilet seat. His feet will track stray bits of litter onto the floor.

Keep a whisk broom and dustpan in the bathroom to clean up litter messes. Be patient. After your cat has completed this step of training, you may never have to buy litter again.

Duration—Spend at least 1 week on this step of training. If you're training a young kitten, spend at least 2 weeks.

Keep the toilet insert filled with at least 1 inch of litter. Don't try to rush your cat into Step 4 before he's comfortable with Step 3.

Your cat is comfortable with Step 3 when he confidently jumps onto the bathroom toilet seat and eliminates his wastes in the toilet insert. He should do this without loud complaining. He should do it without first scratching the floor where the training toilet used to be.

Your cat should eliminate his wastes in the toilet insert whether you are home or not. He should not depend on the discipline of your watchful eye.

Use your own good judgment to determine the time when your cat is ready to proceed to Step 4. You gain nothing but problems by rushing him into a toilet situation he is not ready to accept.

STEP 4. PHASING OUT LITTER

Litter is phased out gradually, so your cat doesn't notice the small reduction in litter each day.

Begin on a Saturday morning. Reduce the amount of litter you put in the toilet insert. Use 3/4 inch of litter instead of 1 inch. Continue to supply your cat with a 3/4-inch level of litter each time you change the litter. Because so little of the litter remains, you may want to change the litter at least twice a day.

On Sunday morning, reduce the litter level to 1/2 inch. On Monday, reduce it to 1/4 inch. Continue making minor reductions each day until by Friday you are supplying your cat with only 1 teaspoon of litter.

On Saturday morning of the second week, after your cat has eaten breakfast, put only 1/2 teaspoon of litter in the toilet insert. Use the clicker to cue for elimination. Apply transition techniques until your cat eliminates his wastes in the toilet insert. Offer him his usual food reward.

On Sunday morning, don't put any litter in the toilet insert. Use transition techniques until your cat eliminates his wastes in the empty insert.

Let your cat watch as you transfer his wastes to the toilet water and flush them away. Clean the insert with aerosol bathroom cleaner, and rinse it with clear water before you replace it in the toilet.

Continue to use transition techniques until your cat feels comfortable about eliminating his wastes in the empty toilet insert. Allow him to use the empty insert for at least 1 week before you proceed to Step 5 of training.

Misplaced Scratching—Your cat's urge to scratch in dirt or litter to cover his body wastes is a strong natural instinct. After you phase out his litter, he may scratch the toilet seat, a nearby wall, a hanging towel or the bathroom floor.

Don't be concerned about misplaced scratching. It's triggered by the smell of body wastes. The act of scratching helps your cat psychologically adapt to the empty toilet insert.

Your cat may scratch the floor around his food dish. This is not a sign he is having psychological problems due to toilet training. It's a normal behavior that's probably inherited from wild ancestors who occasionally buried their excess prey.

Misplaced scratching becomes less frequent as your cat proceeds in his toilet training. He forgets his old instinct, and the smell of body wastes no longer automatically triggers the scratching response. Don't be concerned if your cat occasionally reverts to his original scratching behavior, however. Scratching activity continues to give him psychological satisfaction.

Perch-Squat Training—Continue to practice the perch-squat at least five times a day. Do part of the drills with the insert in the toilet and part of them without it.

At this step of training, stop giving food rewards during drills on the perch-squat. Continue to use the clicker to make your cat jump onto the bathroom toilet seat. Click it again when he goes into the perch-squat position on his own. Stroke your cat and speak softly to him, but don't offer him

Obstacles encourage cat to use perch-squat position.

a food reward unless he eliminates his wastes into the toilet water or the empty toilet insert.

At first your cat may complain about not receiving the reward he has come to expect when he goes into the perch-squat. Don't let his loud meowing persuade you to give him a food treat. At this point in training, he should go into the perch-squat position because it's a well-learned behavior. He no longer needs the reinforcement of a food reward.

It's important to make your cat understand you expect him to combine the perch-squat with the act of elimination. You do this by drilling him on the perch-squat immediately after he has eliminated his wastes in the toilet insert. If your cat begins to eliminate his wastes from the perch-squat position, offer him an extra reward. He can't go to Step 5 of training until he has begun to eliminate his wastes in the perch-squat position at least part of the time.

Encourage your cat to eliminate his wastes from the perch-squat by clicking the clicker to cue for the position when you suspect he needs to eliminate. If he tries to descend into the toilet insert, gently maneuver him back into the perch-squat. He should be relatively willing to accept this guidance, because the toilet insert no longer affords him the satisfaction of having litter under his feet.

Extra Food Reward—Let your cat know that eliminating his wastes in the perch-squat position is a special behavior that pleases you. Show him this by offering him two food rewards instead of one when he does so. Stroke him and praise him. Let him know you are proud.

Don't offer the extra food reward when your cat eliminates his wastes with one or more feet in the toilet insert. Give him his usual single reward. Don't stroke or praise him.

Add Obstacles—If you cat persists in descending into the toilet insert to eliminate his wastes on all fours, it may be necessary to discourage this behavior by adding obstacles. Try placing two rulers or narrow slats of lumber at right angles on top of the toilet insert. Masking tape or pieces of string affixed at right angles also make good obstacles.

After you add obstacles to the toilet insert, your cat will no longer be able to descend into it to eliminate his wastes. He will be forced to eliminate from the perch-squat position on the toilet seat.

STEP 5.
REMOVING INSERT

The toilet insert can be removed in three ways. The first is sudden removal. The other two methods involve an intermediate step of placing water in the insert or making a hole in the insert.

Try sudden removal first. If it causes your cat to have repeated accidents, try one of the other two approaches. If all three methods described in this book fail, you may have to devise your own special method to solve problems unique to your cat.

SUDDEN REMOVAL

This is the fastest, easiest way to handle this difficult step of training. Unfortunately, it's unsuccessful with many cats.

When and How—Remove the insert on the morning of a day when you can be home all day. Do it immediately after your cat has eaten breakfast.

Let cat watch you remove insert.

Let your cat watch you take the insert out of the toilet and put it in a closet or outdoors. Be sure he doesn't have access to the place where you put it.

Reread the section on transition techniques on pages 116 and 117. The two main techniques involve patiently confining yourself in the bathroom with your cat, and using a variety of methods to elicit elimination. You are going to have to apply these techniques often during the course of the next few weeks. Your cat is unlikely to easily accept this major change in his toilet facility.

Increase Perch-Squat Drills—During the first week after you remove the toilet insert, increase your cat's unrewarded perch-squat drills to at least seven a day. Do perch-squat drills at times when you can fairly accurately predict your cat will have a bowel movement.

If he complains and jumps down to the place where the training toilet used to be, firmly put him back up on the toilet seat. Use transition techniques until he eliminates his wastes in the toilet from the perch-squat position. Click the clicker, and give him *two* food rewards when he does.

Leg Support—During bowel movements and occasionally during urination, your cat may put one leg down onto the sloping side of the toilet bowl. This gives him support while he is thrusting his muscles to eliminate.

Don't discourage your cat from doing this until he has used the toilet without accidents for at least 1 month. He may make wet tracks on your bathroom floor, but this problem is minor compared to repeated bowel-movement accidents.

Raise Seat—If your cat refuses to eliminate his wastes in the toilet, try raising the seat so he can perch on the toilet's porcelain rim. He is now much closer to the toilet bowl. This may give him a greater feeling of security.

The porcelain rim of the toilet bowl is slippery, especially when wet. Your cat may not be able to balance on the slippery rim. If you see he's having trouble balancing, allow him to jump down. Lower the toilet seat. Click for him to perch-squat on the seat and apply transition techniques. If he still resists, consider a more gradual method of insert removal.

WATER IN INSERT

If your cat has repeated accidents after you remove the toilet insert, you will have to try a more gradual method.

When and How—This method works with two types of toilet inserts—a rimmed mixing bowl and a sitz bath. It does not work with a patented toilet-training device because the device is too shallow.

Add water to the insert on the morning of a day when you can be home all day. Do it immediately after your cat has eaten breakfast.

Let your cat watch you take the insert from the toilet and fill it with 1 inch of cool water from the tap. Replace the insert in the toilet, and encourage your cat to investigate it.

Click the clicker to cue for the perch-squat when you suspect your cat has a need to eliminate. If your cat is a water-hater, he will eliminate his wastes from the perch-squat to avoid wetting his paws. Click the clicker, and give your cat *two* food rewards if he does so. Let your cat watch you as you empty the waste-containing water into the toilet.

Raise Water Level—Each day add 1/2 inch of water to the toilet insert. Continue to do this until the water is 2 inches below the rim of the insert.

Your cat should begin to regularly eliminate his wastes in the perch-squat position to avoid the discomfort of getting wet. When he does, give him *two* food rewards. After he has eliminated his wastes in the perch-squat for 3 days, go back to offering him a single food reward.

Water-Lovers—Contrary to popular belief, some cats love water. In jungles, tigers often take afternoon swims. Domestic cats have been known to enjoy their owners' swimming pools.

If your cat is a water-lover, he may descend into the water-filled toilet insert to eliminate his wastes. He may scratch the surface of the water after he has eliminated. He may begin to scratch the water in the water bowl at his eating place. He may put his feet in his water bowl because he enjoys getting wet.

Training Collar—Solve the problems of water play and scratching by using a round training collar cut from a sturdy piece of cardboard. The collar should fit exactly over the porcelain rim of your toilet bowl. It should have a hole in the center about 5 inches in diameter.

Place the training collar over the water-filled toilet insert. Lower the toilet seat. Your cat can no longer descend into the insert because the hole in the center of the collar is too small to allow him to pass through. He is forced to perch-squat on the training collar to eliminate his wastes in the toilet insert.

Use transition techniques for 7 days while your cat is using the training collar. At the end of the week, remove the collar. Your cat will probably begin to perch-squat on the toilet seat, at least for the act of urination.

Training collar stops water play.

Remove Insert—When your cat has begun to regularly eliminate his wastes from the perch-squat position on the toilet seat, remove the water-filled toilet insert. Use the techniques described in the section on sudden removal of the insert.

Because your cat has become accustomed to eliminating his wastes into water, he should accept the removal of the water-filled insert with relative ease. He will now eliminate his wastes directly into the toilet water.

HOLE IN INSERT

This is another gradual method for removing the toilet insert.

When and How—This method works with two types of toilet inserts—a sitz bath and a patented toilet-training device. It does not work with most rimmed mixing bowls because they are made of stainless steel or heavy-duty plastic.

Cut a hole 2 inches in diameter in the center of the toilet insert. If you use a sitz bath, use a jigsaw to cut the hole. If you are

When Step 5 is complete, cat no longer requires psychological aid of insert.

using a patented toilet-training device, cut the hole with a pair of kitchen scissors.

Cut the hole in the insert on the morning of a day when you can be home all day. Do it immediately after your cat has eaten breakfast.

Let your cat watch you put the insert into the toilet. Encourage him to investigate the hole in it.

Click the clicker to cue for the perch-squat when you suspect your cat has a need to eliminate. If he has a bowel movement, let him watch you use the litter scoop to push the bowel movement through the hole in the insert. Remove the insert so your cat can see his bowel movement in the toilet water.

When your cat urinates, he may show surprise when he hears the sound of his urine passing through the hole in the insert to the toilet water. Let him watch you remove the insert and empty the remainder of his urine in the toilet water. Encourage him to investigate the urine-smelling toilet water.

Give your cat *two* food rewards and lots of stroking when he eliminates his wastes in the perch-squat position. Allow him to use the insert with a 2-inch cutout for at least 1 week.

Enlarge Hole—Do this on the morning of a day when you can be home all day. Use a jigsaw or kitchen scissors to enlarge the diameter of the hole to 3 inches. Empty urine and bowel movements into the toilet water as instructed above. Allow your cat to use the insert with the 3-inch hole for at least 1 week.

At the end of the week, enlarge the diameter of the hole in the toilet insert to 4 inches. Nothing is left of the insert but a small rim. When your cat eliminates his wastes into it, most of them go into the toilet water. Allow him to use the insert with the 4-inch hole for at least 1 week.

Remove Insert—When your cat is regularly eliminating his wastes into the hole from the perch-squat position, remove the toilet insert. Do this in the presence of your cat. Choose a day when you can be home at all times.

Because your cat is accustomed to eliminating his wastes into the toilet water through the hole, he should accept the removal of the insert with relative ease. He no longer requires the aid of the insert.

TOILET-TRAINING OPTIONS

If your cat resists using the toilet after you have removed the insert, consider several training options. Even partial toilet training can save you considerable litter expense and mess.

Almost all cats can be trained to urinate in the toilet without the aid of the insert. Some cats find bowel movements difficult or impossible. If your cat is resisting the toilet for bowel movements, you may want to settle for one of the toilet arrangements described below.

Litter Box and Toilet—If you want to keep your cat indoors, this is a logical, convenient arrangement. Your cat urinates into the toilet and has bowel movements in a litter box on the floor beside it.

You must continue to buy litter, but now you buy considerably less than you did before you toilet trained your cat. The litter in the box does not become contaminated by urine. It is easy to scoop bowel movements from the box into the toilet.

If your cat has progressed to Step 5 of toilet training, he is probably comfortably using the toilet to urinate. Encourage him to continue doing this by clicking the clicker and offering him a good-sized food re-

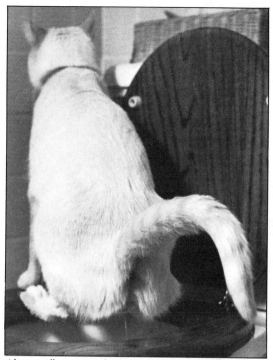

Almost all cats can learn to urinate in toilet.

ward each time he uses the toilet. Continue offering him rewards until he has firmly established the habit of urinating into the toilet.

If you see your cat urinating in the litter box, hiss, place your upraised hand in front of his face, flip him on the nose and firmly say *"No!"* Lift him up immediately, place him on the toilet and guide him into the perch-squat position. He can't stop urinating once he starts, so he should finish his urination in the toilet. Click the clicker, and offer him a food reward.

It is quite common for cats to use a litter box for bowel movements and the toilet for urination. It should take only a little training to coax your cat into this pattern.

Outdoors and Toilet—If you want to allow your cat to roam freely outdoors, this combination of toilet arrangements is a logical solution. While he is outside, he buries his urine and bowel movements in the dirt. When he is indoors, he urinates in the toilet.

If you provide your cat with a constantly opened pet door, he can go outside any time he needs to have a bowel movement. You don't need to provide him with a litter box in your home.

If your cat does not have a constantly opened pet door, you'll have to provide him with an indoor litter box or train him to meow at the door when he wants to go outside to have a bowel movement.

It isn't difficult to train your cat to meow at the door. Let him know you want him to have his bowel movements outside by putting him out at times when he usually eliminates. He soon becomes accustomed to this pattern and meows to be let out when necessary.

If your cat has a bowel-movement accident indoors, discipline him in the usual manner. After the discipline, scoop up the bowel movement with a spoon. With your cat in your arms, take the bowel movement outdoors and put it in the dirt. Set your cat down beside it, so he can see where his bowel movement belongs.

Litter Box, Outdoors and Toilet—This three-part arrangement works if your cat spends part of his time free or on a leash outdoors. When he's inside, he urinates in the toilet. He has bowel movements in the dirt outdoors or in a litter box that you keep beside the toilet.

Encourage your cat to have bowel movements outdoors by emptying his soiled litter in an area where you want him to eliminate. Take him out to the area when you can fairly accurately predict he will have a bowel movement. If he eliminates solid or liquid wastes, click the clicker and give him a food reward.

Continue to reward your cat for urinating in the toilet. Reward him when you see him eliminating his wastes outdoors.

Don't reward your cat when he uses the litter box beside the toilet. He should use the box only for bowel movements he must have when you are not home to let him outdoors.

COMPLETION OF TRAINING

Now that you've removed the toilet insert, a few final steps remain if you want to make your cat's toilet-training behavior perfect.

Don't follow these measures until your cat has used the bathroom toilet without accidents for at least 1 month.

Phase Out Food Rewards—Your cat may begin to show a lack of interest in his food rewards on his own. If this occurs, don't change to another type of reward he will like. Let boredom help you phase out his rewards.

Most cats continue to relish their rewards. If they don't receive one, they may meow loudly near the place in the bathroom where rewards are kept.

Don't allow your cat's complaining to convince you to continue giving him food rewards on an indefinite basis. When he has used the bathroom toilet without accidents for 1 month, stop giving food rewards for the act of urination.

Continue to give your cat food rewards for bowel movements for another month. Learning to have bowel movements in the bathroom toilet has probably been difficult for him. When you give him a food reward, you are thanking him for his effort.

Toilet bowel movements may be difficult.

During the final month of offering rewards for bowel movements, give your cat his rewards by placing them in his food dish. Don't offer treats on the reward can in the bathroom as you did during his training period.

Begin to offer your cat food rewards when you teach him new behaviors, such as flushing the toilet or other tricks in this book. Make him associate food rewards with activities other than having a bowel movement.

If your cat begins to have repeated accidents after you phase out his food rewards, return to giving food rewards for having bowel movements in the toilet. Having bowel movements in the toilet may still be a major effort for him. It may take up to 6 months for him to see the act as completely natural.

Phase Out Clicker—After your cat has used the bathroom toilet for 1 month, you no longer need to use the clicker to cue your cat to eliminate his wastes. He will eliminate when he has the need to do so without any prompting from the clicker.

Store the clicker in a drawer. Don't throw it away. It will come in handy if you want to teach your cat the tricks described in Chapters 7 and 8.

Normalize Bathroom—After your cat has used the toilet without accidents for 1 month, return your bathroom to normal. Hang towels on the rack on the wall beside the toilet, and replace the wastebasket on the floor beside it. Replace the toilet paper on its roller in the wall. Continue to store hazardous substances safely to protect your cat from hazardous objects.

OPTIONAL TRAINING

After toilet training is complete, you may consider progressing to two additional levels of toilet training—toilet training for a second bathroom and toilet flushing. Both of these behaviors require a major investment of your personal time and energy. You should not attempt them unless you are very enthusiastic about cat training and can devote a great deal of time to it.

Training for a Second Bathroom—You may want one toilet in your home that you don't share with your cat. If so, disregard this section. Your cat is unlikely to use a second toilet unless trained to do so. If he uses a second toilet against your wishes, discipline him as you do for accidents.

Training your cat to use a second toilet can be difficult. By urinating in the first toilet, he has made it his familiar territory. He is highly sensitive to its unique odors and textures. A second toilet, with different odors and textures, is foreign to him. He may be nervous and frightened about eliminating his wastes in it.

You may need to use all the techniques in this book to teach your cat to use a second toilet, although you can probably proceed at a faster rate. You may need to do regular perch-squat drilling and offer food rewards. You may need to start at Step 3 and proceed to Step 5 on the second toilet. You may need to keep the door of the first bathroom closed to prevent the use of that toilet. The speed at which you progress and the techniques you use depend on the unique reactions of your cat.

Some cats learn to use any toilet, including strange toilets in gas stations and motels. However, this is rare. You may have to go back to Step 3 of training when you travel with your cat.

Toilet Flushing—Training your cat to flush the toilet makes a spectacular finish to your toilet-training program. However, toilet flushing is more a trick behavior than a part of toilet training. It can be easy to teach some cats, but others find it difficult or impossible to learn.

Don't put hanging towels on the rack beside the toilet if you want to teach your cat to flush the toilet. Hanging towels block his easy access to the flush lever.

Use a toy to teach flushing. Buy a light-weight plastic cat toy. The best type of toy is a cross-hatched plastic ball made by a number of cat-toy manufacturers.

Tie a 14-inch length of strong thread or thin wire to the top of the plastic ball. Tie the opposite end to the tip of the flush lever of your toilet. Wind the thread or wire around the lever several times. After you knot it, secure it to the lever with masking tape or cloth tape.

Flush the toilet by pulling gently on the plastic ball. If it takes more than a gentle pull to flush the toilet, place a 1/2-ounce lead fishing sinker inside the plastic ball. The weight makes it easier for your cat to flush the toilet. The ball remains light enough to allow the lever to spring back up after flushing.

Wait for your cat to eliminate his wastes in the bathroom toilet. When he is finished, show him the hanging ball. Make it sway slightly. Your cat is likely to reach for it in play. He may pull on the ball to depress the flush lever while he is playing. If he does, click the clicker and give him a food reward.

If your cat does not depress the lever on his own, use your hands to place his front paws on the opposite sides of the toy ball. Pull them down gently until the lever triggers the flushing mechanism. Click the clicker, and give your cat a food reward.

Repeat the above procedure each time your cat eliminates his wastes in the bathroom toilet. Don't drill him on flushing at any other time. You don't want him to begin flushing the toilet when he has not eliminated his wastes in it. After a month or more of flush drilling after elimination, your cat should begin to flush the toilet on his own.

If your cat isn't flushing the toilet after a month, add interest to the hanging ball by placing a feather inside it. Wild-bird feathers you find outdoors are the most attractive to your cat. When he smells the wild scent, he begins to bat at the ball. He may attempt to grasp the feather inside it with his claws or teeth. In either case, his activity pulls downward on the ball and flushes the toilet.

If a wild-bird feather doesn't interest your cat, place a small piece of meat inside the ball. As your cat attempts to extract the meat to eat it, he pulls down the ball and flushes the toilet.

Some cats eventually learn to depress the flush lever without the help of the hanging ball, with or without the feather or meat bait. But most continue to need the help of the ball.

People are surprised and impressed when they see your cat eliminate his wastes in the toilet and flush them away. You can be proud of the animal-training skills you learned while you trained your cat to use the bathroom toilet.

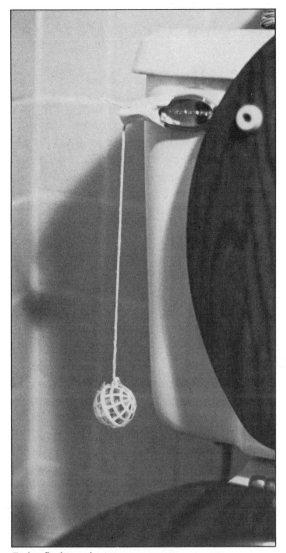

Toilet-flushing device attracts cat.

PINTO THE WONDER CAT

Sometimes a cat learns a behavior so well that he begins to perform it on his own, without a cue. This can lead to trouble, as I learned from my little cat Pinto.

She was given to me when I was assembling my first stable of cats. A friend asked if I would accept a tiny, half-grown, black-and-white female kitten. I took the little girl and named her Pinto.

This little creature's amazing intelligence showed up immediately on the set of "Eye of the Cat," an eerie thriller that cast all 100 of my feline actors as a gang of killer cats. No matter what the situation, Pinto was always the first cat in the group to understand the behavior we were training for.

I was so impressed by Pinto that I made her my almost-constant companion. She soon taught herself to ride around on my shoulder, and from this position she became my assistant trainer in cueing villain cats—she teased them into snarling.

Despite such help, my feline assistant director could be a real brat. She wanted to be in the middle of any scene with cats—regardless of whether she was in the script. If I didn't hold her on my shoulder with a death grip, she would leap off and join the performance. Not only would she join it, she would lead it—front and center.

The director would inevitably shout "Cut!"

Such antics began to cost the studio a lot of film. Pinto was also costing me a great deal of discomfort in my relations with the director. He was a very nice man, but he couldn't stand the sight of Pinto—for obvious reasons.

Because she was always on my shoulder, I decided to work with her between takes and make her a trained feline prototype. This started as a relaxed, fun project, but Pinto took to it with a seriousness I couldn't believe. She learned to sit up and beg, walk on her hind legs (an unnatural behavior for a cat), scamper off in any direction I pointed, stop on command, lie down and roll over. Almost everyone on the set liked to watch the little ham, and she basked in the attention.

Pinto became such a showoff I decided to try teaching something that would surely stump her—the "fetch" or retrieve behavior. However, this brilliant little feline learned to bring back objects almost immediately. No matter what the object, if I tossed it out and told Pinto to "fetch," she'd bring it back—even if it was larger than she was. She would either get behind it and push it, or turn her rear end toward me and drag it, with her tiny little legs digging into the floor.

Pinto was so eager to display her brilliance she started fetching articles from all over the set. She would place them neatly in my canvas chair and sit nearby, beaming with pride. She soon became known as the phantom thief. When something came up missing, such as a cigarette lighter, a fountain pen or even a light meter, I always knew where to look. Returning these articles often brought me some embarrassment—which was bad enough—but I never suspected this little game of Pinto's would cost the movie studio even more money.

One afternoon I flopped down in my chair to wait for the end of a dialogue scene with human actors. I was about to nod off for a nap when an angry shout shook me fully awake.

"Who the *!@#$%¢&*! stole my chalk?" yelled the camera assistant, who chalked up the scene numbers on the scene-marker board.

As I started suddenly in my chair, I felt some uncomfortable little lumps under my behind. The chalk. To the right of my chair sat Pinto, resting on her haunches and looking up at me with a smug expression.

My first instinct was to call out and answer the man, but I stopped myself. Because of her brattiness, Pinto was already on shaky ground. I couldn't bring the wrath of the gods down on her for something I had praised her for and taught her myself. I stayed quietly in the chair, stricken with guilt for half an hour while the prop man ran to a store to buy chalk. The studio's precious money dribbled away with each minute he was gone. When the cameras finally rolled again, I reached under my seat and palmed the pieces of chalk.

Something had to be done, so I decided to try to extinguish the fetch behavior. To do that, I needed a fetchproof article. I dug up some baling wire and constructed a large wire ball. I felt sure Pinto couldn't handle it.

I was right. Try as she might, the wire strands were so close together there was no way she could get a proper grip with her jaws. She tried to push the ball with her paws, but that wouldn't work either, because the thing was lopsided and wouldn't roll straight. After many attempts to move the ball, she gave up. Pinto was one frustrated little cat. Accepting the fact that she could not fetch everything turned out to be a bigger challenge than learning the trick in the first place.

Ray Berwick

Chapter 6:
Solving Toilet-Training Problems

You may not have problems when toilet training your cat. But if they occur, you should be prepared to deal with them.

Accidents present the most common problem. Sometimes you may not be aware that accidents are occurring. Even if you are aware of them, you may not understand why they are happening or how you should handle them.

Elimination disorders in your cat can also interfere with your cat's successful toilet training. When he has physical problems, he cannot control his need to eliminate.

Finally, the greatest obstacle to successful toilet training is your own discouragement. If you give up after a few days of repeated accidents or listen to the discouraging words of skeptical friends, you cannot hope for success. Patience and determination are very important. You must believe in what you are doing!

ACCIDENTS

Several factors influence whether your cat has toilet-training accidents. Some accidents, such as those in the bathroom or around house plants, are precipitated by location. Others reflect psychological or physical problems your cat is having with toilet training.

BATHROOM ACCIDENTS

Accidents in the bathroom are by far the most common. Your cat has grasped the idea that you want him to eliminate his wastes in the bathroom, but he may be confused by a change in his toilet facility. Instead of growing angry about bathroom accidents, clean them and patiently continue to use the training techniques outlined in this book.

When and Where—Bathroom accidents usually occur during Steps 3, 4 and 5 of toilet training. They occur most often during transitions from one step to another.

Your cat may have a bowel movement on the floor where his training toilet used to be. He may urinate in the bathtub or shower stall. He may find a secret place in the bathroom to eliminate his wastes.

What to Do—Discipline your cat in the usual manner. Hold him near his wastes while you hiss, flip him on the nose and firmly say *"No!"* Remember not to rub his nose in his wastes.

Don't remain stern after you administer this brief punishment. Gently pick your cat up, and make him watch as you dispose of his wastes in the toilet. Don't let your disapproval of his accident give him negative feelings about the bathroom.

Clean the area of the accident, and immediately apply a cat repellent. If the accident was on the floor where the training toilet used to be, use only a small amount of repellent. You don't want the odor to waft up to the toilet itself.

If the accident was in the bathtub or shower stall, fill it with at least 2 inches of water. Leave the water standing in the tub or shower stall for at least 1 week. Unless your cat is a water-lover, water should discourage him from having future accidents in the bathtub or shower stall.

Barricades—If your cat persists in having bowel movements in the place where his training toilet used to be, cover the area with an inverted box or bowl. If your cat has accidents on or around the box or bowl, you'll have to barricade the area.

Suitcases make good barricades. Fill in gaps between suitcases and walls with cardboard boxes and full rolls of paper towels. Use materials on hand to make it impossible for your cat to get to the place on the floor where the training toilet used to be.

Persistent cats may have bowel movements on the floor behind the toilet or on the opposite side of the toilet. If your cat does this, you will have to barricade the entire area around the toilet. The barricades must stay up until your cat is thoroughly toilet trained. If your cat has bowel movements on the barricades, treat them with a small amount of cat repellent.

Nighttime Accidents—Cats can see well at much lower light levels than you can, but they can't see in total darkness. If your cat has bathroom accidents at night during a transition stage of training, he may not be able to see his new toilet facility.

Buy a low-level night light, and leave it burning all night. This simple solution sometimes ends nighttime accidents.

If the night light doesn't end your cat's nighttime accidents, adjust his feeding schedule so he will not need to eliminate during the night. If the change in schedule does not stop him from having bowel movements at night, go back to an earlier step of training during the nighttime hours. Replace his toilet facility with the one he used before.

For example, if your cat is using the bathroom toilet without the litter container, provide him with the litter container and a small amount of litter during the night. Remove the container each morning so your cat can adjust to using the toilet without it during the day. Wait until he has become comfortable using the toilet without the litter container during the day before you begin to make him use it at night.

Lid-Related Accidents—Your cat may accidently knock down the toilet-seat lid with his paw. If this happens when you aren't home to lift the lid for him, he will probably have an accident on the bathroom floor.

If your cat habitually knocks down the toilet-seat lid, secure it. A double-sided suction cup works well. Look for one in novelty stores that carry practical joke items.

If you cannot find a double-sided suction cup, create one with two single-sided suction cups. Buy suction cups with plastic hooks attached. These are called *sky hooks* and are available in most hardware, home-improvement and van-modification stores. Hook the two cups together, and secure the bond with strong thread or wire.

Wet one suction cup, and apply it to the front rim of your toilet tank. Wet the second cup, and raise the toilet-seat lid so it makes contact with it.

The suction cups will hold the lid firmly in the open position. You have the strength to break the suction, but your cat does not. Rewet the cups every few days to renew the suction.

ACCIDENTS IN UNUSUAL PLACES

You may be the last to know about some accidents your cat has. Be alert. Investigate the following locations to determine if your cat is eliminating wastes in unexpected places in your home.

Secret Places—Some cats find a secret place in which they occasionally eliminate wastes. This may be under a bed, in a closet, in a wastebasket or under a desk or chair. Because the location is relatively hidden, you may not discover the wastes until the odor becomes very strong.

During toilet training, be alert for the odor of wastes. Frequently check closets, corners and under furniture. Your precautions prevent damage to rugs and furniture.

Fireplace—Some cats insist on eliminating their wastes in the fireplace. They bury their urine and bowel movements in the ashes.

If your cat eliminates his wastes in the fireplace, put a scoop of soiled ashes on top of the litter in his box or litter container. Gradually reduce the amount of ashes until you use none at all. Keep a screen in front of the fireplace.

House Plants—A large plant pot filled with dirt is a very enticing place for your cat to bury his bowel movements. If you find a house plant with disturbed dirt, immediately check for this possibility. Use a spade or a spoon to gently dig up the disturbed area. Your cat's bowel movement may be buried below the surface.

If you find your cat's wastes in the dirt around a house plant, give him negative feelings about the plant by hissing and flipping him on the nose every time he goes near it. If discipline doesn't deter him, protect the soil around your plant with wire window screening or decorative pebbles. You may prefer to transfer the plant to a hanging pot out of your cat's reach. It's important to stop your cat from continuing his habit of burying his wastes in loose dirt.

STRESS-INDUCED ACCIDENTS

Cats are very sensitive to changes in their environment or routine. Sometimes the stress they experience causes elimination accidents.

Disruption of Routine—A sudden disruption in your schedule may cause a setback in toilet training your cat. You may take a job that requires you to be absent from home all day, for example.

Your cat misses your company and objects to changes in his feeding schedule. He shows his objection by refusing to cooperate in toilet training.

Help your cat adjust by sticking firmly to the routine for at least 1 week. Don't go out to a late dinner, for example, leaving your cat to wonder when you'll be home. When he's used to the new routine, he won't feel insecure and anxious. Then you can begin to vary your schedule as you wish.

Try to prevent accidents during the first week of a new routine by offering your cat extra attention when you are home. If accidents occur despite the extra attention, discipline your cat in a firm, gentle manner. Be sure to stroke him soon after the discipline—he needs reassurance and affection while he becomes accustomed to the new routine.

Vacations and Business Trips—Sometimes a trip may intervene during your cat's toilet training. You have three options

regarding his care. You can board him in a kennel, take him with you, or have a family member or friend care for him in your home. All these options are likely to be somewhat stressful for your cat. He may express his bad feelings by having accidents during or after your trip.

Kennel boarding is the least recommended option for cat care. Obviously, accidents won't occur in your home while you are gone. However, cats become psychologically attached to their homes and often become upset when they are suddenly moved.

If your cat has progressed beyond the litter stages of toilet training, he will lose much of what he has learned if he uses a litter box in a kennel. When you return from your trip, you'll have to start his toilet training all over again.

Your cat may not have such a training setback if you take him with you on your trip. Unfortunately, this often isn't practical for several reasons. Whether your cat is traveling by plane, train or car, he'll have to be confined in his portable kennel. Long periods of confinement are likely to upset him. He may have accidents in the kennel, or he may become constipated from the stress of travel.

Your cat may refuse to use strange toilets, either on the road or upon arrival at your destination. He may soil the floors in your hotel or motel. Worst of all, you risk losing him if he escapes from the room.

Home cat care is your best option when you must be out of town during toilet training. Instruct a cat-loving family member or friend about your cat's toilet-training program. Show the person your cat's current toilet facility. Explain how to use the clicker to cue for elimination, and how to reward your cat for depositing his wastes in

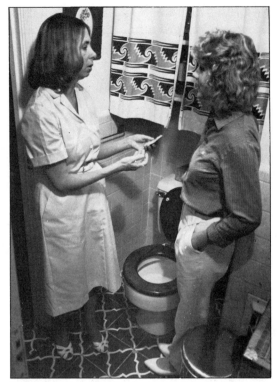
Before trip, instruct friend about toilet training.

the proper place. Give instructions on cleaning and disciplining after accidents.

Your cat may have repeated accidents because of stress due to your absence. If this occurs, tell your friend to go back to an earlier step of toilet training. This book can provide additional guidance.

Make sure your friend visits your cat at least twice a day. Ask the person to offer lots of affection while feeding him and cleaning his toilet facility. Request that your friend retrieve cat toys from corners and under furniture. Your cat needs his toys to play with to relieve his feelings of loneliness and boredom.

Jealousy—A new pet, a new baby or even a house guest can cause your cat to resent the attention you give the newcomer. He expresses his resentment by depositing his wastes in inappropriate places.

Jealousy-caused accidents are usually bowel movements. Most often they occur on the bathroom floor. Your cat is using his misplaced bowel movements as an attention-getting device.

Some jealous cats try to assert their dominance by "marking" the intruder or his belongings with urine. The urine may or may not be the strongly scented type that cats use in spray.

Avoid resentment of a new pet by making a point of not adopting one during toilet training. If you find you absolutely must adopt one, introduce the newcomer gradually.

After the new animal has explored your home, restrict it to one room for several days. Occasionally take it out of the room, and allow your cat in to sniff its scent.

Let the two animals get to know each other through the protection of a screen door. If you don't have a screen door, let them sniff each other through the crack of a slightly open door. Separate the animals if hissing and growling begin.

Give your cat plenty of personal attention to let him know you aren't abandoning him in favor of the newcomer. This rule applies to new babies and house guests as well as to new pets. Always introduce them gradually, and offer your cat lots of love in the process.

Resentment of Punishment—Some trainers can't control their tempers. They become angry with a cat when he does not cooperate in toilet training. They inflict painful physical punishment or loudly scold the cat.

Cats are dignified animals that resent such treatment. They often express their resentment by having bowel movements on the floor. Their owners react by inflicting harsher punishments, and a vicious circle begins.

If you ever are tempted to severely punish your cat, reread the section on discipline on pages 56 to 58. Harsh punishment does *not* have positive results. It's likely to produce a series of stress-induced accidents that is difficult to stop. In addition to creating a serious setback in toilet training, harsh punishment may result in the loss of your cat's friendship.

Fear—Some cats are extremely timid by nature. They fear strangers, loud noises and many other commonplace things. These cats may lose control of their bladders when they are frightened. They are difficult—perhaps impossible—to toilet train.

Normal cats have an adventurous curiosity about commonplace things. They show fear only under abnormal threatening conditions, such as loud electrical storms. Hostile confrontations with other animals can also make them show fear.

Cats often show fear by running and hiding. They crouch submissively and may tremble. The pupils of their eyes may grow large. Their coats may stand on end. If you are around, they may meow loudly.

A cat who has been badly frightened may have a lapse in his toilet training. Discipline accidents, but don't be too severe. Your cat needs comfort and reassurance at times when he is afraid.

HOW TO CLEAN ACCIDENTS

After your cat has a urine or bowel-movement accident in a particular place, he may return to that place to eliminate his wastes again. He is attracted by his lingering body-waste odors. Avoid recurring accidents by thoroughly cleaning and deodorizing each spot where an accident has occurred.

CLEANING AND DEODORIZING

Clean accidents immediately after you discipline your cat. Don't allow the odor of waste to permeate your bare floor or carpet.

If you are dealing with a urine accident, soak up as much urine as possible with an absorbent rag or paper towel. If the accident was a bowel movement, remove all solid matter with a spoon or scoop. Let your cat watch as you dispose of his bowel movement in the toilet.

Vinyl Floors—Aerosol bathroom cleaners are good for cleaning urine and bowel movements from vinyl tile or linoleum floors. They disinfect the area and mask the smell of wastes.

Spray bathroom cleaner on the spot where the accident occurred. Allow it to foam. Soak up the foaming cleaner with a paper towel.

It will probably take several cleanings to eliminate odors to the point that your cat's nose can no longer detect them. His sensitive nostrils detect odors your nose cannot smell.

Repeat the cleaning process until the area of the accident smells strongly of bathroom cleaner. If your cat continues to be attracted to the spot, use cat repellent on it.

Hardwood Floors—If a urine accident occurs on a hardwood floor, soak it up immediately. If you don't, the acid in your cat's urine may damage the finish.

If your hardwood floor has a urethane finish, mix a solution of 1 part vinegar to 3 parts water. Saturate a paper towel with the mixture, and rub it on the floor. Allow the spot to dry, then sponge it with a paper towel dampened in clear water.

If your hardwood floor has a varnished or waxed finish, mix a solution of 1 part turpentine to 3 parts linseed oil. Saturate a cloth with the mixture, and rub it on the floor. Repeat the process several times. When the spot is thoroughly clean, rub it with the wax you normally use on the floor.

Carpets and Upholstery—Foaming rug shampoos are handy for cleaning and deodorizing accidents on carpets and upholstery. You can also use undiluted liquid detergent or a paste made of powdered detergent and hot water.

Sponge the area of the accident with an absorbent rag or paper towel soaked in lukewarm water. Gently rub rug shampoo or detergent into the spot until all smell and discoloration have disappeared. Sponge the spot again with lukewarm water.

Make a solution of 1 part rubbing alcohol to 2 parts water. Use the mixture to give the area of the accident a final sponging. This helps remove the shampoo or detergent and promotes fast drying.

Rub the area partially dry with a towel to prevent mildew. When it is dry, brush the nap.

Deodorants—After you carpet dries, apply powdered carpet deodorant to the area of the accident. Use your fingers to separate the fibers of shag or plush carpets so the deodorant reaches the backing. Leave the deodorant powder down for at least a day to allow its scent to penetrate the carpet.

Remove the powder with your vacuum as directed on the container. If your cat continues to be attracted to the area, apply

Foaming rug shampoos are useful in cleaning accidents.

powdered carpet deodorant every time you vacuum.

Some pet shops and carpet dealers sell special chemicals for removing the odor of animal urine. Medical-supply stores also offer an effective range of products for eliminating the odors of body wastes. These products are relatively expensive, but they are worth the price if ordinary deodorants don't work on your carpet.

REMOVING STAINS

Some spots from accidents don't come out with regular cleaning agents. Give them prompt, special treatment so they don't develop into permanent stains.

Bowel-Movement Stains—Treat stains on carpet or upholstery with a paste made from 1 part meat tenderizer to 2 parts water. Sponge a small amount of this solution on a concealed part of your furniture or carpet. If it doesn't cause discoloration, rub the paste on the stain. Wait half an hour, then sponge the area with lukewarm water. Rub it partially dry with a towel to prevent mildew.

If the bowel movement stain persists after treatment with meat tenderizer, use an enzyme-containing laundry stain remover. Follow instructions on the package.

Urine Stains—Stains from urine accidents are more serious than bowel-movement stains. The acid in your cat's urine can damage hardwood floors and wood furniture and permanently discolor carpets and upholstery.

Treat a urine stain on a waxed-wood surface by rubbing it with a moist rag that has been dipped in silver polish. If the stain persists, put a few drops of ammonia on a damp paper towel, and rub the spot with it. Rewax the area with the wax you normally use on the surface.

Remove urine stains from carpets and upholstery with a solution made from 1-1/2 teaspoon of salt to 1 quart warm water. Sponge a small amount of this solution on a concealed part of your furniture or carpet. If it doesn't discolor the fibers, rub the solution on the urine stain.

If the stain persists, put 1/2 teaspoon of ammonia into 1 cup of water, and sponge the area again. White vinegar may be used in place of ammonia. It has the advantage of preventing mildew.

When you have treated the stain with ammonia or vinegar, rub the area of the accident partially dry with a towel. Wait until it's completely dry, then brush the nap.

PROFESSIONAL HELP

If home cleaning fails to remove an odor or a stain, you will have to hire a professional who has special equipment and chemicals. If you don't, your cat may have accidents in the soiled area for years after he is toilet trained.

Carpet Cleaning—There are many methods of professional carpet cleaning. Most involve some form of steaming, shampooing or dry cleaning. Some companies advertise themselves as specialists in pet stains and odor removal. They usually apply a stain-retarding compound after they clean.

Some companies will come to your home to clean and deodorize a single problem spot. Others try to convince you to allow them to clean the floors of your entire house. Prices may vary greatly from company to company.

The best way to find a reliable cleaning service is to ask your friends for recommendations. When you have a list of recommended companies, call your Better Business Bureau to check their records on consumer complaints. You need a highly competent professional to successfully remove the stubborn stain or odor from your carpet.

Carpet Patching—If professional carpet cleaners fail to remove an odor or stain, your cat's urine has saturated the carpet backing, the padding, the flooring and the wood tack-stripping. The strong-smelling area of the rug will have to be removed and replaced with a patch of clean carpet. The padding and tack-stripping also must be replaced. The floor underneath will have to be washed and disinfected before the clean patch is installed.

Your carpet dealer can send a professional carpet repairman to cut and install the patch. He has special equipment to make seams almost invisible.

If you have remnant pieces left from your original carpet installation, use them to make an exactly matched patch. If your carpet is faded or worn, the remnant pieces must be treated to make them match the existing carpet. Don't try to treat the remnants yourself. Get the advice of a professional carpet repairman.

If you don't have remnant pieces, cut a small sample of your carpet from the corner of a closet and take it to your carpet dealer. He can help you select a piece of carpet to match the sample.

Buy a piece of carpet large enough to give your carpet repairman several options regarding the laying of the nap. A new piece of carpet may appear to match your existing carpet exactly, but it will look considerably different when it's down if both naps are not laid in the same direction.

If your can't find a new piece of carpet to match your existing carpet exactly, your carpet repairman may suggest using a piece of existing carpet from the inside of a closet. He will use the remnant you bought to replace the piece he takes from the closet. He will use the piece from the closet to make a matching patch in the soiled area of carpet.

Backing Cleaning—If you don't have carpeted closets and you can't find a matching remnant to replace your soiled carpet, air and deodorize the backing of the soiled area. Have your carpet repairman cut out the soiled area and remove it from the floor.

Take the piece of soiled carpet outdoors, and lay it on a clean area, backing-side up. *Lightly* spray disinfectant and urine deodorant on the backing. Don't let the backing get very wet, or it may shrink.

Leave the carpet outdoors for 2 sunny days. The rays of the sun help destroy the urine odor. Take the carpet in at night so it doesn't get wet from rain or dew. Disinfect and deodorize the backing again when you lay it outside the next morning.

Airing carpet backing helps destroy odor.

In winter, air the carpet backing in a basement or on a closed porch. Shine a sunlamp on it for two 1/2-hour sessions each day. Disinfect and deodorize it twice, as instructed above.

After the carpet backing is deodorized, have your carpet repairman reinstall the carpet on the floor. Make sure he replaces the urine-soaked padding and tack-stripping. Wash and disinfect the floor before he puts new padding down.

Tile Replacement—If your cat's urine has permanently stained an area of vinyl floor, a professional tile layer will have to remove the stained tiles and replace them with new ones.

If you have extra tiles left from your original tile installation, use them to make a matched replacement. If you don't have leftover tiles, buy tiles that match your flooring as closely as possible.

Hardwood Floor Refinishing—If your hardwood floors have been permanently damaged by acid in urine, you'll have to hire a professional to sand and refinish the spot. Specialists in hardwood flooring are listed in your phone book. Ask friends to recommend a good one.

PREVENTIVE MEASURES

It is easier and less costly to prevent accidents before they happen. If you consistently follow the recommendations below, you can avoid accident problems.

Close Doors—When possible, close the door to a room where an accident has occurred. Keep it closed during the entire period of toilet training.

Your cat may try to follow you into the room whenever you enter it. Be sure to look behind you before you close the door. Many cats are injured by closing doors.

Repellent Measures—If your cat has recurring accidents in a room or hallway where you can't close the door, put chemical cat repellent on the area that is attracting him. If the repellent doesn't work, cover the area with an inverted box or bowl.

Persistent cats continue to deposit their wastes in the forbidden spot, even after it is covered with a box or bowl. They soil the box or bowl, or the floor beside it. If your cat does this, you'll have to give him strong negative feelings about the spot itself.

Watch your cat closely for several days. Discipline him every time he goes near the forbidden place. Hiss, flip him on the nose and say *"No!"* Soon your cat learns to keep away from the spot to avoid discipline.

ELIMINATION DISORDERS

Keep a sharp eye out for elimination disorders while toilet training your cat. Common elimination disorders include urinary problems, constipation and diarrhea. A sick animal cannot learn new habits. If your cat develops an elimination disorder during toilet training, stop training and revert to a litter box until your cat is well. Then begin his training program again.

URINARY PROBLEMS

Because most cats urinate in irregular patterns, urinary problems are sometimes hard to detect. Most urinary problems involve infection or blockage of the urinary tract. These problems are common, and they can become serious if left untreated.

Feline Urologic Syndrome (F.U.S.)—This is the general term vets use for a number of urinary disorders that affect cats. The disorders include infection of the bladder or urinary tract and blockage of the urinary organs by small doughy or gravelly plugs.

If your cat makes frequent false attempts to urinate or you notice blood in his urine, he may have some form of F.U.S. If you see small doughy plugs or flakes of whitish gravel in his urine, you can be sure he has some form of this condition.

Take your cat and a specimen of his urine to your vet as soon as you suspect he has F.U.S. If he is using litter, collect the specimen by putting a saucer in his litter box. If he is at Step 3 or beyond in toilet training, collect the specimen from the insert in the toilet.

After your cat's F.U.S. has been cured by medication or surgery, your vet may advise you to put him on a low-magnesium diet. This may involve prescription-diet cat foods or recommended commercial brands that are especially low in magnesium.

Other Urinary Disorders—Cats can be affected by many of the same urinary illnesses that trouble humans. These range from simple inflammation of the external organs to serious kidney disease.

Take your cat to the vet as soon as you detect any disturbing changes in his urinary patterns. Concentrated, strong-smelling urine and cloudy or watery urine can be symptoms of disease. Constant licking of the external urinary organs or sudden lack of bladder control definitely warrant a trip to the vet.

CONSTIPATION

If you feed your cat the bowel-stimulating foods discussed in Chapter 4, he should have little trouble with constipation. However, good diet is not always a preventive, especially for older cats.

Symptoms and Relief—Constipation is easy to detect. Your cat does not have a bowel movement for a day or more. He strains so hard in his efforts to eliminate that his flanks may tremble. He meows loudly to express his discomfort. He may lick his rectum.

After several days without a bowel movement, your cat's eyes grow dull. He becomes lethargic. He may strain so hard his rectum bleeds.

Never let your cat become seriously constipated. As soon as he misses two regular bowel movements, increase your feeding of laxative foods. If he doesn't have a bowel movement within 12 hours, you will have to take further measures.

Lubricants are the mildest medications for relieving your cat's constipation. The simplest lubricant is petroleum jelly, which you can slip onto the roof of his mouth or smear onto his paw for him to lick off. Use 1/2 teaspoon for a grown cat and 1/4 teaspoon for a kitten.

An infant-sized glycerine suppository can be used in place of petroleum jelly. Use 1/2 a suppository for a grown cat and 1/4 of a suppository for a kitten. Be sure to completely insert it into your cat's rectum.

If petroleum jelly or suppositories don't relieve your cat's constipation, you will have to administer a laxative. Most laxatives made for human beings are too strong for cats, but unflavored liquid milk of magnesia is safe and usually effective. Give 1 teaspoon to a grown cat and 1/2 teaspoon to a kitten.

Milk of magnesia relieves the symptom of constipation, but it does nothing to remove the cause. If your cat becomes constipated a second time, consult your veterinarian.

Hairballs—Constipation caused by swallowed hair requires special treatment. A cat with hairballs has dry, hard bowel movements. Sometimes you can detect undigested hair in them.

Prevent hairballs from forming by brushing your cat for at least 5 minutes each day. Regularly brushed cats have little loose hair to swallow while they groom their coats.

If your cat develops hairballs in spite of regular brushing, buy a special hairball remedy from your vet. Follow the dosage instructions on the package.

Stress-Induced Constipation—A common emotional cause of constipation is stress related to moving or traveling. Your cat may become constipated during his first few days in a new home or on a trip.

When moving or traveling, try to make your cat's new toilet facilities duplicate his old ones as closely as possible. If necessary, use lubricants and laxatives as instructed above. Give your cat extra love until he is over his stress and confusion.

Stress and confusion also are factors in

Licking base of tail may signal infected anal sacs.

constipation that occurs during transition to a new step of toilet training. Your cat doesn't understand the sudden change in his toilet facilities, so he waits until the last possible moment to have a bowel movement. The suppressed movement becomes compacted and hard. When your cat finally tries to go, he cannot.

Lubricants or laxatives may be necessary during major transitions in toilet training. Remember to offer extra love to calm your cat's apprehensions.

Infected Anal Sacs—Your cat has tiny, scent-gland-lined sacs on both sides of his rectum. If they become blocked or infected, he tries to relieve the pain by dragging his rump along the floor. He may also bite at the base of his tail.

Your cat may become reluctant to have a bowel movement because of the pain in his anal area. His suppressed movements become hard and difficult to eliminate.

Take your cat to the vet the moment you suspect he has infected anal glands. He or she will drain the glands and prescribe necessary medicines. Wait until the infec-

tion is cured before you attempt a major new step in toilet training. Unless your cat is thoroughly comfortable with the toilet facility for his current level of training, provide him with a well-filled litter box until his condition is cured.

DIARRHEA

Loose bowel movements can be a sign of serious illness in your cat. Diarrhea may be caused by diet or disease. If nonprescription anti-diarrhea medicines don't cure it, take him to the vet.

Diet-Related Diarrhea—A sudden change in your cat's diet may bring on diarrhea. Introduce new foods gradually along with familiar, well-liked foods.

Milk or other laxative foods, such as vegetables and whole grains, may give your cat diarrhea. If you suspect this is the case, stop giving laxative foods completely until your cat has had several solid bowel movements. Reintroduce them in very small quantities until you determine the correct amounts for your cat.

Meats tainted by harmful bacteria can give your cat diarrhea. Avoid this problem by refrigerating partially consumed canned foods and perishable food rewards.

Eating insects, birds and rodents can give your cat diarrhea. This is usually not a problem if you keep your cat indoors and allow him outdoors only when he is on a leash. If your cat does develop diarrhea, inspect his wastes for undigested bones and fur. This will indicate whether the diarrhea is prey-related. If it is, be extra careful to keep him indoors, and take steps to rid your home of insects, mice or other pests.

Non-prescription anti-diarrhea medications that contain clay usually stop diet-related diarrhea within a day. Give your grown cat 1 teaspoon in an eyedropper every 2 hours. Give your kitten 1/2 teaspoon every 3 hours. Don't offer foods that you suspect might be causing diarrhea.

Disease-Related Diarrhea—If your cat continues to have diarrhea despite the remedy you give him, it may be a sign of serious disease. Diarrhea is a major symptom of feline distemper. It can also signal a malfunctioning pancreas or liver, especially in older cats. Coccidiosis is an illness caused by protozoan parasites. Its major symptom is diarrhea.

Whatever the cause, prolonged diarrhea is dangerous. It severely dehydrates your cat, causing him to become dull-eyed and listless. Severe dehydration can be fatal, especially to young kittens.

Never wait for more than 2 days to take your diarrhea-troubled cat to the veterinarian. Collect a specimen of the diarrhea on a wood tongue depressor or spoon. Take the specimen to the vet, along with your cat. Your rapid action can save his life.

DISCOURAGEMENT

If your cat has repeated accidents or develops an elimination disorder, you may become discouraged. Don't let discouragement cause you to give up his toilet-training program. Each cat has different training-time requirements.

REGRESSION THEORY

Regression means reverting to an earlier stage of development. When regression occurs, it is best to return without guilt to an earlier, more successful stage of training. In many instances, regression leads to progression.

When and Why—Regression can occur at any stage of toilet training, but most often it occurs when you are making the transition from one step to another. Your cat regresses to an earlier step of training to express his frustration with the new step you have introduced.

As already mentioned, the most-common form of regression is a bowel movement on the floor where the training toilet used to be. Your cat is trying to tell you he would like to go back to Step 1 of training, when he had litter to scratch in and was able to eliminate his wastes on all fours. He is telling you he doesn't want to give up his natural instinct to bury his wastes.

What to Do—Be firm with your cat after his first few accidents. Apply transition techniques until he eliminates his wastes in his appropriate toilet facility.

Your cat may refuse to respond to your firm guidance. He may repeatedly have accidents while you are asleep or away from home. If this happens, don't become engaged in a battle of wits with your cat.

Reread the section on timing on pages

114 and 115. Your cat is using his accidents to tell you he needs more time before he can accept the current step of training. He needs a break from the psychological pressure that comes from a toilet situation he's not ready to accept.

Go back to the last step of training. This principle for dealing with regression is discussed in detail in the section on timing. It is mentioned again here because it is one of the most important keys to toilet-training success.

MOTIVATION AIDS TO OVERCOME DISCOURAGEMENT

When toilet training doesn't succeed instantly, it is easy to lose your perspective and decide that your cat's toilet-training program is a failure. Sometimes it is hard to believe that only a few more weeks of work will bring success. The following tips can keep you going when your cat is having repeated regressive accidents during a difficult step of training.

Imagine He's a Toddler—When you become discouraged about a difficult step in toilet training, imagine your cat is a human toddler. A toddler doesn't become toilet trained overnight. It takes weeks or months of care and vigilance to teach a child to use the toilet consistently.

Even after a toddler knows he should use the bathroom toilet, he continues to have occasional accidents in his pants. His mother doesn't give up and allow him to go back to wearing diapers. She patiently goes on with his toilet training until he learns.

Give your cat the same chance a mother gives a child. Continue training until he learns to consistently use the bathroom toilet.

Think of the Future—Your cat is going to live with you for many years. The weeks or months you spend on his toilet training seem brief when you compare them to the years of convenience that lie ahead. When you begin to lose your patience, think about the future. The effort you are making will buy years of thrift and convenience.

Think Positively—The goal you are trying to accomplish isn't impossible. Others have accomplished it. Many cats regularly use the bathroom toilet. Some of them have learned on their own, just by watching the people they live with. Others have been carefully trained by their patient, determined owners.

If you don't give up when your cat temporarily balks at a difficult step of training, you will have success too. You just need a positive attitude.

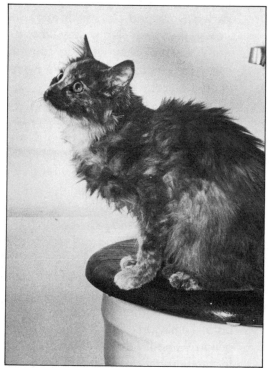

He *can* learn!

DARK DEALING ON THE SET

Every animal has a unique personality, and each deserves to be treated with kindness and respect. Unfortunately, some people in the movie business think of animals as props to be discarded when they're no longer useful. I try to avoid working with these types, but sometimes I get tricked into it. Such an instance cost me two beautiful animals.

One day a production manager called. "We want two black cats who are sweet and loving—the kind that you can hold in your arms," he said.

I chose Dark and Darker, two coal-black cats I'd raised from kittens. Both were gentle, affectionate, sensitive and a little timid.

The scene was to be outdoors at night. The sky was pitch-black just beyond the big movie lights. We were shooting near the edge of the dry Los Angeles River, which was bordered on each side with tangled bushes and trees.

Two actors were to carry the two cats to a simulated patio and place them in a decorative wheelbarrow filled with flowers. The action seemed easy enough as I carried Dark and Darker through the routine. Each time they performed well, I praised them until finally they were full of confidence. By the time the director was ready to shoot, they were so comfortable with their surroundings that they were willing to remain in place in the wheelbarrow until I appeared to take them away when the scene was over.

It all went well in the master shot, which showed the entire set and actors from a wide angle. Next came the close-up of the human actors, and finally the camera rolled around for a close-up of Dark and Darker.

I put them in position among the flowers and scratched them behind the ears. Then I found a hiding place where I could provoke expressive reactions from them as the camera pulled in tight.

When the director called "Action!" Dark and Darker peeked confidently over the flowers in what made a delightful shot. I crouched in my hiding place, totally involved with keeping my actors alert and in place. I didn't see the prop man crawling quietly toward the wheelbarrow. The next thing I remember was a tremendous *Bang!* Dark and Darker flew into the air like they'd been shot. In fact, that was almost what happened.

From the corner of my eye, I saw the prop man backing away with a smoking pistol. Fuming in anger, I realized what the director had done. He had contrived the action without letting me know, realizing I would have no part in deliberately frightening my animals. The prop man had cooperated with the scheme.

I wanted to confront the two of them immediately, but it was more important to find my frightened cats. I ran down the steep bank, smashing my way through the tangled bushes, desperately calling for Dark and Darker.

When I finally came to a halt, breathless and exhausted, I surveyed the pitch-black dry riverbed. If the poor little animals were somewhere in the shadows, I would never know.

I called for another 10 minutes, then realized it was futile. All I could do was hope that I would find the cats in the morning.

By the time I made my way up the riverbank, the director and prop man had disappeared. I didn't get to vent my rage that night, which was good for them and most likely good for me — it's not acceptable to yell at a director.

I spent the next morning searching fruitlessly for Dark and Darker. They were gone forever.

Then I wrote the two men involved. I told them that under no circumstances would I work with either of them again. I feel the same way about any other producer, director or handler who thinks abuse is a legitimate way to provoke an action. My animals perform quite nicely when they're treated with large doses of love and respect — and I intend to keep it that way.

Ray Berwick

TRICK TRAINING

Chapter 7: Beginning Tricks

If the training you have already accomplished has been done by the methods in this book, you and your cat should be well prepared to learn an impressive collection of tricks. Trick training differs from behavior training and toilet training in a major way: you are not modifying an instinctive behavior and replacing it with a new one.

You teach your cat tricks because you want to establish and show off a special kind of communication. You want people to see that your cat can understand and respond to your visual and verbal cues. Trick training displays your skill as a trainer and the intelligence and obedience of your cat. Above all, this kind of training gives the two of you the opportunity to be creative and have fun.

GETTING READY

Before you read this section, go back and reread the general rules of training on pages 50 to 58. A thorough knowledge of these techniques is essential to trick-training success.

Before you begin to teach tricks, your cat should have acquired all of his household behaviors. These are described in Chapter 3. Your cat's toilet training should also be complete, unless you've decided not to teach this behavior or plan to postpone it until he has learned some tricks.

When to Start—Wait until your cat is at

least 4 months old before you begin trick training. By then he has begun to replace his kittenish awkwardness with adult agility. His attention span has lengthened to the point that he can concentrate on learning.

Some cats are not ready to begin to learn tricks at the age of 4 months. If yours is one of these, don't try to force him to do something he's not ready to do. If he constantly tries to run off and play during training sessions, put off trick training for a while. Keep trying until your cat develops the ability to pay attention to instructions long enough to earn at least 12 food rewards at a time. At this point, you can begin teaching him tricks in earnest.

By now your cat should understand the concept of performing a requested behavior on the cue of the clicker to earn a food reward. He should know that the hiss, face-push, nose-flip and a firm *"No!"* are negative cues that mean he's doing something you don't want him to do.

Prepare Training Table—To avoid stooping or kneeling when trick training your cat, you need a training table. Ideally, it should be 2 feet square and exactly the height of your waist. Because few ready-made tables meet these standards, you may have to build one.

If you don't want to build a training table, train your cat on a sturdy card table. If you are tall, you may want to bring yourself down to your cat's level by sitting in a chair directly in front of the card table.

If you prefer to train standing up, you can build up the height of a card table with blocks of wood. Drill shallow holes in the blocks so you can firmly fit the table's legs in them to ensure stability. Your cat must be able to perform his tricks without the threat of a table that wobbles or falls.

Whatever kind of table you choose, cover the top of it with a towel or blanket so your cat won't slip when he's learning new behaviors. You may want to make and decorate a felt table cover to give your cat's trick performances a colorful circus air.

Prepare Props—Some tricks described in the next section require props, such as a hoop or hurdle. Suggestions for making them are included in the instructions for teaching each trick.

If you are training your cat to do his tricks before an audience, you may want to decorate his props so his routines look more professional. Spray paint, glitter, ribbons and other decorations can add a lot to the fun and excitement of your cat's trick performances.

CUES AND REWARDS

You use cues and rewards in a slightly different way in trick training than in household training, but the basic principles are the same. You cue your cat to perform a behavior and reward him when he does it.

You've already learned the value of the clicker. Keep it handy near the training table to use for cueing your cat. But *before* you cue with the clicker, you give a visual and a verbal cue. *After* your cat performs the action, you click the clicker to let him know he has done what you want him to do. *Last,* you give him a food reward.

Cues—Use a different visual and verbal cue to demand each new trick behavior from your cat. For example, when you cue him to wave, you wave your hand and say the words "bye-bye." After your cat performs the wave, you click the clicker to reinforce your verbal and visual cues. Gradually you phase out the sound of the clicker and use only verbal and visual cues

Some difficult tricks look easy.

to demand trick behaviors.

Tricks appear more sophisticated when you cue them from a distance. So 1 week after you phase out the clicker, begin to back farther and farther away from the training table before you give your cat his visual and verbal cues. If you are demanding a trick from a distance of more than 10 feet, you may have to exaggerate the movement of your hand or body so your cat can clearly see his visual cue.

Your cat may become so familiar with his tricks that you can eliminate his visual cues. He obediently performs his behaviors when you cue him with words alone. When your cat reaches this level of sophistication, you are the owner of a very well-trained animal!

Types of Food Rewards—As mentioned earlier, the treats you use to teach tricks are only 1/8-inch square. Prepare at least a week's worth in advance for freshness and convenience. Divide treats into daily portions, and freeze them in plastic sandwich bags. During intensive trick training, you may offer over 100 miniature treats a day. On less-intensive training days, you may give your cat less than 30 rewards.

Pot roast makes excellent trick rewards because it easily divides into narrow strings of tender meat. Cut strings into halves or thirds to produce hundreds of miniature rewards.

Cooked fresh fish can be divided into tiny pieces with your fingers. Use scissors to cut liver, round steak or chicken into miniature rewards, or prepare tiny balls of hamburger or horsemeat, as described in Chapter 2. Never use flaky canned fish products as food rewards when you are training your cat.

Constant Versus Random Rewards— When you introduce your cat to a new behavior, give him a food reward every time he performs it. After he becomes thoroughly familiar with the trick, begin to give him rewards at random intervals.

At first your cat may object to not receiving a reward each time he performs the behavior. He may refuse to cooperate in the training unless he receives constant rewards.

Don't allow your cat to persuade you to return to the constant-reward system. If you are firm and patient, he will eventually decide random rewards are better than no rewards at all.

Introduce the random-reward system gradually. Begin by rewarding 9 out of every 10 performances. After 3 days, reward only 8 out of 10. Continue to reduce the number of rewards until you reach a ratio of 5:10. Your cat is now receiving rewards for only half of his performances.

No matter how many random rewards you give your cat, be sure to offer them at irregular intervals. Reward five performances, for example, then don't reward four. Continue the random pattern until you have given him all the rewards.

Never fall into the pattern of rewarding every other performance. Your cat soon detects the pattern and refuses to perform at times when he thinks he won't be rewarded. You want him to perform the desired behavior on cue, whether or not he receives an immediate reward.

How to Offer Rewards—Place the required number of rewards in a cup, saucer

Cats have no natural need to do tricks like hoop jump.

or shallow bowl. Place the dish on a stool, table or shelf that is behind you as you face the training table. Use your body to block the reward container from your cat's vision. Don't allow him to become distracted by the presence of food rewards.

Offer your cat each food reward by placing it on the reward can and passing it under his mouth. Or put the can down on the training table and let him help himself.

Continue Food Rewards—Trick training differs sharply from training for behaviors that involve a natural need or desire. Your cat has no natural need or desire to do tricks. If you phase out his food rewards, he may soon forget the behaviors you have taught him.

Keep your cat from forgetting his tricks by randomly rewarding at least half of his performances during review drills. Continue review drills at least once a week throughout your cat's lifetime. For years, he will obediently perform on cue to earn his expected treats.

Reward of Stroking—Stroke your cat after—not before—you give him a food reward. When you are rewarding on a random basis, substitute stroking for food rewards.

Don't get involved in long, distracting stroking sessions, but offer frequent pats on the head and scratches on the ears or under the chin. Stroking helps strengthen the bond of love that makes your cat want to learn new behaviors to please you.

TIME AND PLACE

Training schedules depend on feeding schedules. Make it a rule to schedule at least one training session per day. If you don't have time for a full session, settle for a shorter session. Even a few minutes of training will help your cat acquire a new behavior or refresh his memory on an old one.

Schedule major trick-training sessions at times when your cat is really hungry. His hunger makes him anxious to perform to earn food rewards.

If you are feeding your cat one regular meal a day, you can schedule one training session before he eats and another at least 4 hours after his meal. If you feed him a small supplementary meal, schedule an additional training session right before you serve it.

The duration of each trick-training session depends on your cat's level of interest. If his hunger is making him anxious to perform, make him earn up to 24 food tidbits before you give him a break. Let him rest 5 minutes, then make him earn 24 more rewards before he gets his meal.

If your cat seems irritable or bored, make him earn only 12 treats before you give him his meal. Don't schedule another training session until he's really hungry.

To speed up your cat's learning process, you can schedule extra sessions on days you have lots of time for training. Unless he's showing high interest, limit extra-session rewards to 12. Don't disturb your cat for training while he's sleeping or engaged in play with another animal.

Where to Train—Locate the training table indoors in a comfortable, well-ventilated room. It should be a pleasant, quiet place that's free from distractions. Keep other people and animals out of the room during training sessions. You need to command your cat's full attention to teach him to do tricks.

Until your cat becomes thoroughly familiar with his routines, it's helpful to locate the training table in a corner. If he gets restless and tries to jump down, he is blocked on three sides by two walls and your body.

If you want your cat to perform his tricks in places other than the training table, schedule every-other reviewing drill on the floor or a chair. He will soon learn you want him to perform his tricks in any place you demand them—not just on the training table.

MULTIPLE TRICKS

If you are going to teach more than one trick, you will have to make some advance decisions about how many and which tricks you want to teach. Base your decisions on the amount of time you have available and your cat's learning ability.

Look-alike cats solve some training problems.

Learning Ability—Some cats learn fast and have no limit to how much they can learn. Others are listless, slow learners who become resentful about training if pushed too hard. This is why most professional trainers keep some look-alike cats in their kennels. One cat may be trained to do tricks, while a more placid cat is best for holding or carrying onstage. In some cases, the slower cat is a back-up performer for the highly trained cat.

To determine your cat's learning ability, first teach him three simple tricks. As you continue to introduce new trick behaviors, watch for the signs discussed below that indicate he is being pushed too hard. This is the time to stop trick training if you want to keep your cat's friendship.

If your cat seems bored or irritable during training sessions, stop trying to introduce new behaviors for at least 2 weeks. Continue to review his old tricks at least once a day on a random-reward basis. Give him lots of stroking to assure him you still love him.

After 2 weeks have passed, reintroduce the trick your cat was refusing to learn. If he continues to reject the behavior, try to teach him another one. If he becomes bored or irritable, stop trying to add new tricks to his collection for a period of at least 1 month.

To avoid pushing your cat beyond his learning ability, read this chapter and the next completely before you begin to teach him tricks. Select the tricks you want him to learn, and teach these first. In this way, you can be sure your cat acquires the behaviors you want most.

Simple Tricks First—Before you begin, make a list of all the behaviors you want your cat to learn. Plan on teaching him three simple tricks first. This will familiarize you with basic trick-training techniques and acquaint your cat with the principle of performing trick behaviors on cue.

You will want to teach the sit-and-stay and lie-down because these are lead-ins to a number of other tricks. Teach at least one simple trick in addition to these *before* you go on to the advanced tricks described in Chapter 8.

Use Your Imagination—Because of natural agility, the variety of tricks your cat can learn is almost endless. Use your imagination and the general techniques outlined in this book to teach him many behaviors beyond those described here. Tricks can be as simple as shaking his head "no" or as complicated as walking on a rolling barrel. Whatever their complexity, you will find your tricks fun because you devised the training procedures.

TRAINING SESSIONS

Regular training sessions increase the understanding and friendship you share with your cat. Keep things clear and simple by teaching your cat new behaviors one at a time. Never introduce more than one new behavior in a single training session.

Wait until each new behavior is thoroughly learned before you advance to another. A behavior is thoroughly learned when your cat obediently performs it on cue, whether or not he immediately receives a food reward.

Order of Teaching—During training sessions, you do two things—introduce new behaviors and review old ones. You may devote some sessions to teaching a new behavior, while others may be dedicated to reviewing your cat's acquired tricks. Most sessions should involve a little of both types of training.

If you are introducing a new behavior, work on it first. When you or your cat get tired of working on the behavior, begin reviewing him on one or more of his acquired tricks. After a brief drill, go back to the new behavior. Continue alternating new-behavior work and reviewing drills until your cat has earned all of his food rewards.

Order of Reviewing—Review your cat's acquired tricks in a random order. Don't let his performances fall into an unbreakable routine, with one trick always following another in the same predictable sequence.

If your cat seems unsure of a certain behavior, strengthen his performance by offering him extra rewards for that behavior. Drill him on it more often than you do his other tricks during the next week of training sessions.

After your cat has obediently performed a trick on cue for 1 month, cut reviews down to once every 3 days. If he begins to seem unsure of the behavior, go back to reviewing it on a daily basis.

Don't expect your cat to retain his collection of tricks without regular reviewing drills. His practical nature makes him rapidly forget behaviors that appear to have no purpose from his point of view.

Wrong Performances—Sometimes you cue your cat to perform one trick, but he performs another. He may do this frequently until he learns to connect certain visual and verbal cues with certain behaviors. He needs to learn to discriminate cues from each other and not just perform any trick he feels like performing when he hears you say a word and move your hands.

Don't reward wrong performances. Continue to cue for the behavior you are requesting until your cat performs it. At this point, click the clicker and give him his reward.

If your cat doesn't perform the behavior you request, guide him into it with your hands. Do this after your cat has done three wrong performances. Cue him for the behavior you want, then put out your hand to stop him before he does the wrong trick. Firmly say *"No!"* and guide his body into the position you are requesting. Continue to guide your cat with your hands until he performs the correct trick on cue without your help.

After your cat has performed the correct trick at least five times on his own, begin to cue him to perform the trick he had been doing on the wrong cue. Click the clicker, and reward him when he performs it.

During the remainder of the training session, cue for both tricks in a random pattern. Reward your cat *only* when he performs the behavior you cue for. Make him understand he doesn't earn rewards merely for performing his tricks. He must perform them on the proper cue.

Be Patient—Don't get discouraged if your cat seems confused when you introduce a new trick. It may take him time to accept the fact that you reward him for a behavior he thinks has no apparent practical purpose. Even after he understands you want him to perform the behavior, he may have a training session in which he acts like he's forgotten everything he knows about it.

Be patient with your cat—he has bad days just like you. Often when you think he's learning nothing, he'll show you how wrong you are in his next training session.

Never allow your cat's slow progress to make you feel bored during a training session. Even when he's having trouble with a trick, it's fun to try to read his reactions and devise new ways to steer him in the right direction. Soon you'll be feeling pride and excitement when your efforts begin to pay off.

SIMPLE STATIONARY TRICKS

To perform stationary tricks, your cat stays in one place and responds to negative cues. This set of tricks differs from tricks that require your cat to move from one spot on the floor or training table to another to perform a behavior.

Some stationary tricks, including the roll-over, wave and handshake, do involve some body movement. They are included in this section because your cat performs them from the stationary positions of the lie-down and the sit.

SIT-AND-STAY

This behavior is an important lead-in to a number of other tricks. Because you don't use food rewards, you do not need to wait until your cat is hungry to teach him sit-and-stay. You can train him for 1-to-3 minute periods at intervals throughout the day.

Do most of the training with your cat on the training table. If you wish, add variety by training him on the floor, a chair or the lawn outside. Well-trained cats sit and stay wherever they may be.

Positive Cues—The verbal cue for sit is the word *sit*. The visual cue is your hand extended above your cat's forehead. Hold your palm downward in the traditional signal for "down."

After your cat has assumed the sitting position, move your hand into the visual cue for "stay." To do this, place your hand in front of your cat's face. Hold your palm at a right angle to your wrist in the traditional signal for "halt." The verbal cue for stay is the word *stay*. After your cat has stayed in the sitting position for 5 seconds, lower your hand to your side.

The sound cue you use to release your cat from the sit-and-stay position is a sharp hand clap. At first you may have to follow the clap with the repeating chant that you use when you call your cat by name.

The visual cue for release is your cupped hand moving toward your chest in a beckoning gesture. After your cat has come to you, lower your hand to your side.

Negative Cues—Keep your cat in the sit-and-stay position by using the hiss. Use it along with the hand signal for "down" if he tries to rise from the sitting position. Use it along with the hand signal for halt if he tries to walk away from a stay.

At first you may have to extend the halt signal so it's an actual push in the face. If this proves necessary, don't exert enough pressure to cause your cat pain or discomfort.

Guide His Body—You will only have to guide his body during the initial period of training. Your cat will soon learn the sit command and go into the position on his own.

With your cat standing on all fours on the training table, give the verbal and visual commands for sit. If your cat does not respond to them, put your hand on his neck, and move it down his back in a stroking gesture. When you come to his rump, exert gentle pressure, and push him down into a sitting position. Say the word "sit" the moment he assumes the proper position.

Gradually lessen the pressure you put on your cat's rump to guide him into the sit. When he begins to sit down with the encouragement of only a stroke, phase out the stroke. Your cat is ready to perform the sit to visual and verbal commands alone.

Keep Him in the Stay—During the first week of training, your cat will probably repeatedly try to walk away from the sit-and-stay position. When he meets with a hiss and your upraised hand in one direction, he'll try to walk away in a different direction.

If your cat gets by you and jumps down to the floor, pick him up, and put him on the table again. No matter what direction he turns to try to escape, put your upraised hand in his face, and stroke him back down into the sit.

During the next few weeks of training,

repeat the hiss and hand signal each time your cat tries to jump down from the table. Use your hands to gently, but firmly, put him back into the sit. Immediately repeat the cues for stay. Wait at least 10 seconds before you release him from his position with a hand clap. Gradually increase the time of the stay until your cat obediently remains in position for 1 minute for more.

Grooming—During the first 2 weeks of sit-and-stay training, allow your cat to groom himself while he's holding the sitting position. If he attempts to lie down to groom, hiss and firmly replace him in the sit.

As your cat's training progresses, you'll begin to use the sit-and-stay position as a lead-in to other tricks. At this point, hiss and manually stop his grooming behavior. Your cat must learn you want his full attention while he is maintaining the sit-and-stay posture.

LIE DOWN

Teach your cat to lie down on his haunches, not on his side. The verbal cue for this behavior is the phrase *lie down*. The visual cue is your hand extended palm downward above your cat's head.

The release from the lie-down is a sharp hand clap, as it is for the sit-and-stay. If you want your cat to come to you after his release, call him by name and beckon him with your hand moving toward your chest.

Food rewards are not used in lie-down training, but praise and stroking are. They help make lying down a pleasurable behavior that your cat wants to perform.

Start from Sit—Cue your cat into the sit-and-stay position on the training table. Make him stay for at least 1 minute before you give him the cues to lie down. This helps him perceive the lie-down as a be-

Use negative cues to keep cat in lie-down position.

havior in itself, not merely an extension of sit-and-stay.

Training Procedures—Give the verbal cue "lie down," and extend your hand 3 inches over your cat's head. Lower your palm until it touches his head, then exert a gentle pressure. If your cat goes down on his haunches, begin to stroke and praise him.

When your cat is first learning to lie down on cue, stroke and praise him for at least 1 minute before you give him his cue for release. After the behavior becomes established, gradually reduce the amount of stroking you give him. When he has learned to consistently lie down on cue, confine your stroking to a quick single pass down his back.

Possible Problems—If your cat hunches his back and refuses to lie down when you press his head, take his front paws in your hand. Gently lift and lower his forepaws until he is lying down on his haunches.

If your cat begins to move into a lying position on his side, use your hands to nudge him back onto his haunches. Gently restrain him with one hand on his flank while you stroke his back with the other. Repeat this correction as often as necessary until your cat understands you want him to lie on his haunches.

Even when you are stroking him, your cat may grow restless and try to get up from the lying position. If this happens, extend your upraised hand in front of his face in the halt position and hiss. If the hiss doesn't stop him, use the other hand to exert gentle pressure on his rump. When he is comfortably lying down again, stroke and praise him for at least 1 minute before you give him his cue for release.

Make Trick Perfect—When your cat begins to understand the verbal and visual cues for the lie-down, gradually exert less

Cue for roll over.

pressure on his head when you cue him. When the pressure has been reduced to a light brush, stop touching his head.

Gradually raise your palm higher above your cat's head. When he responds to the cue of your palm-down hand at a height of 2 feet, begin to back away from him, and phase out the visual cue. The trick is perfect when your cat lies down on command when you cue him with the words "lie down" from a distance of 5 feet or more.

ROLL OVER

Teach this trick on the floor until your cat grasps the idea of doing a quick single roll. If you use the training table, he may fall off.

Cues and Rewards—The verbal cue for this trick is the phrase *roll over*. The visual cue is your hand extended palm downward above your cat's forehead, moving horizontally across a distance of 2 feet in the direction you want him to roll.

Teach this trick by using food rewards. Because it's an easy trick, you'll soon change from constant to random rewards. Load the reward can, and put it on a chair or stool behind you, along with a good supply of food rewards. You'll need both hands free when you begin to teach the roll.

Start from Sit—Start this trick from the sit-and-stay position. The roll is not impressive unless your cat obediently performs it from a sit.

Use the appropriate verbal and visual cues to make your cat assume the sit-and-stay position on the floor. After he has been sitting for 30 seconds, cue him to lie down. When he has been lying for 30 seconds, you can begin to cue him to roll.

Training Procedures—Kneel on the floor in front of your cat. Give the visual and verbal cues for the roll, as described above. Use one hand to gently lift your cat's forepaws. Hold the clicker in your other hand while you exert a slight pressure on the side of his rump that is opposite the direction in which you want him to roll.

Guide your cat onto his back with the motion of your hands on his rump and forepaws. He may feel so uncomfortable in this unnatural position that he will roll onto his opposite side on his own. If he doesn't, continue to guide him through the roll with your hands. Click the clicker, and give him a treat as soon as he's comfortably lying on his side.

As your cat becomes familiar with the verbal and visual cues for the roll, he'll begin to perform the action without your help. At first you may have to continue to push him on his back, but he'll soon get the idea that rolling is the action that's being rewarded.

Reward each roll until your cat no longer needs your help. When he obediently performs the action on cue, stop using the clicker, and begin offering random rewards. You can also begin to drill your cat up on the training table, and reduce the amount of time he spends in the introductory sit and lie-down to 3 seconds for each.

Make Trick Perfect—Your cat may get up into the sitting position to comfortably swallow his reward. Take advantage of this natural desire to add polish to the trick. Give your cat the visual and verbal cues for the sit. When he gets up and swallows his reward, it will appear that he is obeying the command that you gave him. Make him stay sitting for at least 5 seconds before you cue him to roll again.

If your cat doesn't go into the sit on his own, you'll have to cue him into it. At first you may find it necessary to guide him with your hands. Don't begin to cue for the sit until after his roll-over behavior has become firmly established. Don't offer him his treat until he gets up into the sit.

After your cat has learned to combine the roll-and-sit, begin to teach him to roll in the opposite direction. Reverse the direction of your visual cue, and use your hands to guide him until he understands the action you are training for. Drill him in alternating directions until he understands what each cue means.

Begin to back farther away from your cat when you cue him to roll. When he obediently rolls over when you are standing at least 5 feet away, begin to teach him the multiple roll on the floor. Do this by cueing for a second roll immediately after he has completed his first one—before he goes up into the sit. Reward him only *when* he's sitting up after his second roll.

Use the same technique to teach your cat to roll three times or more in rapid succession. Save his reward for the sit-up after his final roll. The trick is perfect when your cat performs multiple rolls in either direction when you cue him from a distance of 5 feet or more.

WAVE BYE-BYE

This is an easy beginner's trick. Your cat instinctively bats his paw at a food reward that's waved in front of his nose.

Start from Sit—Use the appropriate verbal and visual cues to make your cat assume the sit-and-stay position on the training table. After he has been sitting for 10

Cue for wave.

seconds, begin to cue him to wave.

Don't allow your cat to move out of the sit-and-stay position while you are teaching him to wave bye-bye. If he tries to walk away, cue him back into the sit with a hiss and a push in the face. You have to make him keep his body in one position so he'll reach out to bat at the food reward with his paw.

Cues and Rewards—The verbal cue for this trick is the word *bye-bye*. The visual cue is your hand waving from side to side. At first you hold the loaded reward can in your waving hand. Later, give the cue for the wave with your hand in the upraised halt position, just as you do when you are waving to a friend.

Training Procedures—Hold the clicker in one hand. Hold the loaded reward can in the other. Lower the treat to a position directly in front of your cat's nose, so he knows it's there.

Move the reward can to a position just out of reach of your cat's front paws. Give the verbal cue "bye-bye." As soon as your cat reaches a paw out to bat at the reward, click the clicker, bring the reward can to a position just under his mouth and allow him to eat his treat. Repeat this exercise until he has earned all his food rewards.

As soon as your cat shows you he has learned that extending a paw will earn him a reward, it's time to teach him to wave. Hold the loaded reward can, and give the verbal cue "bye-bye." When your cat reaches out to bat at the reward, begin to move it back and forth in a teasing wave. Continue to wave it back and forth until he makes at least two passes at it. Immediately click the clicker, and give him his reward.

As your cat becomes familiar with the waving motion of your hand, he'll begin to

wave his paw repeatedly until he gets his reward. Continue this level of training until your cat understands that three or four repeated waving motions are the behaviors you are requesting when you say the word "bye-bye."

Once your cat understands the verbal cue, stop using the clicker. You can also stop holding the reward can in your hand, and begin moving your upraised hand in a natural waving motion.

Make Trick Perfect—Gradually move farther away from your cat when you cue him for the wave. If he steps out of the sit or tries to jump for his reward, correct him with a hiss and the hand cues for down or stay. The trick is almost perfect when you can cue him to wave bye-bye when you are standing 5 feet or more away from him.

To make your cat's wave really impressive, teach him to perform it off the training table. Start by kneeling directly in front of him and cueing him with the loaded reward can in your hand. Gradually start to stand up, eliminate the reward can and begin to offer rewards on a random basis.

If you frequently hold reviewing drills beside your front door, this trick becomes a good one to show off to friends. Whenever you leave home, you can call your cat and wave bye-bye—and he'll wave back!

HANDSHAKE

Shaking hands is a cute behavior that is easy to teach once your cat has learned the wave. He has already grasped the basic principle of extending his paw to earn a food reward.

Cues and Rewards—The verbal cue for this trick is the word *shake*. The visual cue is your extended hand, palm upward, 3 inches from your cat's chest. After he learns to respond by placing his paw in your hand, complete the trick by shaking his paw, then releasing it.

Use food rewards in training for this behavior in the same way you did for the wave. However, don't go through the step of waving the reward can back and forth.

Training Procedures—Cue your cat into the sit-and-stay position on the training table. If necessary, use negative cues to keep him in the sit, just as you did when you taught him the wave. Wait 10 seconds before you cue him to shake hands.

Hold the clicker in one hand and the loaded reward can in the other. Lower the treat to a position directly below your cat's nose to let him smell it, then take it back to your side.

Extend the hand holding the clicker toward your cat's chest, and give the verbal cue "shake." Immediately move the hand with the reward can to a position directly behind your extended hand. When your cat reaches out to bat at his treat, grasp his paw in your extended hand and shake it.

After three shakes, click the clicker and allow him to eat his treat from the can. Repeat this exercise until your cat has earned all his food rewards.

Make Trick Perfect—As soon as your cat has learned that placing his paw in your hand will earn him a treat, stop using the loaded reward can. Begin to demand the shake with the verbal cue alone. Reward the behavior on a random basis.

This trick is cute if you teach your cat to perform it off the training table, as you did the wave. If your cat isn't shy, you may be able to teach him to shake hands with a friend who extends a hand and gives the appropriate cue. If you lead into this performance by formally introducing the two of them, your friend will be impressed with your friendly, hand-shaking cat.

Trainer Karl Mitchell and "cat biker" Mitten.

CAT BIKER

Teaching your cat a really unusual behavior can be a ticket to animal-training success, as my friend Karl Mitchell proved with his remarkable cat.

The first time I saw his cat, I was headed for the parking area on the upper lot at Universal Studios. A motorcycle roared by me up the hill with the rider hunched over against the wind. Between the handle bars in front of him was a small black cat. His ears were flattened against his head and he leaned skillfully with the turns.

"How in the heck does the fellow have that cat tied on?" I wondered.

They skidded to a stop. The cat adjusted his position and began purring and licking the base of one of his own back legs that was pointing straight up in the air. It was evident that he hadn't been tied on at all—the cat had been holding himself in position on the bike!

The young man introduced himself as Karl. I realized he was the young man who had been phoning me persistently for several days—the same one I had just as persistently been avoiding. He wanted me to help him become a professional trainer.

He and Mitten, his cat, had finally decided to try to surprise me with a performance in the parking lot.

I liked the fellow's pleasant smile and his open admission that he had engineered this meeting. I held and examined Mitten. He was gentle and friendly—a very good cat—but he had one big disadvantage. "Black cats aren't all the rage for television and movies," I said. "They're hard to light."

"Gee, I never thought of that. I thought Mitten was something special. I'm sorry I bothered you, Mr. Berwick. I won't waste any more of your time." Karl's shoulders slumped in dejection as he turned away.

"Hang on a minute," I said. "Black cats are not exactly in demand, but . . ."

The shoulders quickly straightened—a touch of hope.

"But a black cat on a motorcycle, that may be something else," I finished.

"I was hoping you'd say that," Karl said, smiling and turning back to me. "Would you show me how to train my cat for the movies?"

"Well, now, let's make a deal," I countered. "You show me how you got him to ride that motorcycle, and I'll show you how to train him to perform on camera."

Karl's gamble paid off. Motivation and persistence can be far more valuable than "lucky breaks." Karl soon became a regular trainer on the Universal Studios tour, and within two months Mitten was a first-rate actor. He subsequently appeared in two movies and in several television series, including "Fantasy Island."

Ray Berwick

Chapter 8:
Advanced Tricks

By now you have a good idea of the theory of cat training. If your cat has learned the tricks in Chapter 7 and still seems to learn readily, you and your cat are ready for the adventure of learning sophisticated tricks.

This chapter will introduce you to advanced tricks that include communication behaviors, location behaviors, jumping behaviors and working behaviors. Don't be disappointed if your cat cannot learn these advanced behaviors. They are fun but difficult.

Read the chapter through and decide which tricks or behaviors you want your cat to learn. Prioritize them, teaching the most important ones first. If your cat reaches the limits of his learning ability, he will have learned the behaviors you consider most important.

During this stage of training, it's important to bear in mind that only a few very intelligent and agile cats can learn all the behaviors presented in this chapter. You are not a failure if your cat learns only one or two.

COMMUNICATION BEHAVIORS

This set of behaviors gives the impression your cat is trying to tell you something. *Speak* and *beg* are two communication behaviors discussed in this chapter. Communication behaviors not discussed here include a nod of the head to say "yes" or "no" and an affectionate nose rub or kiss.

If you want to teach these additional communication behaviors, devise your own visual and verbal cues. You will know the basic principles of training from your experience in teaching speak and beg.

SPEAK

This is a simple trick to teach a dog, but it can be difficult to teach a cat. Except for a few cats who meow habitually, cats usually meow much less often than dogs bark. Don't try to teach this behavior if your cat is a habitual meower. It will reinforce a behavior that can be annoying.

Cues and Rewards—The visual cue is your upraised hand over your cat's forehead. At first, hold the loaded reward can in your upraised hand. Later, stop using the reward can, and cue for the speak behavior with only your upraised hand. Extend your index finger in a pointing gesture as you give the verbal cue.

The verbal cue for this trick is the word *speak.* If your cat has trouble understanding the behavior you're training for, imitate his meow after you say the verbal cue. Continue to do this until he begins to consistently respond to the cue with a meow of his own.

Training Procedures—Teach the speak when your cat is really hungry. He must feel frustrated enough to meow when you

tease him with the loaded reward can.

Put your cat on the floor near the training table. Put a halter and leash on him, and tie one end of the leash to a leg of the table. Follow this training procedure even if your cat isn't trained to lead on a leash. Your goal is to frustrate him just enough to make him give a little protesting meow.

Hold the clicker in one hand and the loaded reward can in the other. Pass the reward can under your cat's nose to let him smell his treat.

Step back 3 feet and give the verbal cue "speak." At the same time, hold the reward can out to him so he can clearly see his treat.

Your cat may respond to your teasing with the reward can by pulling on his leash. He may meow to express his frustration at being restrained. If he does meow, immediately click the clicker and give him his food reward. Stroke and praise him to let him know he has done something you want him to do. Repeat this exercise until he has earned at least 10 rewards by meowing.

If your cat does not meow when you tease him with the reward can, call him by name immediately after you give him the command to speak. If he's been well-trained to come to the sound of his name, he should pull on his leash and meow.

If your cat doesn't meow when you call him by name, walk 10 feet away from him and turn your back. In a short time, he may meow to get your attention.

If you have a very patient leash-trained cat, you may have to use your imagination to find a way to frustrate him enough to provoke a meow. Playing with another animal in front of him often works. So does making an elaborate show of serving a dish of his favorite food.

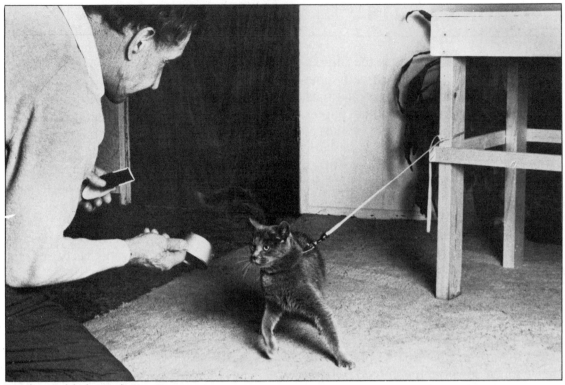

Teach *speak* behavior by teasing.

Whatever you do to provoke a meow, *don't resort to causing him pain* and don't frustrate him so much that he becomes angry. Stop teasing if he begins to snarl, hiss or strain hard on his leash. It's important to make sure the training experience remains fun for both of you.

After your cat has earned 10 rewards, end your first training session. Continue to drill on the speak behavior with a 10-reward session at least once a day. Maintain this schedule until your cat begins to meow regularly on the cue of "speak."

Make Trick Perfect—When your cat is regularly meowing on the cue of "speak," phase out the clicker and begin to offer random rewards. Eliminate the leash and begin to cue for the behavior when he's on the training table. Step farther away from the table until he responds to your command from a distance of 10 feet or more.

Because meowing is a natural behavior, follow two rules to keep your cat from becoming a nuisance meower. First, never reward him for meows he gives without a cue. Second, never cue him to meow when he's not on the training table. The meow is not a trick unless it's performed obediently at your command.

BEG

Cats vary in their ability to learn to beg. Most take longer to learn it than dogs, but once they learn to balance, they do quite well. Count on at least 1 week to teach the beg trick.

Cues and Rewards—The verbal cue for this trick is the word *beg*. At first, the visual cue is to hold the reward can with a treat 1 foot or more above your cat's forehead. Later, the cue is to raise your arms and hands in a begging position that imitates the begging paws of your cat.

After the behavior is well-established, you can begin to offer random rewards. When you are cueing for the beg without a food treat, use the visual cue of your two hands raised in the begging position.

Training Procedures—Cue your cat into the sit-and-stay position on the training table. Hold the clicker in one hand and the loaded reward can in the other.

Pass the reward can under your cat's nose so he can smell his treat. Then raise it until it's 3 inches above his forehead.

Give the verbal cue "beg." At the same time, use the hand that's holding the clicker to gently guide your cat into the begging position. Do this by grasping his forepaws and gently lifting them until his body is vertical to the floor.

Release your cat's forepaws and click the clicker. Give him his reward while he's still in the begging position.

If your cat lowers himself into a sit, use your hand to guide him back into the begging position before you give him his reward. If he tries to jump for the treat while it's over his head, correct him by pushing him down by the forehead. Guide him back into the begging position before you give him his treat. Continue this exercise until he has earned at least 10 rewards.

Make Trick Perfect—As your cat becomes familiar with the verbal and visual cues for the beg trick, he'll begin to perform the action without the help of your hand. At first you may have to help him to balance in the begging position, but he'll

Mimic begging position to cue for a beg.

soon learn to balance on his own.

Reward each beg until your cat no longer needs the help of your hand. Continue to use constant rewards and the clicker until he understands the verbal and visual cues. At this point, you can stop using the clicker, and begin to offer random rewards.

Begin to lengthen the span of time that elapses between the moment your cat rises into the beg and when he receives his reward. The trick looks like part of a circus act when you can make him balance in the begging position for 5 seconds or more.

Expand Trick—Rising on his haunches is cute, but you may want to teach your cat to move his forepaws up and down in an expanded begging gesture.

Hold the clicker in one hand and the

loaded reward can in the other. Cue your cat into the begging position, but don't reward him. Instead lower the reward can until it's just out of reach of his paws, then move it up and down. If he tries to follow it with his paws, click the clicker and give him his treat.

If your cat doesn't follow the moving reward can with his paws, use the hand holding the clicker to guide him into the action. Or have a training partner move his paws until your cat understands the behavior you are teaching.

When your cat has learned to combine the rise to his haunches and the movement of his paws into one smooth action, stop using the clicker and begin to offer random rewards.

Hind-Leg Walking—If your cat learns easily, you may decide to expand the beg behavior into one of the most difficult of all cat behaviors—walking on his hind legs. This is not a natural cat activity, but it can be successfully taught.

This trick is taught on the floor. Hold the clicker in one hand and the loaded reward can in the other. Kneel in front of your cat and cue him into the beg position. Lower the reward can as if you're going to give him his treat. As soon as he tries to eat it, give the verbal cue *up high,* and move backward on your knees. Move the hand holding the clicker toward your chest in a beckoning gesture.

If your cat follows you on his haunches, click the clicker and immediately give him his reward. If your cat drops to all fours, guide your cat back into position with the hand that's holding the clicker.

The hind-leg walk can be taught more easily if you have a training partner, and your cat is trained to lead on a leash. Attach his leash to his halter and coax your cat

Hind-leg walking is difficult but impressive.

along gently. Your training partner guides him into position on his haunches and helps him balance as he walks along. If you use this training technique, be sure there is never any painful tension on the leash.

If you successfully teach your cat to walk forward on his hind legs, you may want to expand the behavior to include the action of walking backward. You can begin to give him his cue from a standing position. If your cat reaches this level of training, don't allow him to walk on his hind legs for a distance of more than 10 feet, and don't demand performances more than three times a day. Because your cat's body is designed to walk on all fours, too much hind-leg walking can be harmful.

LOCATION BEHAVIORS

Fetch and *go up* are tricks—or location behaviors—that require your cat to go off on his own to whatever location you specify. To some people, these tricks may not seem difficult—but they are. Professional animal trainers know that if you can train your cat to perform these location behaviors, you and your cat can be considered professionals.

FETCH

Unlike the majority of dogs, most cats don't have a natural retrieving instinct—but some cats are exceptions. Before you begin the training procedures below, test your cat to see if you have a natural retriever.

Cats without a retrieving instinct usually take at least 1 month to learn to fetch. If the test shows that your cat is a natural retriever, you can bypass these long weeks of training.

Test Your Cat—For the test, use a soft toy that your cat can easily grasp in his jaws. Toss it 3 feet away from you, and give the verbal cue "fetch." If your cat retrieves the toy, click the clicker and reward him from the loaded reward can. Be sure to hold out your hand to catch the toy before he eats his treat.

Test your cat's understanding by substituting other small, soft objects for the toy. If he doesn't begin to bring these objects back to you on his own, you'll have to teach him the retrieve behavior described below. Plan on spending several weeks or more training your cat to fetch.

Cues and Rewards—The verbal cue for this trick is the word *fetch*. The visual cue is a small rag you may later replace with a variety of other small, soft objects. During the first part of training, a cereal bowl provides a second visual cue. As your cat progresses, your stretched-out palm replaces the cereal bowl.

If your cat has shown some retrieving instinct, you may try to proceed through the steps below using your outstretched palm in place of the cereal bowl. Most cats need the visual aid of the cereal bowl, however, to help them understand the fetch behavior.

In the beginning your cat receives two forms of rewards. The first is 1/2 teaspoon of soft-meat baby food smeared on the rag. The second is the food treat he receives when he performs the required behavior.

Bait Folded Rag—Cut a soft, clean rag into the size of a small handkerchief. Fold it and tie it in the middle, so it stays in a neat rectangle. The knotted rag should fit easily into your cat's mouth.

At a time when your cat is really hungry, spread 1/4 teaspoon of soft-meat baby food on the rag. Call your cat to the training table. Give him a lie-down cue. While he is in that position, place a cereal bowl directly in front of him. Next place the baited rag inside the bowl. Show him the food on the rag.

After he finds and eats the food, repeat the same process six times. On the sixth time, pick up the rag as you have done before. Don't put additional food on it. Place it back in the bowl. Your cat will expect to eat as before. He will look for the food but only find the leftover flavor. At this point, he will probably pick the rag up and try to chew the flavor from it.

The instant he picks up the rag, click the clicker and drop a regular reward into the bowl. As he eats the reward, pick up the rag and repeat the process. He should soon get the idea that he is being rewarded for picking up the rag.

STEPS IN TEACHING CAT TO FETCH

(1) Grasping object in jaws.

(2) The pick-up.

(3) Drop to cereal bowl.

(4) Drop into hand.

After your cat has accomplished this much, switch the rag to a fresh one. This one should be clean, without food flavor or odor. Your cat should then pick up the new rag just as he did the flavored one. If he does this, you will know that he understands he's getting the reward for the pick-up behavior.

If your cat does not pick up the new rag, you will have to go back to the rag with meat flavor until he gets the idea more fully. Repeat this process until your cat is picking up the rag with regularity.

Your cat may start to get a fixation about chewing the rag. If that happens, pull the rag away from him and drop the reward plainly in sight inside the bowl. Continue to do this until he learns to let go of the rag the moment he hears the clicker and sees the reward.

Teach Pick-Up and Drop—Tie or sew a metal washer to the clean rag. This causes a distinctive "ping" sound when it hits the bowl. This noise becomes another cue to your cat. It teaches him that when he hears that sound, he is performing properly.

With the bowl still in front of your cat, place the rag close to one side, but not inside, the bowl. When your cat picks it up and his head turns back toward the bowl, click the clicker and reward him.

If the rag falls in the bowl when your cat drops it to eat his reward, your cat will hear the ping of the washer hitting the bowl. If he misses the bowl, try to reposition him so that when he hears the clicker and drops the rag, it falls inside the bowl.

If your cat continues to miss the bowl, take hold of the rag with your free hand, guide it to the bowl and drop it in. Do this even if your cat releases the rag from his jaws. Let him hear the metal hitting the bowl.

It is critical at this point that your cat be reinforced almost every time he picks up the rag. Don't allow too many tries to pass without a reward. Your cat is beginning to use his reasoning and is slightly stressed. He may want to give up the training if his attempts to learn go without reward.

Lengthen Distance—When your cat is regularly picking up the rag and dropping it in the bowl, put the rag 1 inch farther from the bowl. Keep gradually moving it away until he actually has to take a step to retrieve. If he misses the bowl, coax him by repeating the verbal cue "fetch" and gesturing with your hands in the direction that you want him to move.

At this point you may make your cat pick up the rag without a reward. Continue to do so until he drops it into the bowl. You may also use your hands to guide the rag to the bowl.

You are now at a very important stage of fetch training. Your cat may get confused and want to quit. You may have to back up and use a baited rag again. Be patient. As the rag is moved farther and farther away from the bowl, your cat will suddenly understand the behavior you are training for. He will know that the required behavior is to pick up the rag and place it in the bowl. When this time comes, your cat will race for the rag wherever you throw it, pick it up, and return to place it gently inside the bowl.

Make Trick Perfect—At this point, you may begin to hold the bowl in your hand and let your cat place the rag inside it. When he is doing this consistently, place your outstretched palm over the top of the bowl when he fetches. Take the rag without letting it hit the bowl.

Cats—like most animals—learn things from associating each step with the next.

This is an animal reasoning process you will understand as you continue training your cat. It will become even clearer when you change the rag for another article.

You will probably have to tie a small piece of the rag, or even the entire rag, to an article you want your cat to fetch. Following the formula of graduation, reduce the portion of rag until your cat learns to fetch the new article.

When your cat's retrieval behavior is perfect, you may want to try giving him food rewards on a random basis. Do this gradually. If his performance level begins to fall, go back to offering him rewards on a constant basis. Most cats need regular food rewards to retain this difficult trick.

GO UP

People are impressed when they see your cat walk off and jump up onto whatever surface you point to. The trick becomes even more impressive if you explain that his behavior is an important part of an animal movie star's collection of tricks. The director tells the trainer that he wants the animal to walk over to a specific raised surface and jump up on it. The trainer points his finger, and the animal performs the action on cue.

If your cat becomes really good at the go up behavior, you can train him to walk off and stop at a mark, such as a stick or a chalk mark. In this case, he does not end his walk with a jump up onto a raised surface. Instead he stops at the mark and waits for his reward. This is another simple but important movie-star routine.

Cues and Rewards—The verbal cue is the phrase *go up*. The visual cue is your arm extended, with your index finger pointing toward a raised surface, such as the training table or the seat of a chair.

Point with index finger to cue for *go up*.

Reward your cat for performing this trick with his usual food treats on the reward can. At first you follow him over to the raised surface and immediately give him his reward. Later you train him to wait on the surface while you walk over and give him his treat.

Training Procedures—Stand beside the training table with your cat on the floor beside you. Load the reward can with a food treat, and pass it under his nose.

Point to the top of the table and give the verbal cue "go up." At the same time, use your free hand to hold the loaded reward can above the table.

When your cat jumps up on the table to go after his treat, use your pointing hand to pick up the clicker and click it. Lower the

Go-up trick is important if your cat is to perform in films.

reward can, and let your cat eat his treat. Repeat this process until he has earned at least 10 food rewards. Continue this level of training for at least 1 week.

Make Trick Perfect—Gradually move yourself and your cat farther from the training table when you cue him to go up. At first, step 1 foot away and stretch out your hand to hold the loaded reward can over the table's surface. Continue to do this as you step farther away from the table.

When the table's surface is beyond the reach of your outstretched hand, stop using the lure of the reward can. Begin to request the behavior with visual and verbal cues alone. In the beginning, follow your cat as he walks over to the table. As soon as he jumps up on it, click the clicker and give him his reward.

When your cat is consistently performing the go up behavior on cue, stop following him to the table to give him his reward. Stand in place until he jumps up onto the table. Then walk over and give him his reward. If he jumps down before you get there, put him back up on the table. Cue him into the sit and make him wait 5 seconds before you give him his treat. Continue this drill until he begins to obediently walk off, jump up onto the table and wait there for you to come with his reward.

Gradually phase out the clicker, and begin to offer random food rewards. At this point, you can begin cueing your cat with each of you in various locations in the room. Once he is consistently walking off and jumping up onto the training table, use the procedures described above to teach

194   Advanced Tricks

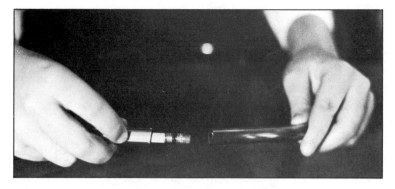

Connect ends of plastic tubing with pencil stub to make hoop.

him to walk off and jump up onto another raised surface, such as the seat of a chair. The trick is perfect when he walks off and jumps up on any raised surface you point to.

JUMPING BEHAVIORS

Your cat's natural agility is a big advantage in teaching jumping behaviors. You can teach your cat over-and-through jumps using hurdles, sticks and hoops. You can also teach your cat to jump to you—either into your arms or onto your shoulder. For very advanced jumping behaviors, you can teach two cats to do jumps together or one cat to perform a backward somersault.

OVER-AND-THROUGH JUMPS

These jumping behaviors are classic circus routines. Everyone has seen a lion or tiger jumping through a hoop—but how many have seen the same thing done by a domestic cat? Teach your cat these tricks, and you can show your friends something they have never seen before.

Cues and Rewards—The visual cues for this group of tricks are the props described below. Your cat sees you holding a hoop, for example, and knows that you want him

to jump through it. He knows this because you have trained him to jump at the sight of the hoop.

The verbal cue for all jumping behaviors is the word *jump.* Your cat learns to choose the type of jump you want by recognizing the prop you select.

Props—One or more hurdles are necessary for the first trick, *jump over hurdle.* The hurdles may be as simple as tied-together stacks of books or blocks, or as elaborate as weight-filled shoe boxes decorated with colored felt. Adjustable height and stability are important. If your cat knocks over a hurdle in the act of jumping it, he may become nervous about learning this behavior for the next several training sessions.

At different steps of training, the height of the hurdles varies from 9 to 12 inches or more. The height of the hurdles when the trick is perfect depends on the size and agility of your cat.

The hurdle you use during the first step of training must be wide enough to block a doorway. During later steps, the width may vary from 9 to 18 inches.

The second trick, *jump over stick,* requires a stick about 3 feet long. A cane, broom handle or yardstick is good for this behavior. You may want to decorate it with ribbon or felt to give it a circus look.

The third trick, *jump through hoop,* requires three different-sized hoops. Start your cat out with a large plastic hula hoop available in a variety or toy store. Graduate him to a 16-inch hoop you make according to directions given. Unless your cat is unusually large, you can perfect the trick with a hoop that is 1 foot in diameter.

Hoops can be made from many types of flexible tubing available in hardware stores. Polyethylene tubing is the least expensive and easiest to work with. Ask for 5/16-inch-interior-diameter size. Four feet of tubing makes a 16-inch hoop, while 3 feet makes a 1-foot hoop.

Cut the point off the stub of a pencil and insert one end into each opening of the tubing. The pencil stub now connects the two openings, making a neat, clear-plastic hoop you can decorate as you wish.

If you choose to make a hoop of copper or aluminum tubing, ask for the same 5/16-inch-interior-diameter size. Stiff steel wire in a 14-gauge width is another possible hoop material. All hoops made of metal tubing or wire require a clamp for connecting ends.

Over Hurdle—Set up a 9-inch-high hurdle in the doorway between two rooms. Position your cat on one side of the hurdle, then step over it and kneel on the other side. Load the reward can, and pass it under his nose.

Hold the can at your cat's eye level, and give the verbal cue "jump." If he jumps over the hurdle, click the clicker, and give him his treat. Repeat this exercise until he has earned at least 10 rewards.

If your cat doesn't jump over the hurdle, gently lift his forepaws, and guide him over it with your hands. Continue doing this until he understands the jumping behavior

Over hurdle in center of room.

you are training for.

If your cat is slow at learning this trick, ask for help from a training partner. You kneel on one side of the hurdle and cue your cat, while your partner starts him from the opposite side and guides him through his jump.

Continue to practice with the hurdle in the doorway until your cat begins to consistently jump over it when he hears the cue "jump." At this point, move over to his side of the hurdle, and start him from a run at 3 feet away. Reach over the hurdle to reward him when he jumps to the other side.

When your cat is consistently running to the hurdle and jumping over it on cue, you can increase the height of the hurdle to 1 foot or more. When he is consistently jumping the higher hurdle, you can move it to the center of the room. Train him to jump over it by beckoning him with the loaded reward can. At this point, phase out

After hurdle, jumping over stick is easy.

the clicker, and begin to offer random rewards.

If you wish, you can add polish to the trick by raising the hurdle to a height of 2 feet or more. When your cat is consistently jumping it on cue, you may want to place one or more additional hurdles on the floor in front of it. Allow at least 5 feet between them, so your cat can get good running starts. Start with two hurdles, then use three or more. At first you may have to use the lure of the loaded reward can to get him to jump each hurdle. Reach over each hurdle to reward him when he jumps to the other side.

When your cat is consistently jumping all the hurdles, begin to withhold his reward until he jumps the final one. Another variation involves eliminating the hurdles altogether and having your cat jump horizontally from station to station.

Jump Over Stick—If your cat is consistently jumping hurdles, this trick is easy. Squat on the floor 2 feet away from the training table, and call your cat to your side. Hold a 3-foot stick 1 foot off the floor in front of him. Give the verbal cue "jump," and he should jump over the stick to the surface of the table.

If your cat jumps to the floor on the other side of the stick instead of to the surface of the table, move the stick close to the table. Click the clicker, and offer a reward as soon as your cat jumps up onto the table. Continue this exercise until your cat has earned at least 10 rewards.

If your cat doesn't jump over the stick, ask a training partner to help you by manually guiding him over it, then carrying him up to the table top. Continue to do this until he understands the jumping behavior you are training for.

When your cat is consistently jumping over the stick at a height of 1 foot, begin to back farther away from the training table when you start him. Continue to increase the distance between you and the table until your cat is leaping as far as he is able. The trick is perfect when he makes a big leap over the stick to the surface of the table whenever he hears the cue "jump."

Jump Through Hoop—Teach your cat this trick in a way that's similar to the way you taught him to jump over a hurdle. Start him in the same doorway you used for the hurdle behavior.

Position your cat on one side of the doorway, then walk through it to the other side. Hold a hula hoop against the door jamb, with its bottom part on the floor. Load the reward can, and pass it under your cat's nose.

Hold the can at his eye level, and give the verbal cue "jump." If he walks through the hoop, click the clicker and give him his treat. Repeat this exercise until he has

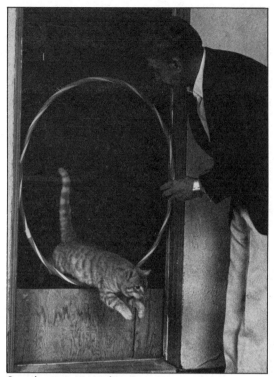

Start hoop jump in doorway.

Variation: a "human hoop."

earned at least 10 rewards.

If your cat doesn't walk through the hoop, use your hands to gently guide him through. Continue to do this until he understands the behavior you are training for.

As soon as your cat is consistently walking through the hula hoop on the cue of "jump," begin to gradually raise the hoop to a height of 1 foot or more. If he tries to walk under it, put a hurdle in the doorway below the hoop to block his passage.

If your cat is slow at learning this behavior, ask a training partner to help you in the same way he or she helped you train your cat to jump the hurdle. When the hoop-jumping behavior is firmly established, ask you partner to hold the hoop while you move to your cat's side of the

hoop to start him from a run 3 feet away. Have your partner click the clicker, and reward him as soon as he jumps through the hoop.

When your cat is consistently running to the hoop and jumping through it when he hears the cue "jump," move away from the doorway. Practice with the hula hoop in the center of the room. You can also phase out the clicker, and begin to offer random food rewards.

Cue him to jump through the hoop when you hold it 1 foot above the floor. Gradually increase the height to 3 feet. When he is consistently jumping through the hoop from his position on the floor, you can introduce a simple variation. Position two sturdy tables 3 or more feet apart. Cue your cat to jump through the hoop that you

Jump into arms.

hold between the tables. Instead of jumping from the floor through the hoops, your cat jumps from table to table.

When your cat becomes really good at jumping through hoops, you may discard your props to achieve an interesting variation on the trick. This involves forming a circle with your arms, and cueing your cat to jump through a "human hoop."

Introduce smaller hoops when your cat is consistently jumping through large ones. You may want to set up a series of hoops and train him to jump through them in sequence, as you did with the hurdles. The trick is perfect when your cat jumps through one or more hoops of 1-foot diameter when he hears the cue "jump."

JUMPS TO YOU

Because these tricks are likely to cause accidental scratches, *you should not teach them unless your cat has been declawed.* If your cat's declawing does not include his back paws, wear a heavy jacket for protection when you teach these tricks.

Into Your Arms—Stand in front of your declawed cat as he sits on the training table. Load the reward can, and pass it under his nose. Step back a foot, open your arms and give the verbal cue "jump."

Because your cat is now familiar with this cue, he may jump on your chest. If he does, catch him securely, click the clicker and give him his treat. Cuddle him and stroke him, so he feels secure in your arms.

If your cat does not jump onto your chest, get the help of a training partner. When you give the cue "jump," he or she should carry him into your arms. After he has "earned" 10 rewards in this manner, have your partner nudge him off the table by his rump.

If your cat still doesn't jump onto your chest for his treat, review him on the jumping behaviors he has already acquired. Eventually he will understand the be-

Jump to shoulder.

havior you are training for.

When your cat is consistently jumping into your arms from a distance of 1 foot, gradually lengthen the distance you stand from the training table. Phase out the clicker, and begin to offer random rewards. The trick is perfect when your cat jumps onto your chest from a distance of 3 feet or more.

Onto Your Shoulder—Stand in front of your cat as he sits on the training table. Load the reward can, and pass it under his nose.

Turn your back, and squat down until your shoulders are level with the height of the training table. Now give the verbal cue "jump."

If your cat jumps on your shoulder, click the clicker and give him his treat. Stroke him, and speak softly to assure him he won't fall off.

If your cat doesn't jump on your shoul-

der, ask a training partner to help you the same way he or she did when you taught your cat to jump into your arms. When he's consistently jumping to your shoulder with you in the squatting position, gradually begin to stand up. When he is consistently jumping up to your shoulder with you in the standing position, begin to lengthen the distance. Gradually move away from the table until you are cueing your cat to jump on your shoulder from a distance of 3 feet or more.

The trick is impressive at this level of training, but if your cat is particularly agile, you may want to add even more polish. Use the training procedures described above to teach him to jump on your shoulder from the floor. Once he becomes comfortable on your shoulder, begin to walk around the room with him. Eventually he may become a shoulder-riding cat who takes walks with you indoors and out.

VARIATIONS ON JUMP

If you are an ambitious trainer, you can teach two cats who know and like each other to perform together. You can also teach your cat to do a spectacular backward somersault.

Simple Jump—Teach each cat to stand on his hind legs and jump at least 1 foot into the air. Do this separately with each cat in different training sessions. The cats should *not* be together when you teach them to do the simple jump. Review them separately on the behavior for at least 1 week before you begin to drill them together.

To teach the simple jump, stand in front of the cat on the floor. Load the reward can, and pass it under his nose. Hold it 1 foot over his head, and give the verbal cue "jump." If he jumps, click the clicker, lower the reward can and let him eat his treat. Continue this exercise until he has earned at least 10 rewards.

If the cat doesn't jump for his treat, have a training partner guide him up into the jumping motion. Continue to work with your training partner until your cat understands the behavior you are training for.

Drill the cats separately as you teach them to jump higher and higher by gradually raising the height of their reward cans. At the end of 1 week, they should be jumping 1 foot into the air. When both cats are consistently jumping at least 1 foot high on cue, begin to drill them in training sessions together.

Two at a Time—To get two cats to perform together, you must have a good training partner. He or she cues and rewards one cat, while you cue and reward the other. Until tandem behavior is firmly established, use the lure of the reward can over the cats' heads to elicit the jumping behavior. Continue to click the clicker before you give the cats their food rewards.

At first, allow an interval of at least 10 seconds to pass between the time your partner cues his or her cat and the time you cue yours. Gradually decrease this interval to 5 seconds or less. Stop decreasing it when the cats become confused and begin responding to each other's cues.

When the cats are consistently jumping in tandem on separate verbal cues, phase out the clicker, and stop using the lure of the reward can over their heads. Offer frequent random rewards to maintain this difficult behavior.

Backward Somersault—This challenging trick can be learned by a small, agile cat who already knows how to fetch and do a simple jump. If your cat doesn't meet these qualifications, don't try to teach it.

Stand 3 feet away from your cat as he sits on the training table. Give the verbal cue "flip over," and toss him a small, soft object he likes to fetch. If his fetching behavior is strong, he may catch the object in his mouth. If he does, hold out your palm, so he can drop the object into it. Immediately click the clicker, and give him a reward.

If your cat doesn't catch the object in his mouth, pick it up and place it between his jaws. Hold out your palm for the drop. Continue to do this until your cat understands the catching behavior you are training for.

When your cat is consistently catching the object in his mouth, begin to back farther from him when you toss the object. Gradually increase the height of your throw.

When he consistently reaches up to catch the object, begin to toss it so high he must jump to reach it. Increase the height

Only a small, agile cat can do backward somersault.

still more, so he must tilt his head backward to see it. Continue to increase the height of your throw until he must do a backward somersault to catch the object in his mouth.

When your cat is consistently doing a complete backward turn over, stop tossing the object. Begin to demand the behavior on the cue of "flip over." Don't get discouraged if your cat won't perform without the help of the tossed object. The backward somersault is a difficult behavior that few cats can ever completely master.

WORKING BEHAVIORS

The first working behavior described below, the hearing-ear behavior, gives you and your cat a chance to assist a hearing-handicapped person. The second set of working behaviors, on-camera behaviors, are for performing cats. These give you and your cat the opportunity to be creative together.

HEARING-EAR CATS

If you are hard of hearing, you may be able to train your cat to be your ears. If a friend or family member has this problem, you can help him or her train a cat to provide reliable hearing help.

The hearing-ear behavior is suitable only for an intelligent, owner-devoted cat. Likewise, only a trainer with lots of time and patience can successfully teach it. Don't begin a hearing-ear training program unless you and the cat fully meet these qualifications.

Cues—The cue for each hearing-ear behavior depends on the sound you are training the cat to hear for the hard-of-hearing person. It may be a bell, such as a telephone ring or doorbell. It may be a buzzer, such as an alarm clock or the timer on a clothes dryer or microwave oven. It may even be the thud of the newspaper as it lands on the front porch.

Hard-of-hearing people often have trouble noticing dropped objects because they don't hear the sound of the fall. A cat can be trained to alert his owner to the noise of an object dropping on the floor.

Rewards—During the first part of training, most food rewards are the same easy-to-eat fresh treats you used during household and trick training. Later, offer non-perishable treats you keep in a jar near the

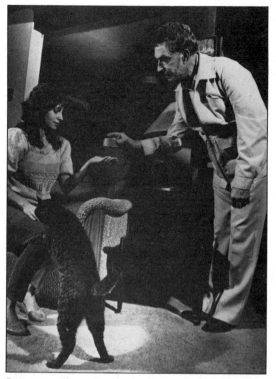

Pass reward can to hard-of-hearing owner, so she can give reward.

First Level of Training—Because you may help train another person's pet, in this section the term "the cat" has been used in place of "your cat." The pronoun "her" has been used to refer to the hard-of-hearing person for the sake of convenience and clarity.

For hearing-ear training, many basic procedures you used to teach your cat to come to the sound of his name or the call of the clicker are used. Review these techniques on pages 81 to 83 before you begin hearing-ear training.

This type of training requires three people. The first is the hard-of-hearing person, who offers rewards. The second is a helper, who sets off the sound of the cue. The third is the person who handles the cat. The following section is written with you as the handler. But if you are the hard-of-hearing person, you take the reward-giving role instead.

No matter how many sound cues you plan to teach the cat to respond to, train him to react to only one cue at a time. Because it's such an important hearing need for many people, the ring of the telephone is usually the best cue to begin with.

Ask your phone caller to ring the phone every 3 minutes. Position the hard-of-hearing person in a chair by the phone. Position yourself beside the cat in his kennel, 10 feet away.

Load the reward can, show it to the cat, then close the door of his kennel. As soon as the phone rings, let him out and carry the reward can over to the phone. The cat will probably follow you because he's anxious for a treat. When the two of you have reached the ringing phone, gently lift the cat's forepaws and place them on the knees of the hard-of-hearing person. Pass the reward can to this person, who should let the

source of a sound cue, such as the telephone.

Pet stores carry a variety of tasty, nonperishable treats. Choose one that's nourishing, but not too filling, so it doesn't spoil the cat's meals or interfere with other training.

To ensure reliability in the performance of hearing-ear behaviors, offer food rewards on a constant basis during the entire period of training. After a behavior is firmly established, stroking and praise can occasionally be given in place of food. Don't eliminate the food treat more than 1 out of 10 times. A hearing-ear cat will perform faithfully year after year if he knows his efforts will usually be rewarded with the pleasure of a small bite of special food.

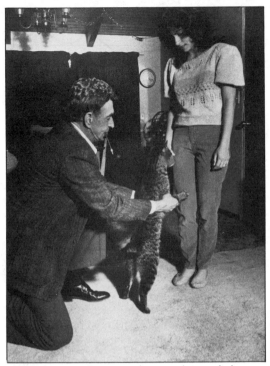
Place paws on knees until cat understands how to signal owner.

cat eat his treat before she answers the phone.

Once she is alerted to the ring of the phone by the gesture of the cat, the hard-of-hearing person may hold a conversation with the aid of a voice amplifier or telephone typewriting device. However, keep conversations brief during training.

Repeat this exercise at least 10 times each drilling session. Schedule at least three sessions at intervals throughout the day.

Rules of Timing—The amount of time you take on each level of training depends on the learning ability of the cat. Make sure each behavior is firmly established before you go on to the next one.

A fully trained hearing-ear cat must respond to a variety of sound cues by seeking out the hard-of-hearing person wherever she is in her home. The cat must then place his paws on her knees, whether she is sitting, standing up or lying down. Finally, he must lead her to the source of the sound cue—whether it's the phone, doorbell or timer on an appliance.

This is a complicated set of behaviors. It may take months before the cat learns to perform the whole set to perfection. Perfection is necessary, however, so take time to help the cat achieve it. A hearing-ear cat must alert his hard-of-hearing owner every time he hears a sound cue—not just when he's in the mood for it.

Learning Limit—If the cat seems unable to learn a new step of training, he may have reached his learning limit. If you suspect that this has occurred, go back to an earlier level of training. When he feels comfortable with this level, introduce the new level a second time. If he is still unable to learn the new step, he may be trying to tell you he has reached his learning limit. Instead of trying to push him beyond his capacity, find another cat to train for the hearing-ear behavior.

Second Level of Training—When the cat consistently responds to the telephone bell by jumping out of his kennel, walking to the hard-of-hearing person and placing his paws on her knees, begin to lengthen the distance of the kennel from the phone. Continue to do so until the cat performs the behavior from any point in the room.

It's time to add variety. Instead of positioning the hard-of-hearing person by the phone, have her take positions at various points in the room. Do this by gradually moving her farther and farther from the phone. Continue to position the cat's kennel at other places when you start him to the cue of the phone bell.

Vary location and position of hard-of hearing owner.

Have the hard-of-hearing person hold the loaded reward can. When the cat comes to put his paws on her knees, have her carry the can over to the ringing phone. When the cat follows, she should give him his treat beside the phone. This tells him that he is required to accompany the hard-of-hearing person *all the way to the phone* before he gets his treat.

If the cat does not come to the hard-of-hearing person, carry him to her, and place his paws on her knees with your hands. Continue to give him this guidance until he begins to understand the behavior you are training for.

When the cat consistently walks over to the hard-of-hearing person at any point in the room and places his paws on her knees,

it is time to teach him to *lead her* to the ringing phone.

Instead of walking over to the phone to reward the cat, the hard-of-hearing person should stay in her position. The cat may walk over to the phone on his own in hopes of receiving his treat. If he does so, the hard-of-hearing person should follow him and reward him. If he does not walk to the phone, pick him up and carry him to it until he begins to understand the behavior you are training for. Always have the hard-of-hearing person follow you and the cat to the phone and offer him his reward there.

Third Level of Training—At this point, the cat should consistently alert the hard-of-hearing person to the phone bell by placing his paws on her knees. He should

Cat is stroked for alerting owner to oven buzzer.

then lead her to the ringing phone, where he receives his reward.

Perfect this behavior in the room with the phone by adding variety. Have the hard-of-hearing person lie down on a couch or stand in a corner instead of sitting in a chair. Drill the cat until he understands he must always alert her to the sound of the phone bell by placing his paws on her knees, no matter what position she is in.

Instead of starting the cat from his kennel, have him start on his own from various points in the room. Continue this level of training until he consistently responds to the cue of the phone bell by immediately walking over to the hard-of-hearing person and placing his paws on her knees.

Now is the time to completely perfect the hearing-ear behavior. Begin by starting the cat from his kennel placed in other rooms in the home. When he consistently walks over to the hard-of-hearing person in the room with the phone, eliminate the kennel and have him start on his own.

When the cat responds to the phone bell from any room in the home, begin to position the hard-of-hearing person in other rooms. Start the cat in the same room she's in until he consistently walks over to her, places his paws on her knees and leads her to the phone.

The final step of training involves starting the cat from a different room from the hard-of-hearing person, who should be positioned in another room without a phone. The behavior is perfect when the cat seeks her out, alerts her with his paws on his knees and leads her to the ringing phone.

When the hearing-ear behavior is firmly established for the sound cue of the phone bell, begin to use the same procedures to train the cat to respond to additional cues. Each new behavior should be easier to teach than the previous because the experienced cat quickly understands the activity you are training for.

Remind the hard-of-hearing person to continue to offer non-perishable food treats near the source of every sound cue on an almost continuous basis. Reinforcement with rewards will be necessary for the cat to continue the hearing-ear behavior. Ask her to reinforce the food treats with stroking and praise. The cat will enjoy the pleasure of having a special purpose in life, and his hard-of-hearing owner will have a well-trained helper and friend.

WORKING ON CAMERA

Your cat may never go to Hollywood to do his tricks for a major studio, but he can perform a cute routine for your home movie or videotape camera. Use the same techniques professionals use to give these performances polish.

Types of Performances—If you have a shy cat who won't perform in front of strangers, a film or videotape of his tricks will make it possible for your friends to see him in action. You can take the film or tape almost anywhere to show off your trained animal act.

Review your cat for at least 1 week under whatever supplemental lighting you need for proper lens exposure. It is helpful to acquaint him in advance with the sight and sound of a camera.

When the time comes to film or record his performance, ask another person to operate the camera for you. This leaves you free to concentrate on cueing and rewarding your cat.

Ask your camera person to keep the camera steady and avoid frequent zooms (rapid close-up-to-long-shot or long-shot-to-close-up lens movements). Shots of you giving cues are important so the viewer can see the activity as a whole, not just the performance of your cat. If you have editing facilities, you can select the best shots and edit them together to create a professional-looking show.

In addition to trick-performance routines, you can create another type of on-camera cat performance that develops a gimmick or tells a story. Write a script that describes each camera shot on the left side of the page. Write the corresponding narration, sound effects and music on the right. Shoot and edit your production according to the script directions.

You can create a wide variety of clever productions with a few simple costumes, props and some imagination. A cat detective story, a practical joke or a musical performance with a prop instrument are some examples. The possibilities are endless. If you keep things simple and carefully follow your script, you may produce a piece that gets accepted by a TV variety show that runs unusual home film and tape clips.

Getting Him to Perform—Use the basic trick-training techniques described in this book to teach your cat to perform special actions you write into your script. In many cases, one of the tricks he already knows can be quickly modified to produce the action you have in mind. His "wave bye-bye" can be modified into a guitar-strumming movement, for example.

If you are working with a story script, you may have to get your cat to walk a particular route. He may have to go in or out of a real door or the door of a stage-set building you have made. He may have to stop his action at a particular point on the set.

By this time, you should know enough about cat training to devise your own ways of getting him to do things on cue. But it's helpful to have at least one assistant so he or she can start your cat while you work him from a distance.

Use food treats and the security of your cat's portable kennel as rewards at the end of a route to be covered. Use the clicker as a calling device and as a sign he's performed a desired action. The hiss is a helpful negative cue for getting your cat to stop at a designated point.

Dangle food rewards and interesting toys just outside of camera range to produce anything from an alert expression to a jump. Put food rewards in doorways or at other stop points to lure your cat to these locations. Use your imagination to think up other off-camera tricks to trigger specific performances. Don't worry if some of your devices look silly—it's what the scene looks like on camera that counts.

More than One Cat—Working with two or more animals can be very difficult. If you do decide to try to get multiple cats to work together, make sure they know and like each other. Each cat should have two trainers to help him start and respond to cues.

You may want to use several look-alike cats separately, as professionals do. Train each look-alike so he's strong on two or three behaviors. In your final edited production, it will look like one very well-trained cat is performing them all.

Going Professional—Very few cat owners end up having their pets perform in a professional TV or film studio. This is because it takes a lot of patient effort to accustom a cat to working in a strange place filled with lights, moving scenery and other distractions. It is possible to get around this barrier, however. If you are willing to put in lots of work, you may be able to make your pet a star.

First, put your cat in his portable kennel and take him for car rides all over town. Continue to do this until he begins to show you that he feels as comfortable on the road as he does at home. This may take days or weeks, depending on your cat.

After he is accustomed to riding in your car, begin to let him out of his kennel in many different indoor and outdoor locations. Lure him out of his kennel with the clicker and reward system described in Chapter 3. Soon he will lose his apprehension about strange places.

Be creative. Use training techniques to devise new tricks.

Your next step is to take your cat into a film or TV studio, if possible. If you do not have access to a studio, take him to a series of other busy, brightly lit places. Leave him in these environments for several hours a day. In a short time, he will cease to be bothered by noisy distractions.

At this point, you can begin to put your cat through his trick routines in a studio or studiolike environment. Keep his hunger level high, so he is anxious to earn his rewards. When he becomes accustomed to performing, he may no longer need the motivation of the food drive. Instead, he may begin to work simply for the feeling of accomplishment that it gives him.

When your cat reaches this point, he is ready for his first booking. You don't have to go to Hollywood to prepare your cat's debut. It is possible to get him started right in your own home town. A well-trained cat is still a novelty all over the world, because many people remain convinced that cats can't be trained.

Call your local television stations and make dates to present your future star to the program directors. Most likely one of them will offer you a spot on a newscast or a talk show. After all, you have something different, and your trained cat will be sure to cause comment.

From this start, who can tell? More than one animal star has been discovered in such a way. Good luck!

THE MAKING OF A GENTLEMAN

Sometimes you have to use trickery to get a desired behavior from a cat. Such was the case with Ouch, our attack cat, who learned to behave like a gentleman — with a little help from a pane of glass.

We would not have used Ouch had it not been for the insistence of a smart advertising producer. He wanted to produce a sequel to an award-winning commercial featuring one of our cats. In the commercial (pictured on our back cover), a handsome cat is so engrossed in eating his bowl of delicious food that he fails to notice a band of uniformed birds who parade in front of him with musical instruments blaring.

Now the ad agency was looking for a cat to star in another spot in the same campaign. When the producer arrived at our kennels, he began examining every cat. My trainers and I tried to focus his attention on Beverly Hills, a gorgeous animal we'd been grooming for the part. He was so unusually handsome, we thought he'd be a natural.

"He's got shifty eyes," the producer declared. "What about that big guy on the second shelf at the far left?"

"Darn!" I thought.

"You don't want to use him," I said. "His name is Ouch. We were going to name him Attack Cat, but that sounded a little long. Here, I'll show you."

A trainer dropped Ouch at my feet, and immediately — ouch! He lunged into the air, landed with his claws wrapped around my leg, and began chewing my pant leg.

"That's the way he is," I said, gritting my teeth. "He was raised with a Doberman, and he thinks he's a dog."

"I like him — he's the one," the producer declared.

Sighing, I pried Ouch off my pant leg.

As soon as the producer left, I studied the plan for the commercial. The 30-second spot called for a big cat to chow down on cat food while three masked mice, dressed like bandits, entered the scene. The mice were to hold a quick conference directly under the big cat's nose, and then disappear. The cat would have to love that brand of food! He would have to continue paying no attention when the mice re-entered, dragging a monstrous hunk of cheese as the final gimmick.

How could we get Ouch the attack cat to ignore those three tasty mice? I cupped his chin in my hand and looked at him eyeball to eyeball. "Ouch," I said, "you're going to learn all about the nicer things in life."

Before we could teach Ouch manners, we had to get him hooked on the cat food. Lucky for us, he loved it.

Next we placed a screen of wire mesh around him and let three mice scamper about almost under his nose. *Crash!* He burst right through the wire, and we barely saved the terrified mice.

Obviously we needed a different approach. After a quick conference, we set up a pane of thick glass in front of Ouch's eating place. We cleaned it until it was as clear as could be. Then we released our three reluctant mice on the side opposite the cat.

Ouch immediately crouched and sprang into an attacking leap. Pow! His body crashed awkwardly into the glass. When he recovered his balance, he shook his head as if to say, "What happened?" Then he began compulsively grooming his tail, covering his embarrassment in typical cat fashion.

Ouch was a bully, but he was definitely no dummy. He soon settled down to his cat food, deciding he preferred it to mouse meat. To further save face, he ignored the mice completely. No matter how many times we put him through this exercise while filming the commercial, he never looked up at them again.

Ray Berwick

Berwick's Animals with Hollywood Friends

Isabel Sanford of "The Jeffersons" presents Berwick with the 1983 Patsy Award from the American Humane Association for training Boomer, selected best dog actor of the year.

Betty White — TV personality, author and animal advocate — with Boomer.
Courtesy of Pets Are Wonderful Council

Opposite and above: Strawberry, an orangutan trained by Berwick, clowns with "Little House on the Prairie" stars (left to right) Victor French, Michael Landon, Landon's daughter Leslie, and Melissa Gilbert. *NBC photos*

Melissa Gilbert as a youngster with "little sister" Sidney Greenbush and Berwick's dog Bandit, both "Little House on the Prairie" regulars.

Jake, a dog trained by Berwick assistant Steve Berens, attacks Lane Novack on cue in a recent movie, "Up the Creek."

Above: Berwick and Robert Blake discuss a scene with Fred, the cockatoo on "Baretta."
Copyright © by Universal City Studios, Inc.
Courtesy of MCA Publishing Rights, a Division of MCA Inc.

Left: Fred and Ray enjoy each other's company.

Fred rides his customized bicycle.

Berwick's animals, Whitey the Cat and Willie the Goat from TV series "Helltown."

Berwick's Animals with Hollywood Friends **219**

Actor Terrance Stamp and Berwick's orangutan Locke, stars of recently released movie, "Link."
Courtesy of THORN EMI Screen Entertainment Limited

Index

A

Abstract thought in cats 30
Accidents in toilet training 151-155
Accidents, how to clean 155-159
Activity levels in cats 14
Adding toilet insert 135
Adding training-toilet seat to litter box 127
Advance preparation of treats 52
Advanced tricks 184-211
Affection, cat's feelings of 31
Age of grown cats for training 39
Age of kittens for training 39
Aggressive behaviors 71-75
  Aggression toward people 74
  Catching prey 74
  Darting outdoors 71
  Fights with other animals 74
Anal sacs, infected 161
Attitudes and emotions in cats 31

B

Backward somersault 26, 201
Bad-tasting repellents 65
Balance, cat's sense of 27
Baldness 44
Balking on leash 87
Barricades in toilet training 151
Basic behaviors 49, 81-91
  Come when called 81-83
  How to teach three basic behaviors 80-91
  Kennel training 83-85
  Lead on leash 85-91
Basic characteristics of cats 13
Basic corrective techniques 56
Basic techniques of toilet training 112-114
Basics of training 50-58
  Corrective techniques 56-58
  Food rewards 51
  Stroking rewards 50
  Training cues 54, 56
Bathroom accidents 151
Bathroom distractions during toilet training 110
Bathroom hazards 107-110
Bathroom preparation for toilet training 107-114
Beg trick 186-188
Beginning tricks 168-183
Behavior, aggressive 71-75
Behavior, changing your cat's 64-91
Behavior, hyperactive 31
Behavior-modification techniques in toilet training 113
Behaviors, basic 49, 81-91
Behaviors, communication 185-188
Behaviors, desired 49
Behaviors, devices to change undesirable 65-69
Behaviors, how to eliminate undesirable 69-75

Behaviors, how to teach three basic 80-91
Behaviors, jumping 195-202
Behaviors, location 189-195
Behaviors, self-taught 30
Behaviors, working 202-209
Berwick on cats 5-36
Bites 52
Bitter-tasting repellents 65
Boarding in kennel 153
Body language, cat's 33
Body, getting to know your cat's 25
Bolting on leash 87
Booby traps 67
Bowel-movement accidents, discipline for 114
Bowel-movement patterns 99
Bowel-movement stains 156
Bowel-stimulating foods 98
Brain structure 28
Breed-related characteristics 14
Breeds for training 12
Bringing cat home 22
Brushes for grooming 45
Business trips, leaving your cat for 153
Bye-bye wave 179-181

C

Call cat to come 81-83
Camera performances 207-209
Carpet cleaning 156
Carpet patching 157
Carpet-backing cleaning 158
Cat bites 52
Cat-care equipment 20
Cat-care items 21
Cat food 20
Cat repellents 65-67
  Bad-tasting substances 65
  Booby traps 67
  Chemical preparations 65
  Noise-making devices 65
  Snapping devices 67
  Water 67
Cat repellents in toilet training 106
Cat skeleton 25
Cat talk 33
Cat treats, commercially prepared 52
Cat's body, getting to know your 25
Cat's health 40-46
Cat's mind, getting to know your 28-33
Catnip 22, 53, 78
Changing your cat's behavior 64-91
Characteristics of cats, basic 13
Characteristics, breed-related 14
Checkups 25
Chemical repellents 65
Choosing a cat 10
Choosing the right foods 20
Claw clipping 79

Claw trimming 46
Clean accidents, how to 155-159
Cleaning and deodorizing aids in toilet training 106
Cleaning carpet 157
Cleaning of carpet backing 158
Clicker, teaching cat to come to 83
Clickers, kinds of 54
Clickers, where to buy 54
Combs for grooming 45
Come to clicker 83
Come when called 81-83
Commercial litter 105
Communication behaviors 185-188
Completion of toilet training 144
Constant versus random rewards 171
Constipation 160
Constipation, stress-induced 118
Contaminated water, drinking 112
Control feedings 51
Coordination, muscle 28
Corrective discipline 69
Corrective techniques, basic 56-57
  Discipline with sharp sounds 57
  Imitate mother cat 57
  No pain or humiliation 57
  Stroke and make up 57
Cosmetics in bathroom 109
Cueing in toilet training 106
Cues and rewards for appropriate scratching 78
Cues and rewards for trick training 169-172
Cues for hearing-ear training 202
Cues for training 54, 56
Cues, negative 56
Cues, visual and verbal 56, 169

D

Daily grooming 44
Dangers in bathroom 109
Deaf cats 13
Declawing 79
Declawing, psychological reactions to 80
Delayed discipline 58, 114
Deodorants, carpet 156
Deodorants, litter 105
Deodorizing accidents 155
Deodorizing aids in toilet training, cleaning and 106
Desirable behaviors 49, 76-80
Devices to change undesirable behaviors 65-69
Devices, snapping 67
Diarrhea 161-162
Diarrhea from eating prey 74
Diet changes, sudden 20
Diet, milk in 99
Diet-related diarrhea 161
Dietary supplements 98-99
Digestive system, cat's 26

Discipline 38
Discipline, delayed 58, 114
Discipline in toilet training 113
Discipline, no pain or humiliation 57
Discipline, stroking after 57
Discipline with sharp sounds, 57
Discouragement in toilet training 162
Disease-related diarrhea 161
Disruption of routine 153
Distractions in bathroom 110
Dogs, training techniques for 59-61
Domestic shorthairs 14
Double-cat jump 201
Double-cat performances 208
Double-cat training 58
Dousing with water 74
Dousings as repellents 67
Dragging on leash 87
Drapes, protection of 69
Dreams, cat's 32
Drinking from toilet 130
Drooling and sucking 70
Dry skin 44

E
Ear mites 41
Eating grass 98
Eating house plants 98, 109
Eating, messy 70
Eczema 44
Electric shock 109
Eliminating undesirable behaviors
  69-75
Elimination disorders 159
Elimination, how to elicit 118-119
Elimination patterns 99
Elimination signals 117
Emotions and attitudes, cat's 31
Equipment for cat care 20
Excessive meowing 70
Exploration of toilet 130, 136
Extrasensory perception, sense of 28

F
Factors in timing 58
Falling into toilet 130
Feeding for regularity 97
Feedings, control 51
Feelings of affection, cat's 31
Female cats, training 12
Fetch trick 189-193
Film performances 207
Fireplace accidents 152
First impressions, cat's 20
Fleas 40
Flushing toilet 146
Follow-up techniques in toilet train-
  ing 124
Food rewards 51-54
  How to offer food rewards 52
  Types of food rewards 52
Food rewards in toilet training 106,
  113
Food rewards in trick training 170
Food treats 38
Foods, bowel-stimulating 98
Foods, choosing the right 20

Forbidden places, keeping cat from
  69-70
Furniture, protection of 69

G
Garbage containers, keeping cat
  from 69
Getting to know your cat's body 25
Getting to know your cat's mind
  28-33
  Brain structure 28
  Instincts 29
  Reason & memory 30
  Abstract thought 30
Getting wet in toilet 131
Go-up trick 193-195
Grass, eating 98
Grooming 25, 44-46
  Brushing and combing 45
  Claws 46
  Eyes, ears & rectum 45
  Tools 45
Grown cats, age for training 39
Grown cats, meal schedules for 97

H
Habits, infantile 70
Habits, cat's personal 70
Hair, cat's 26
Hairballs 44, 160
Handshake trick 181
Hardwood-floor cleaning 155
Hardwood-floor refinishing 158
Harmful substances in bathroom 107
Hazardous objects in bathroom 109
Health, cat's 40-46
  Daily grooming 44-46
  Parasites 40-41
  Skin diseases 41, 44
Hearing, sense of 26
Hearing-ear training 202-207
Heeling 89
Hind-leg walking 188
Hissing, cat talk 33
Hole in toilet insert 141
Hollywood Cat Tales
  Caste of Cats 34-35
  Cat Biker 183
  Click, Click — The Sound of Suc-
    cess 55
  Dark Dealing on the Set 164-165
  Home Sweet Homes 42-43
  Jerry's World 18-19
  Lights, Camera, Ouch! 60-61
  No Sitting Pigeons 120-121
  Pinto the Wonder Cat 148-149
  The Giant 72-73
  The Pro 90-91
  The Making of a Gentleman
    210-211
Hoops for jumps 196
Hot-sauce repellents 65, 67
House plants, accidents in 152
House plants, eating 98, 109
Household routines 25, 100
Household training 49
How cat sees you 32
How to clean accidents 155-159

How to eliminate undesirable be-
  haviors 69-75
How to offer food rewards 52
How to offer rewards in trick train-
  ing 171
How to promote desirable behaviors
  76-80
How to teach three basic behaviors
  80-91
Howling, cat talk 33
Human hoop 199
Humiliation in discipline 57
Hybrid vigor 12
Hyperactive behavior 31

I
Imagination, cat's 30
Imitating mother cat 57
Infantile habits 70
Infected anal sacs 161
Instinctive behavior 29
Internal organs, cat's 25
Introducing cat to home 20-25
Introducing perch-squat on training
  seat 129
Introducing yourself to your cat 22

J
Jealousy-caused accidents 154
Jump-from-table-to-table trick 199
Jump-into-arms-trick 199
Jump-onto-shoulder trick 200
Jump-over-hurdle trick 196
Jump-over-stick trick 197
Jump-through-hoop trick 197
Jump-to-you trick 199
Jump trick, simple 201
Jump, variations on 201
Jumping behaviors 195-202
Jumps
  Human hoop 199
  Over-and-through 195-199
  Props for 195
  Two cats 201

K
Keeping records of elimination pat-
  terns 99
Kennel boarding 153
Kennel, portable 21
Kennel training 83-85
Kittens
  Age for training 39
  Meal schedules for 97
  Sources for 15
  Training 10
Kneading 70

L
Lead on leash 85-91
Learning ability 12, 173, 204
Leash training 49, 85-91
Leash training, equipment for 85
Lice 41
Lid-related accidents 152
Lie-down trick 173, 176-178
Litter 20 105, 123
Litter box 20
Litter box, moving 125-127

Litter, commercial 105
Litter container for training toilet 101
Litter deodorants 105
Litter-mate play 16
Litter mess 128
Litter substitutes 105
Location behaviors 189-195
Location of training toilet 122

M

Making a training toilet 102
Male cats, training 12
Mantles, protection of 69
Marking with scent 50-51
Meal schedules for grown cats 97
Meal schedules for kittens 97
Medicines in bathroom 109
Memory, cat's 28, 30
Mental problems in cats 13
Meowing, cat talk 33
Meowing, excessive 70
Messy eating 70
Milk in cat's diet 99
Mind, getting to know your cat's 28-33
Mixing bowl, rimmed 102, 103
Moods, cat's 31
More than one cat, training 58
Mother cat, imitating 57
Mother figure 32
Moving litter box 125-127
Multiple tricks 172-174
Muscle coordination, cat's 28

N

Naming cat 81
Negative cues 56
Neutering 39
Neutral-smelling litter 123
Nighttime accidents 151
Noise-making repellents 65
Nose-rubbing in wastes 114

O

Obstacles in toilet insert 138
Older cats, training 12
Options in toilet training 143, 146
Order of reviewing tricks 174
Order of teaching tricks 174
Organs, cat's internal 25
Other pets and your cat 23-25
Outdoor safety 88
Over-and-through jumps 195-199
Over-hurdle jump 196

P

Pain in discipline 57
Parasites 40-41
Partner, training 82
Patching carpet 157
Patterns of elimination 99
Perch-squat on bathroom toilet, step 2 of toilet training 129-134
Personal habits, cat's 70
Personality factors 13-14
    Activity levels 14
    Basic characteristics 13
    Breed-related characteristics 14
    Shyness and friendliness 14

Pet psychology 48
Phasing out litter, step 4 of toilet training 137-139
Physical problems in cats 13
Place and time for trick training 172
Plants in bathroom 108
Plants, eating 98, 109
Plants, protection of 68-69
Poisonous substances 107
Portion control 98
Praise 38
Preparing for general training 38-62
Preparing for perch-squat 130
Preparing for toilet-training 94-121
Preparing props for trick training 169
Preparing training table 169
Preparing your bathroom for toilet training 107-114
Preparing your cat for toilet training 96-101
Preparing yourself for toilet training 95
Prevention of toilet accidents 158
Prey, stalking and eating 74
Principles of training 38
Problems in cats, mental 13
Problems in cats, physical 13
Problems with training toilet 128
Problems, solving toilet-training 150-165
Problems, urinary 159
Professional training 208
Props for jumping tricks 195
Props for trick training 169
Protective measures 68-69
    Closed doors 68
    Covers and barriers 68
Psychological reactions to declawing 80
Psychology, pet 48
Pulling on leash 87
Purring, cat talk 33

R

Random versus constant rewards 171
Reason and memory, cat's 30
Records of elimination patterns 98
Regression theory 162
Regular household routines 25
Regularity, feeding for 97
Removing insert, step 5 of toilet training 139-143
Removing stains 156
Removing training toilet 135
Repellents, cat 65-67
Replacing litter box with training toilet 127
Reviewing tricks 174
Reward of food in general training 51-54
Reward of stroking in trick training 172
Rewards 38
Rewards, constant versus random 171
Rewards for appropriate scratching, cues and 78
Rewards for hearing-ear training 202

Rewards for trick training, cues and 169-172
Rewards in toilet training 106, 113
Rewards, stroking 50
Rewards, types of food 52
Roll-over trick 178
Routine, disruption of 153
Routines, household 100
Rubbing cat's nose in wastes 114
Rules of timing for hearing-ear training 204
Rules of timing in toilet training 114

S

Safety outdoors 88
Scent marking 50-51
Scented litter 123
Scratching 44, 69
Scratching habits, good 76-80
Scratching posts 77-79
Scratching tree 78
Scratching, cues and rewards for appropriate 78
Scratching, misplaced in toilet training 138
Second bathroom, training for 146
Secret places, accidents in 152
Self-taught behaviors 30
Sense of time, cat's 30
Senses, cat's 26-28
    Balance 27
    Extrasensory perception 28
    Hearing 26
    Smell 26
    Super 26
    Taste 27
    Touch 28
    Vision 27
Shelves, protection of 69
Shock, electric 109
Shorthairs, domestic 14
Shots 25
Shyness and friendliness 14
Sick cats 75
Signals of elimination 117
Signs of suppression 118
Simple jump trick 201
Simple stationary tricks 175-182
Sit-and-stay trick 173, 175
Sitz bath 102, 104
Skeleton, cat 25
Skin diseases 41, 44
    Baldness 44
    Dry skin 44
    Eczema 44
    Mange 41
    Ringworm 41
Skin, cat's 26
Smell, sense of 26
Snapping devices 67
Soft treats 52
Soiling training toilet 128
Solving toilet-training problems 150-165
Somersault, backward 26, 201
Sounds, discipline with sharp 57
Sources for kittens 15
Speak behavior 70
Speak trick 185

Special training situations 58-61
Spraying 39, 71
Stain removal 156
Stains, bowel-movement 156
Stains, urine 157
Stationary tricks 175-182
Stay behavior 173, 175
Step-by-step toilet training 95, 122-149
   Step 1 122-129
   Step 2 129-134
   Step 3 134-137
   Step 4 137-139
   Step 5 139-143
Steps in teaching fetch 190-191
Stress-induced accidents 153
Stress-induced constipation 118, 160
Stroking 24, 38
Stroking after discipline 57
Stroking rewards in general training 50
Stroking rewards in toilet training 113
Stroking rewards in trick training 172
Stroking techniques 50
Substitute litters 105
Sucking and drooling 70
Sudden diet changes 20
Sudden removal of toilet insert 139
Super senses 26
Supplements, dietary 98-99
Suppression, signs of 118

T
Table, preparing training 169
Tapeworms 44
Taste, sense of 27
Teaching order of tricks 174
Teaching perch-squat 131
Techniques for training dogs 59-61
Techniques of toilet training, basic 112-114
Tests for training ability 16
Tether training 85, 90
Ticks 41
Tile replacement 158
Time and place for trick training 172
Time, cat's sense of 30
Timing factors in general training 58
Timing in toilet training, rules of 114
Timing rules for hearing-ear training 204
Toilet accidents, discipline for 113
Toilet-bowl cleaners 107-108
Toilet exploration 130
Toilet flushing 146
Toilet insert 102
Toilet insert, adding 135
Toilet insert, removing 139-143
Toilet insert, step 3 of toilet training 134-137
Toilet seat for training toilet 101
Toilet training
   Aids 106
   Basic techniques of 112-114
   Bathroom preparation for 107-114
   Commercial device for 104

Completion of 144
Cueing in 106
Discipline in 113
Food rewards in 106
Long-term pet 125
Options 143
Preparation 94-121
Problem-solving 150-165
Rewards in 113
Tools 101-107
Tools of grooming 45
Touch, sense of 28
Toxoplasmosis 40
Toys 21
Trainers, how many 46
Trainers, unqualified 47
Training ability, tests for 16
Training aids in toilet training 106
Training, behavior 62-91
Training, breeds for 12
Training collar in toilet insert 141
Training cues 54, 56
Training decisions 46-50
   How many trainers? 46
   Unqualified trainers 47
   What to teach 49
   Who should train? 46-48
Training factors, age and sex 38
Training female cats 12
Training for a second bathroom 146
Training for urination only 143
Training, household 49
Training kittens 10
Training, leash 49
Training male cats 12
Training older cats 12
Training partner 82
Training preparation 38-62
Training principles 38
Training situations, special 58-61
Training table, preparing 169
Training techniques for dogs 59-61
Training toilet 101-103, 122-129, 135
Training-toilet problems 128
Training toilet, removing 135
Training-toilet seat 101
Training toilet, step 1 of toilet training 122-129
Training tools for toilet-training 101-107
Transition techniques 116
Transition training 114-119
Treats, preparation and storage 52
Trick-performance errors 174
Trick training 49
Trick training, cues and rewards for 169-172
Trick training, food rewards in 170
Trick training, how to offer rewards 171
Trick training, props for 169
Tricks
   Beg 186-188
   Fetch 189-193
   Go up 193-195
   Handshake 181
   Jump from table to table 199
   Jump into arms 199

Jump onto shoulder 200
Jump over hurdle 196
Jump over stick 197
Jump through hoop 197
Jump through human hoop 199
Lie down 176-178
Multiple 172-174
Order of reviewing 174
Order of teaching 174
Roll over 178
Simple jump 201
Sit-and-stay 175
Speak 185
Stationary 175-182
Two-cat jump 201
Wave bye-bye 179-181
Trimming claws 79
Tug-and-follow behavior 86
Two-cat jumping trick 201
Two-cat performances 208
Two-cat training 58

U
Undesirable behaviors 65-75
   Aggression 69
   Devices to change 65-69
   Getting into forbidden places 69
   How to eliminate 69-75
   Irritating personal habits 69
Upholstery cleaning 156
Urinary problems 159
Urination patterns 99
Urination, inappropriate 71
Urination, training for 143
Urine accidents, discipline for 114
Urine stains 157

V
Vacations 153
Variations on jump 201
Verbal cues 56, 169
Videotape performances 207
Vinyl-floor cleaning 155
Vision, sense of 27
Visual cues 56, 169

W
Walking, hind-leg 188
Water as a repellent 67
Water consumption 99
Water in toilet insert 140
Water, drinking contaminated 112
Water-hating cats 67
Water-loving cats 67
Wave bye-bye trick 179-181
What to teach 49-50
Where to buy clickers 54
Who should train? 46-48
Working behaviors 202-209
Working on camera 207-209
Worms 40
Wrestling response 51, 74
Written records of elimination patterns 98
Wrong trick performances 174